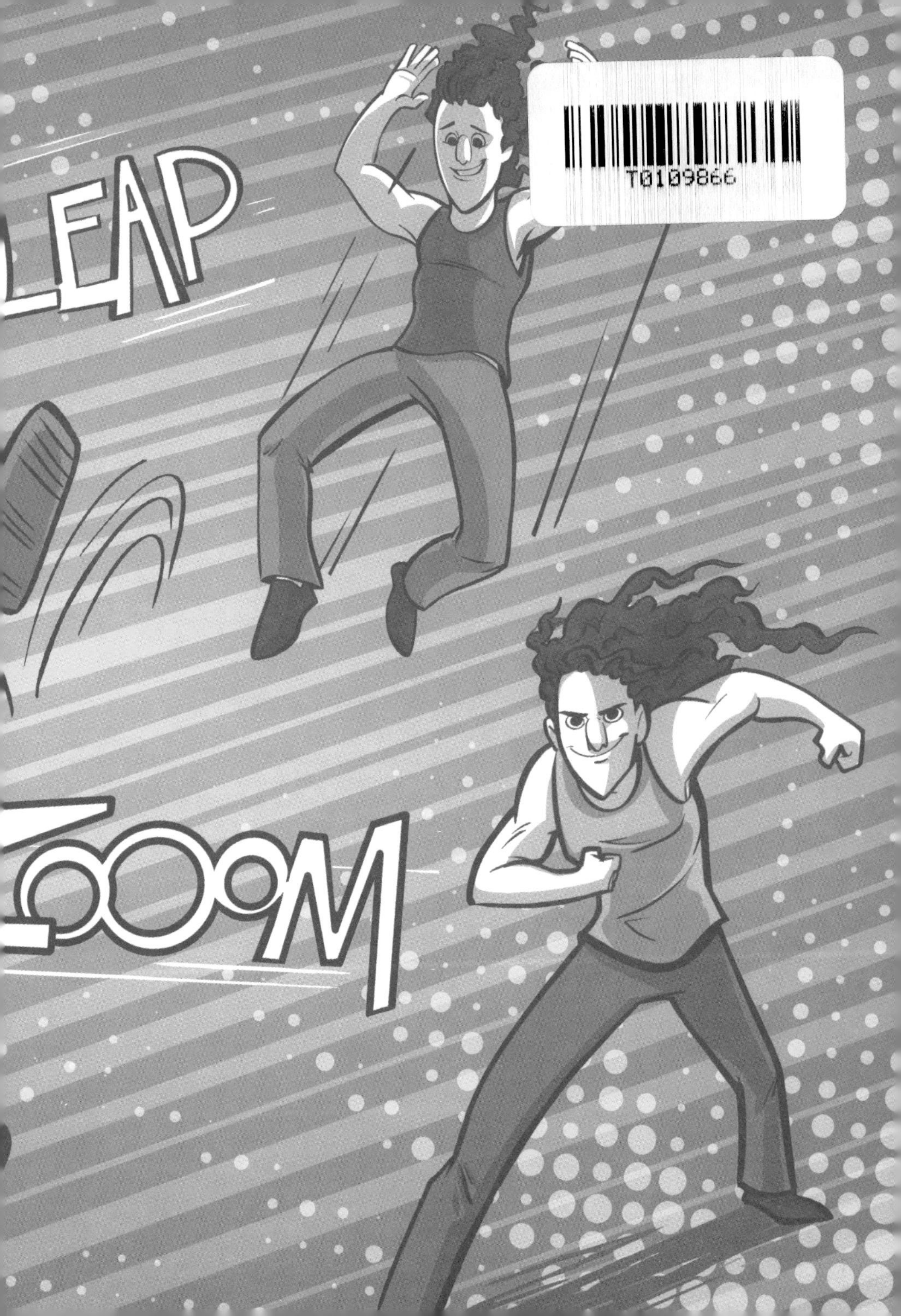
LEAP
OOM

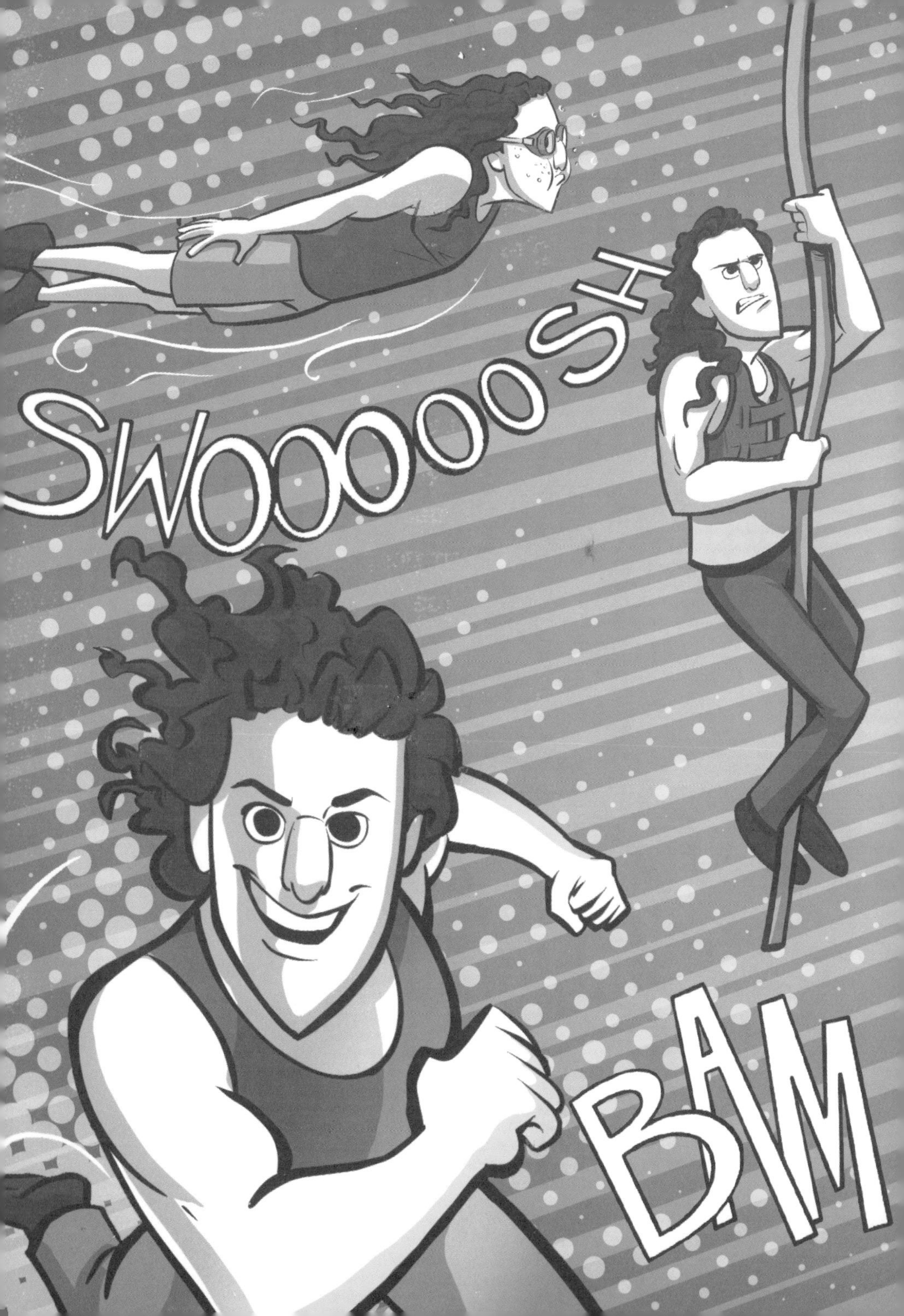
SWOOOOOSH
BAM

HOW
TO BE A
KINGDOM
NINJA

Art by Brad Smith

TEN PEAKS PRESS®
EUGENE, OR

Cover design by Bryce Williamson
Cover images © vkulieva, Anna Pylypets/Getty Images
Interior design by Chad Dougherty
Author photo by Jay Eads

For bulk or special sales, please call 1-800-547-8979.
Email: CustomerService@hhpbooks.com

TEN PEAKS PRESS
TEN PEAKS PRESS is a federally registered trademark of the Hawkins Children's LLC. Harvest House Publishers, Inc., is the exclusive licensee of this trademark.

HOW TO BE A KINGDOM NINJA

Published by Ten Peaks Press, an imprint of Harvest House Publishers
Eugene, Oregon 97408

ISBN 978-0-7369-8716-5 (hardcover)
ISBN 978-0-7369-8717-2 (eBook)

Library of Congress Control Number: 2023951880

Printed in Colombia

24 25 26 27 28 29 30 31 32 / NI / 10 9 8 7 6 5 4 3 2 1

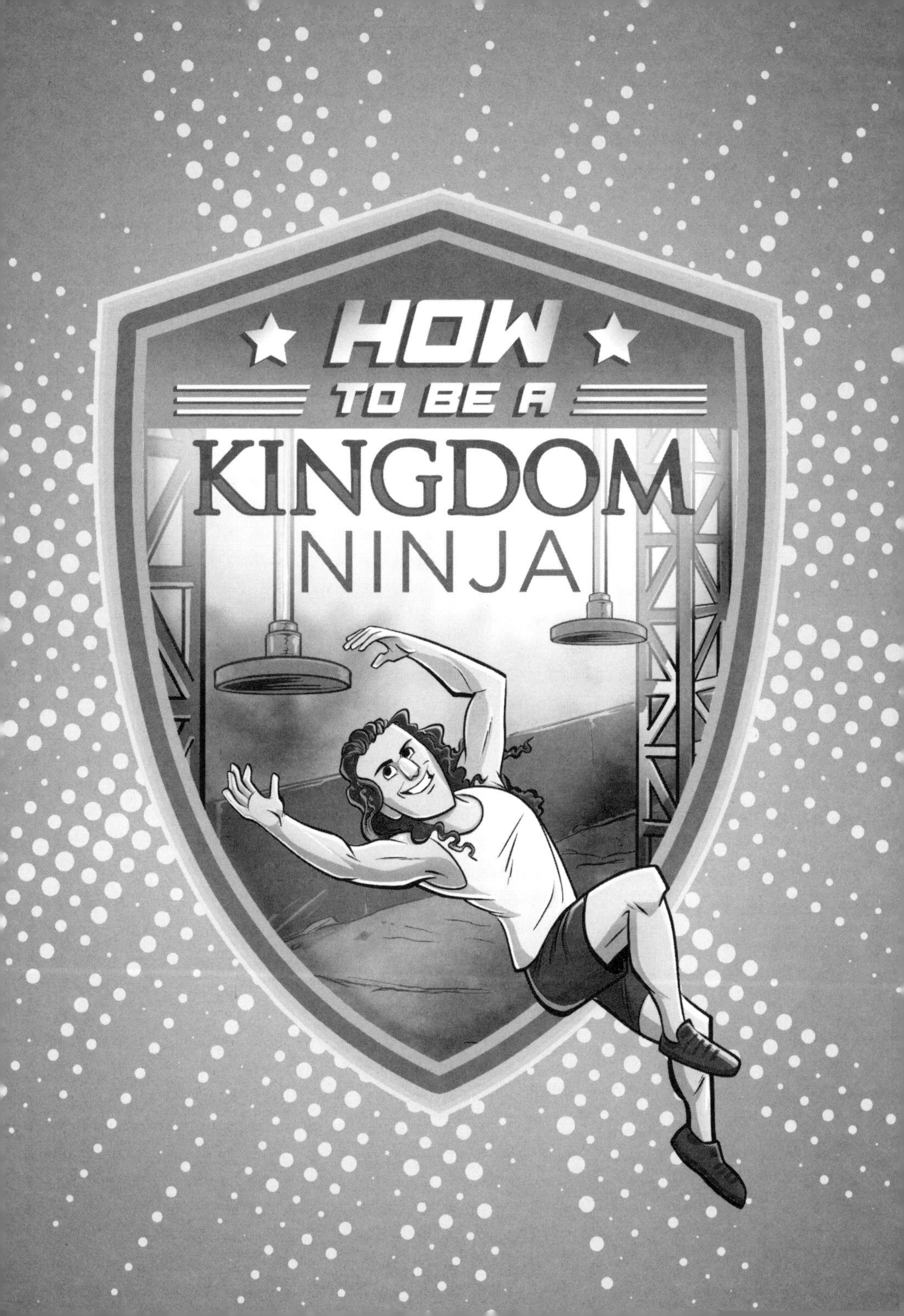
HOW
TO BE A
KINGDOM
NINJA

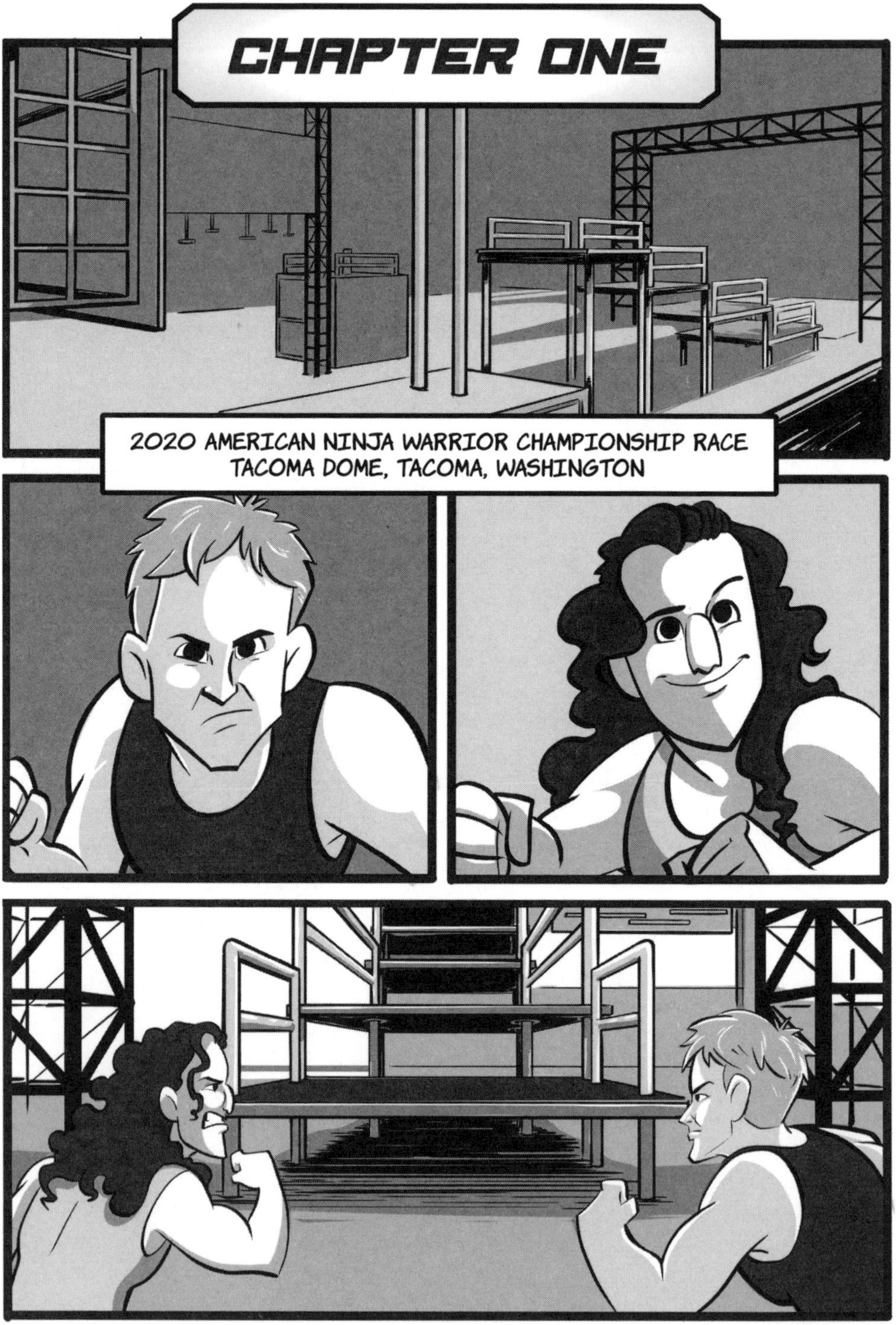
CHAPTER ONE
2020 AMERICAN NINJA WARRIOR CHAMPIONSHIP RACE
TACOMA DOME, TACOMA, WASHINGTON

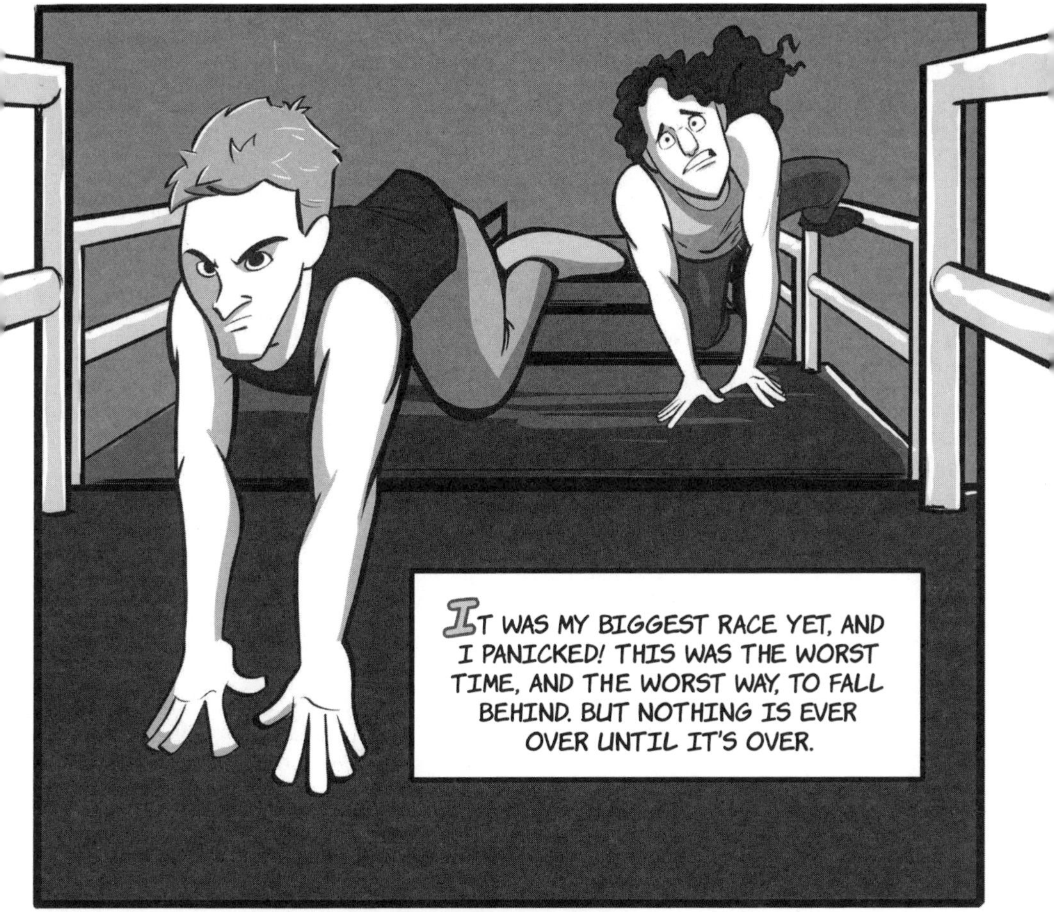
IT WAS MY BIGGEST RACE YET, AND I PANICKED! THIS WAS THE WORST TIME, AND THE WORST WAY, TO FALL BEHIND. BUT NOTHING IS EVER OVER UNTIL IT'S OVER.

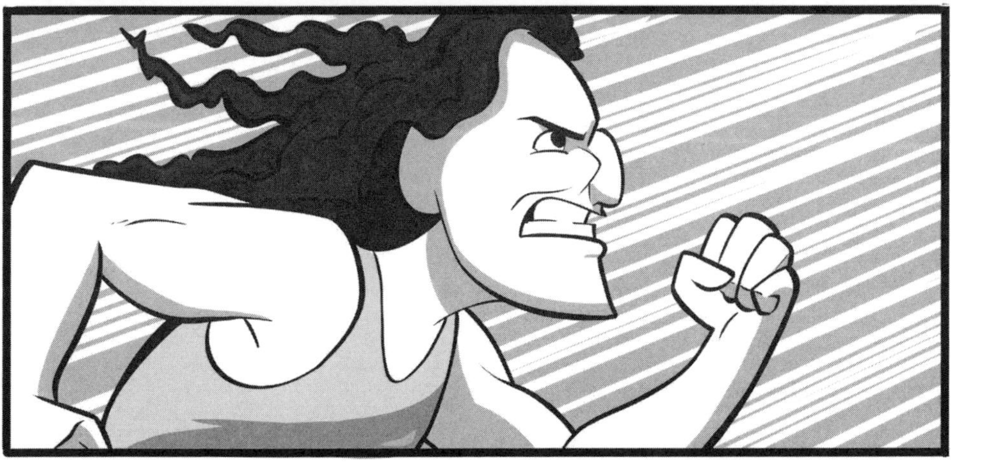

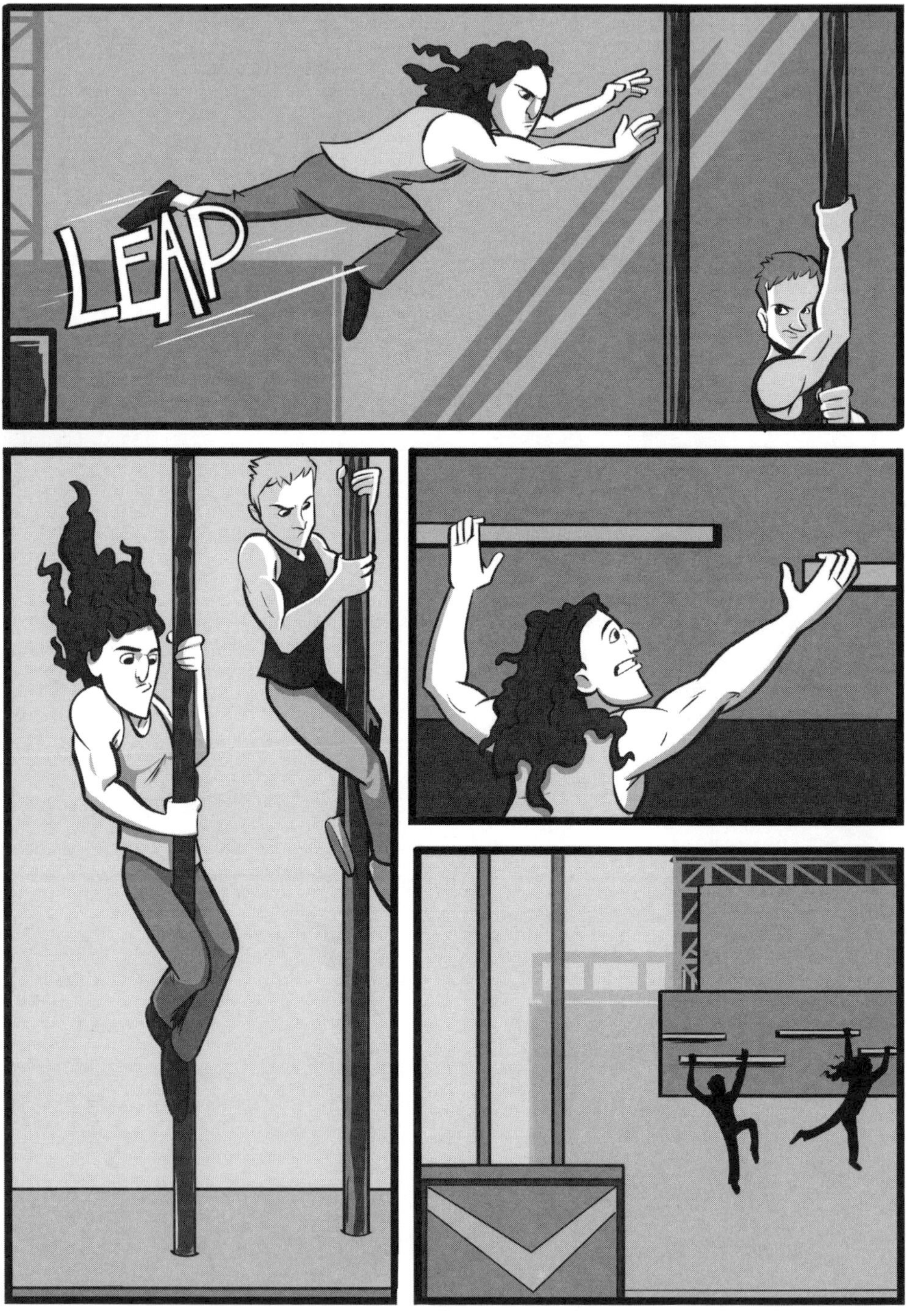
LEAP

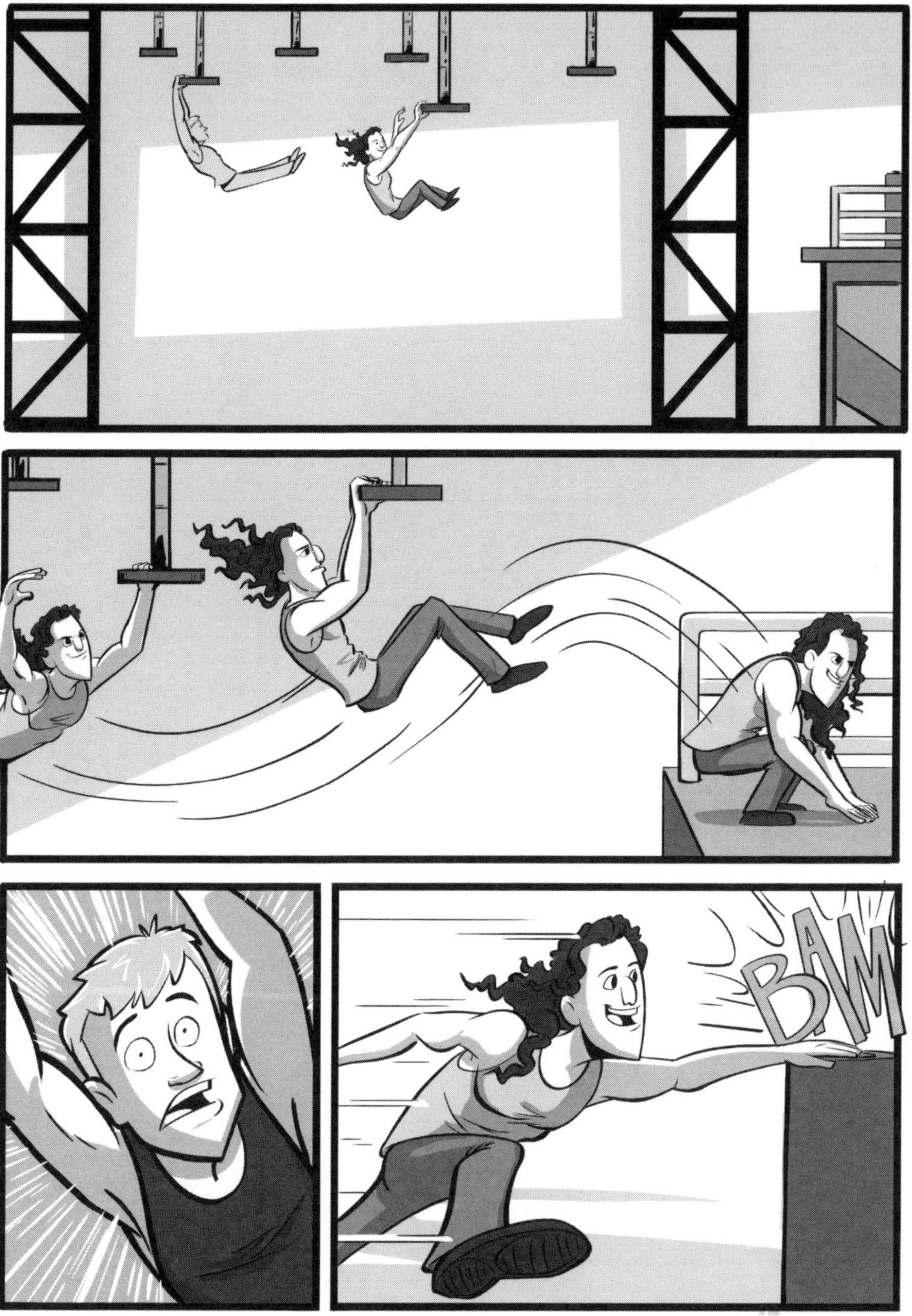
BAM!

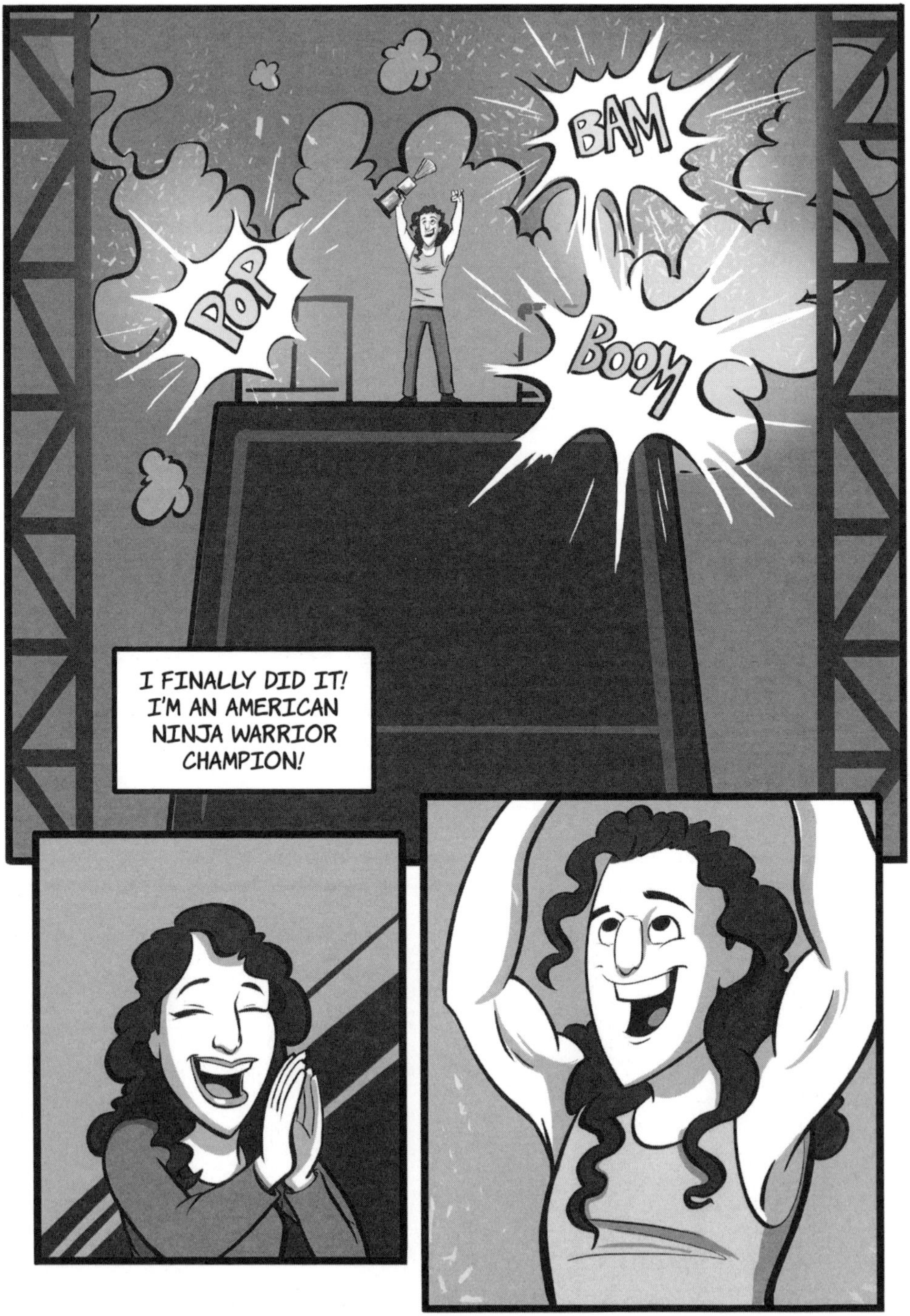
BAM
POP
BOOM
I FINALLY DID IT! I'M AN AMERICAN NINJA WARRIOR CHAMPION!

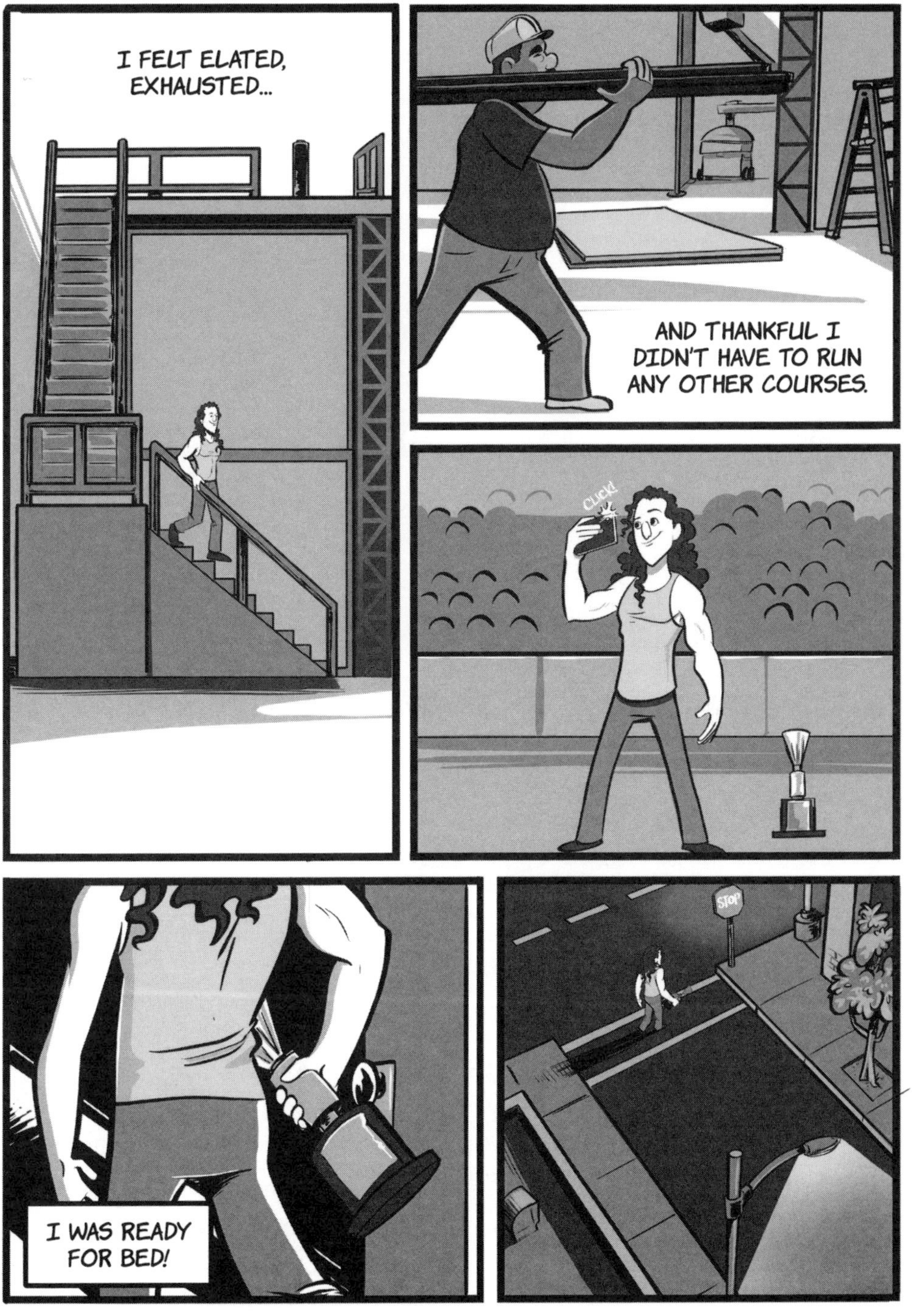
I FELT ELATED,
EXHAUSTED...
AND THANKFUL I
DIDN'T HAVE TO RUN
ANY OTHER COURSES.
CLICK!
STOP
I WAS READY
FOR BED!

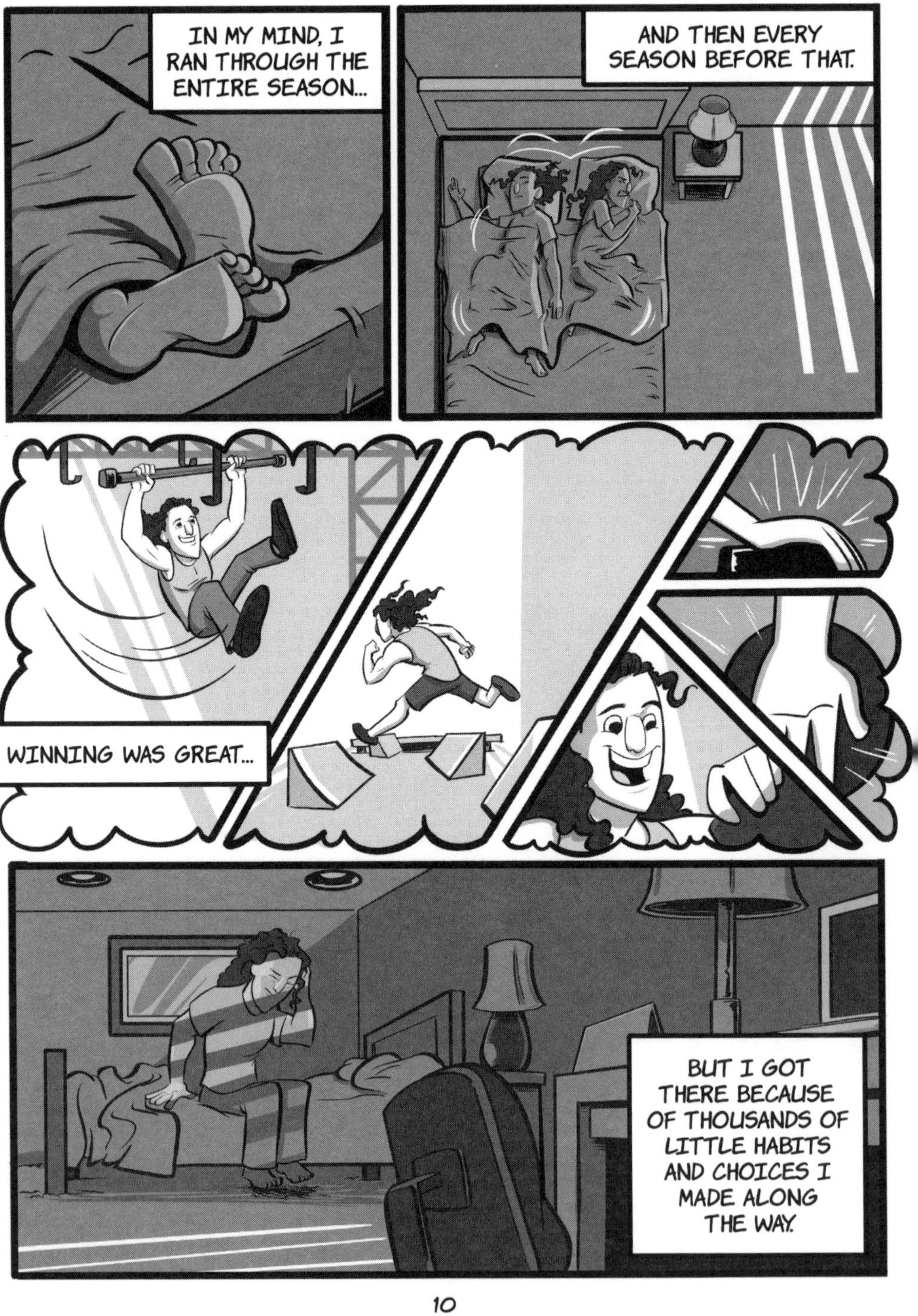
IN MY MIND, I RAN THROUGH THE ENTIRE SEASON...
AND THEN EVERY SEASON BEFORE THAT.
WINNING WAS GREAT...
BUT I GOT THERE BECAUSE OF THOUSANDS OF LITTLE HABITS AND CHOICES I MADE ALONG THE WAY.

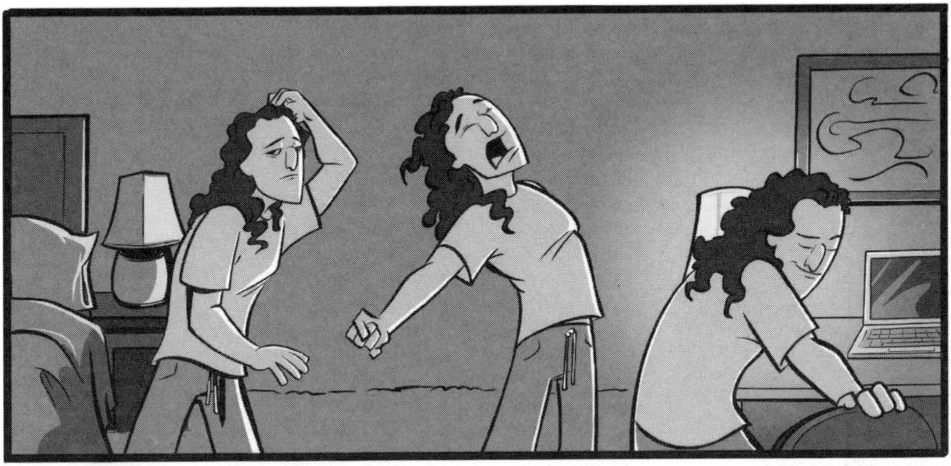

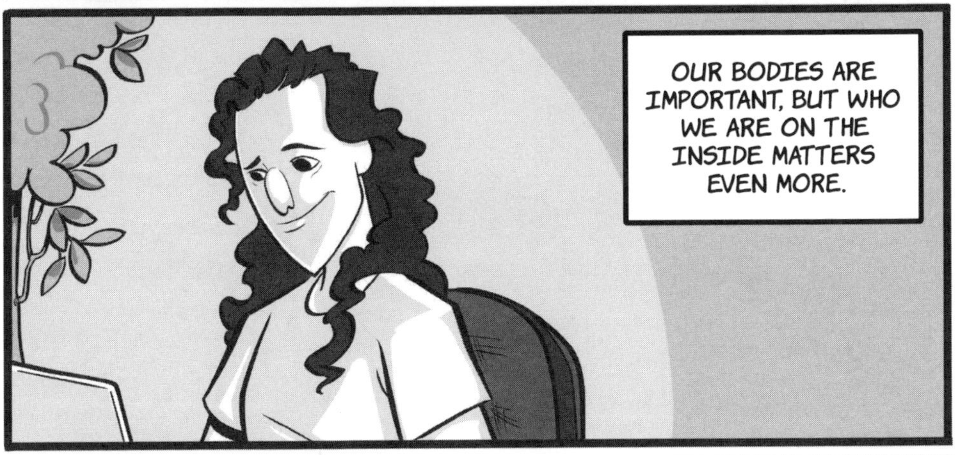
OUR BODIES ARE IMPORTANT, BUT WHO WE ARE ON THE INSIDE MATTERS EVEN MORE.

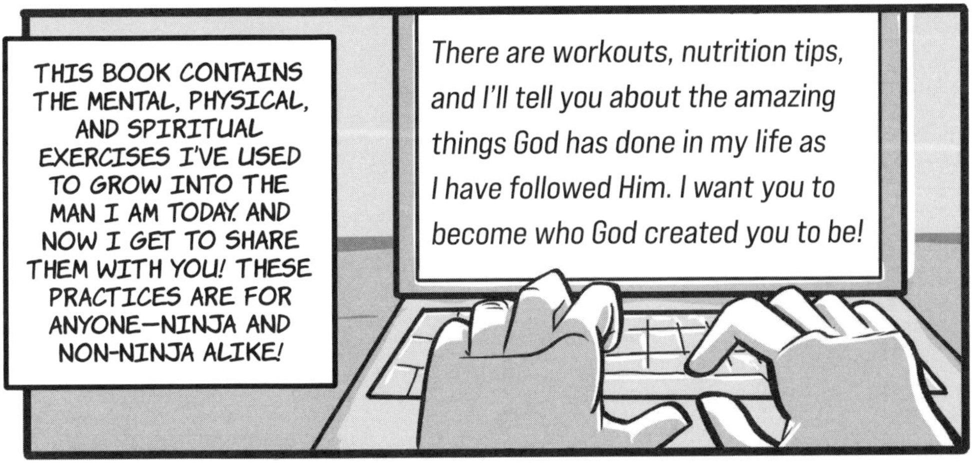
THIS BOOK CONTAINS THE MENTAL, PHYSICAL, AND SPIRITUAL EXERCISES I'VE USED TO GROW INTO THE MAN I AM TODAY. AND NOW I GET TO SHARE THEM WITH YOU! THESE PRACTICES ARE FOR ANYONE—NINJA AND NON-NINJA ALIKE!
There are workouts, nutrition tips, and I'll tell you about the amazing things God has done in my life as I have followed Him. I want you to become who God created you to be!

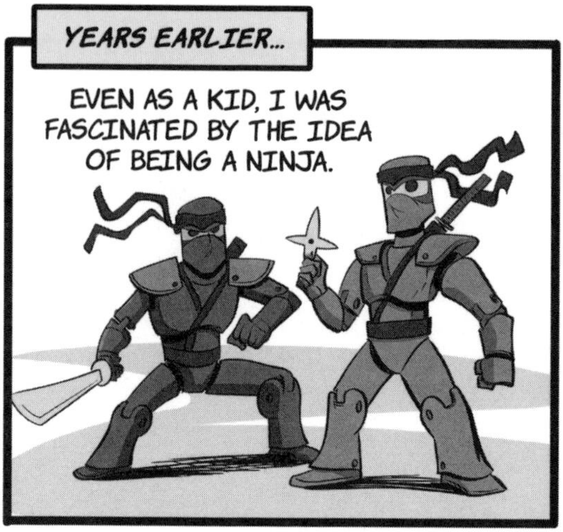
YEARS EARLIER...
EVEN AS A KID, I WAS FASCINATED BY THE IDEA OF BEING A NINJA.

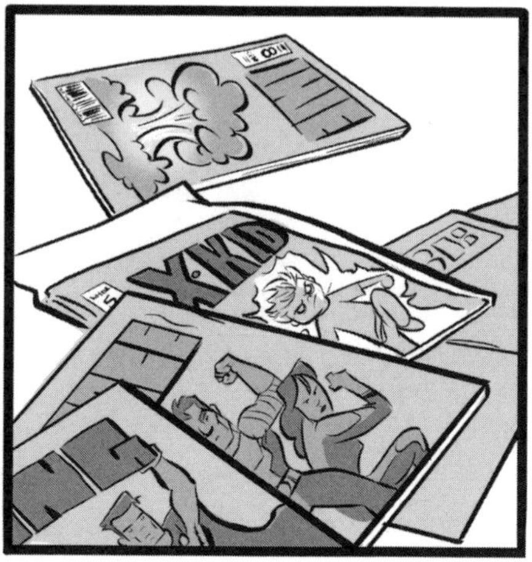

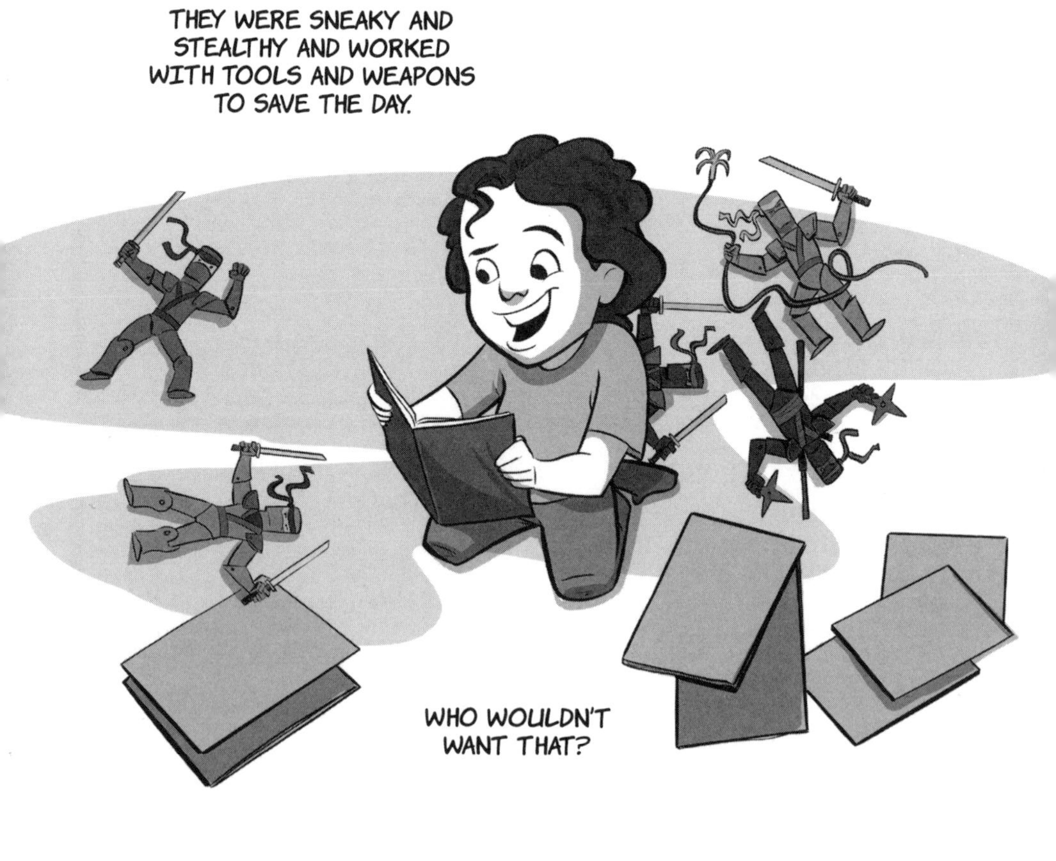
THEY WERE SNEAKY AND STEALTHY AND WORKED WITH TOOLS AND WEAPONS TO SAVE THE DAY.
WHO WOULDN'T WANT THAT?

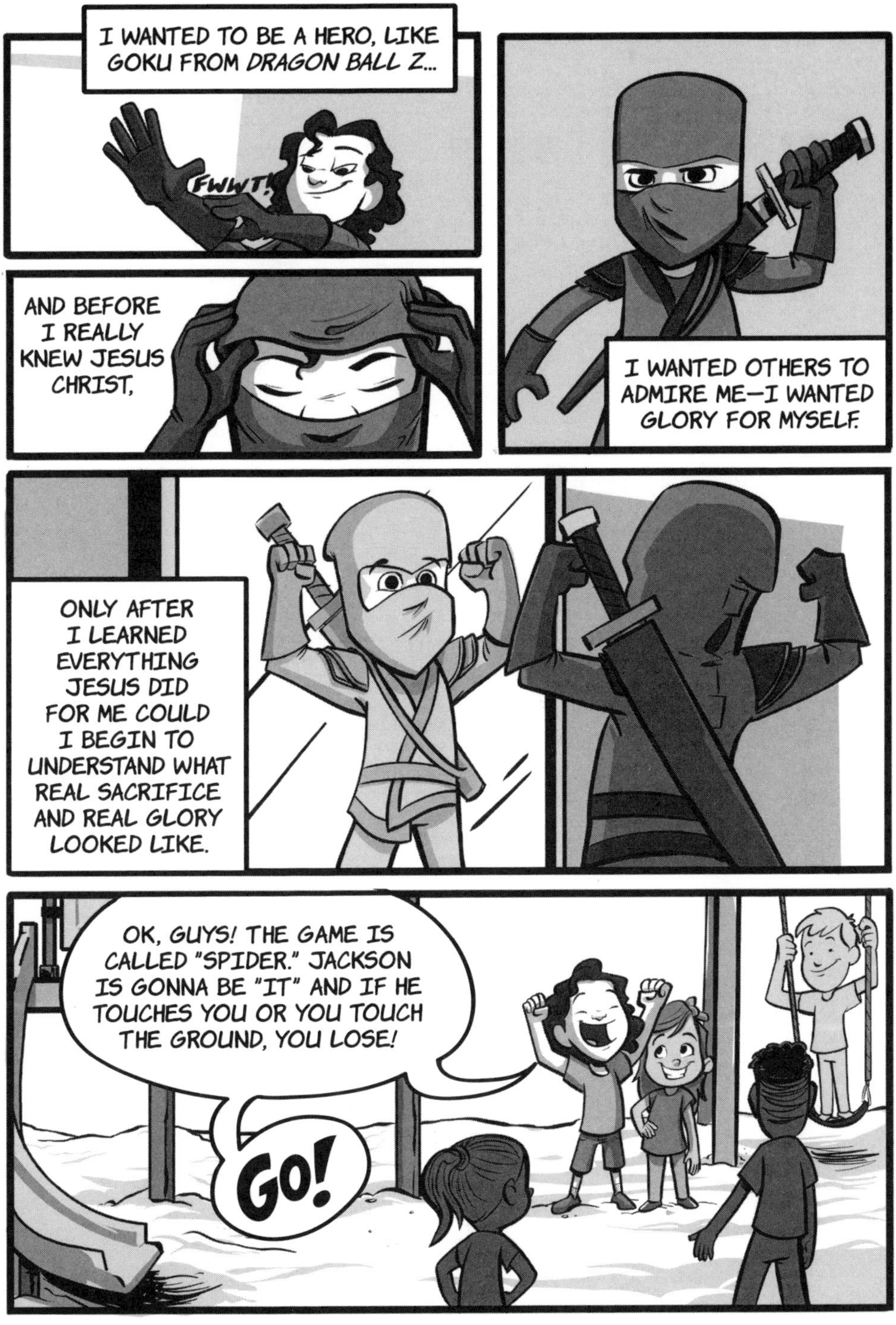

I WANTED TO BE A HERO, LIKE GOKU FROM *DRAGON BALL Z*...
FWWT!
AND BEFORE I REALLY KNEW JESUS CHRIST,
I WANTED OTHERS TO ADMIRE ME—I WANTED GLORY FOR MYSELF.
ONLY AFTER I LEARNED EVERYTHING JESUS DID FOR ME COULD I BEGIN TO UNDERSTAND WHAT REAL SACRIFICE AND REAL GLORY LOOKED LIKE.
OK, GUYS! THE GAME IS CALLED "SPIDER." JACKSON IS GONNA BE "IT" AND IF HE TOUCHES YOU OR YOU TOUCH THE GROUND, YOU LOSE!
GO!

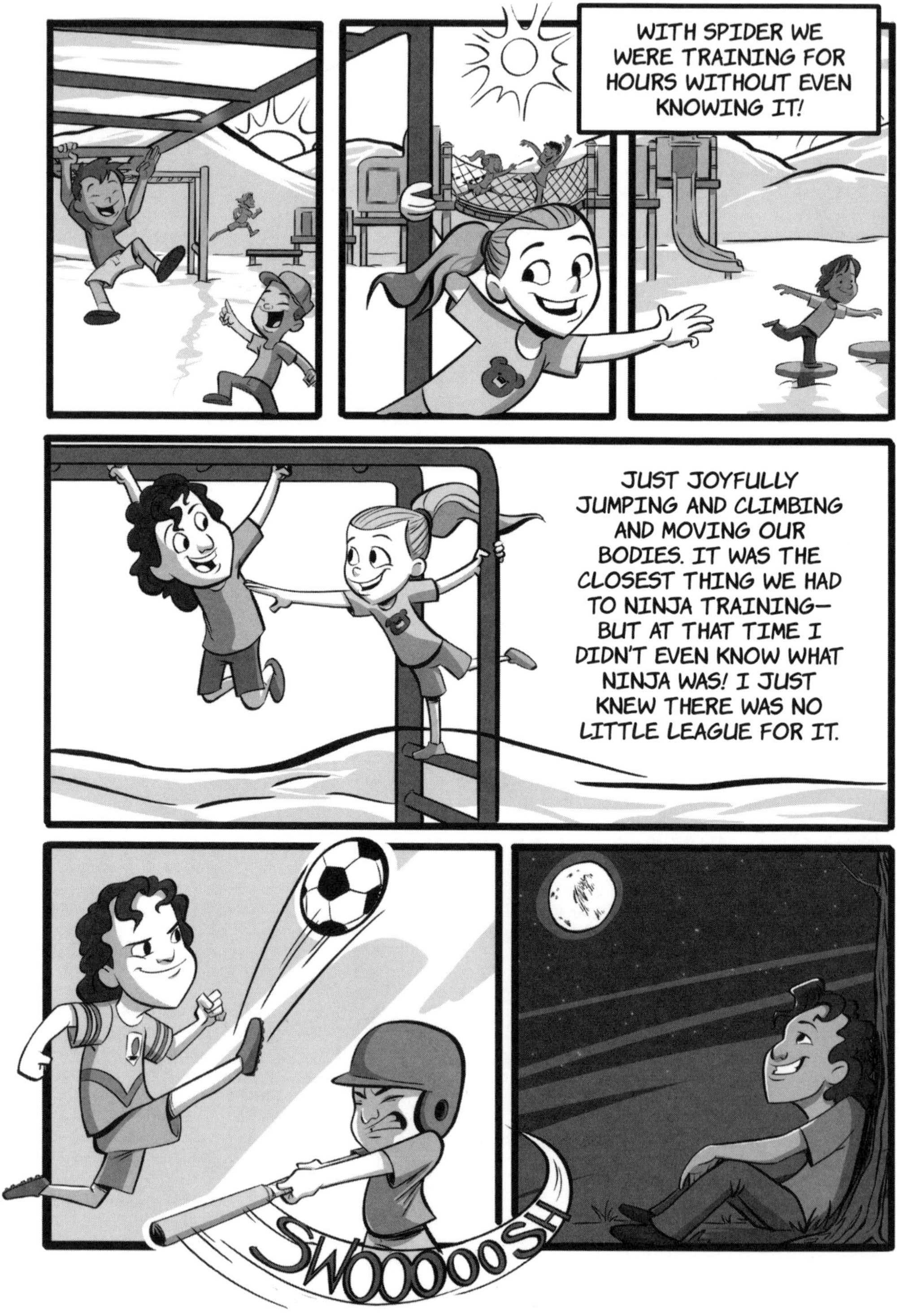
WITH SPIDER WE WERE TRAINING FOR HOURS WITHOUT EVEN KNOWING IT!
JUST JOYFULLY JUMPING AND CLIMBING AND MOVING OUR BODIES. IT WAS THE CLOSEST THING WE HAD TO NINJA TRAINING— BUT AT THAT TIME I DIDN'T EVEN KNOW WHAT NINJA WAS! I JUST KNEW THERE WAS NO LITTLE LEAGUE FOR IT.
SWOOOOOSH

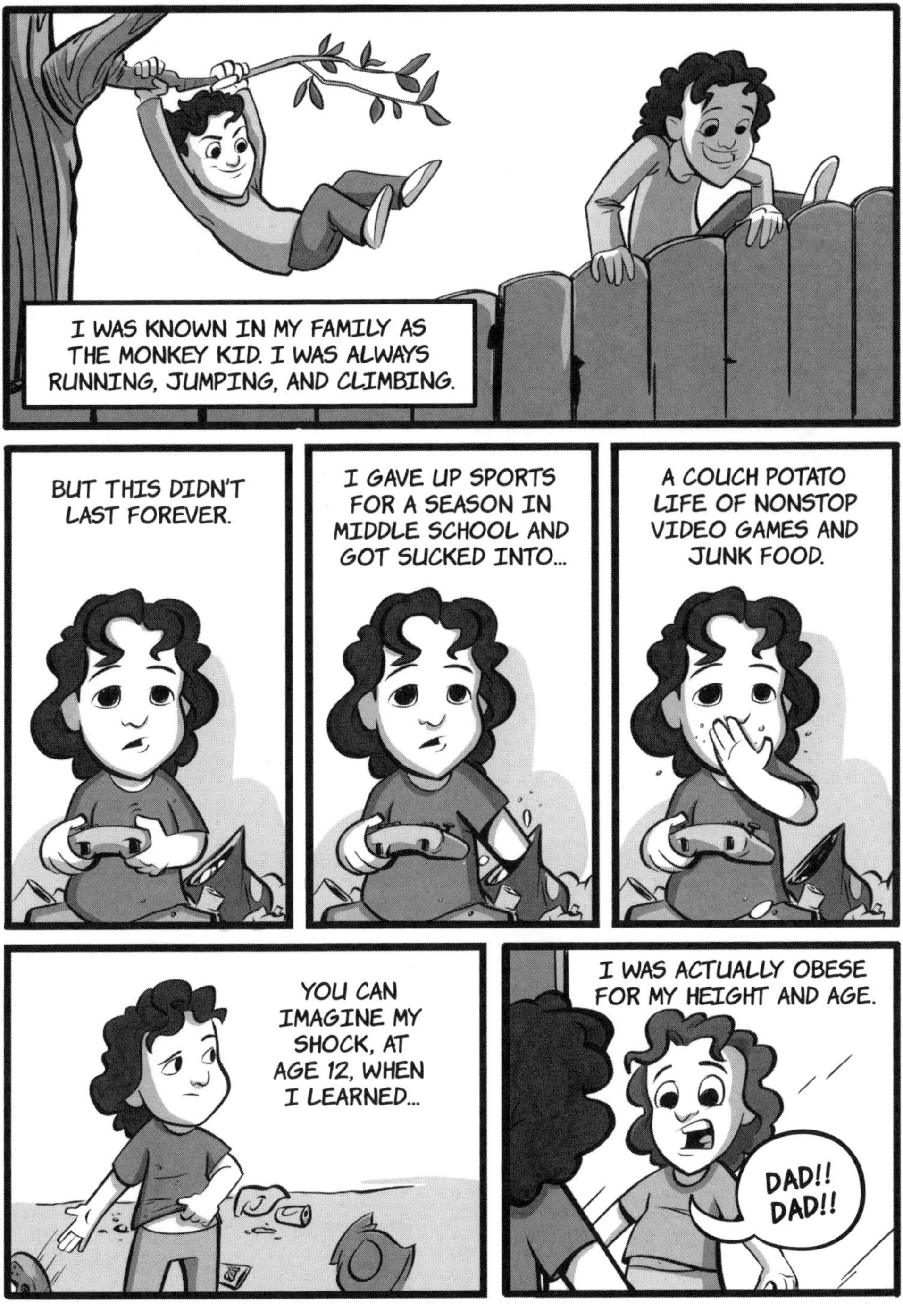
I WAS KNOWN IN MY FAMILY AS THE MONKEY KID. I WAS ALWAYS RUNNING, JUMPING, AND CLIMBING.
BUT THIS DIDN'T LAST FOREVER.
I GAVE UP SPORTS FOR A SEASON IN MIDDLE SCHOOL AND GOT SUCKED INTO...
A COUCH POTATO LIFE OF NONSTOP VIDEO GAMES AND JUNK FOOD.
YOU CAN IMAGINE MY SHOCK, AT AGE 12, WHEN I LEARNED...
I WAS ACTUALLY OBESE FOR MY HEIGHT AND AGE.
DAD!! DAD!!

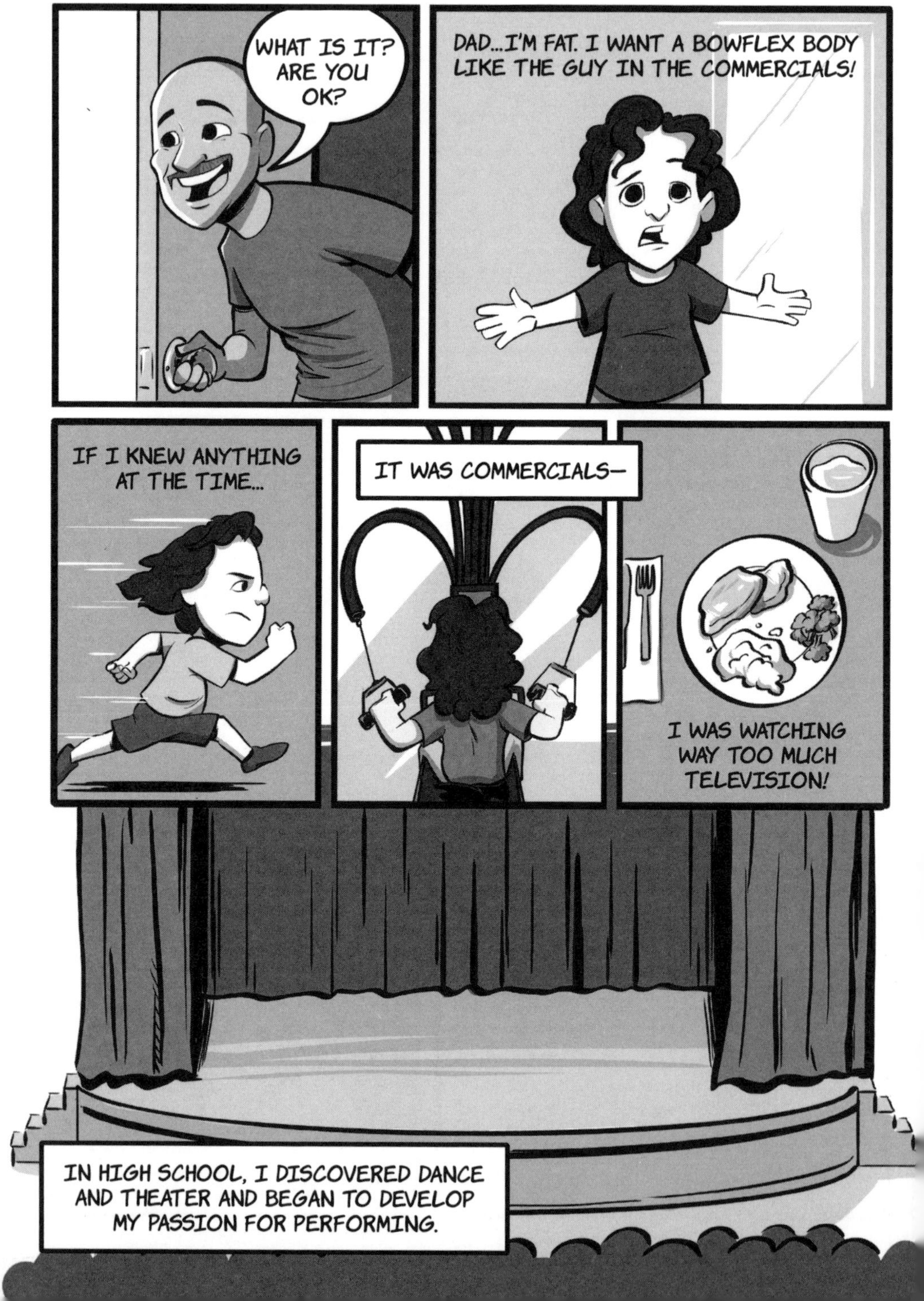
WHAT IS IT? ARE YOU OK?
DAD...I'M FAT. I WANT A BOWFLEX BODY LIKE THE GUY IN THE COMMERCIALS!
IF I KNEW ANYTHING AT THE TIME...
IT WAS COMMERCIALS—
I WAS WATCHING WAY TOO MUCH TELEVISION!
IN HIGH SCHOOL, I DISCOVERED DANCE AND THEATER AND BEGAN TO DEVELOP MY PASSION FOR PERFORMING.

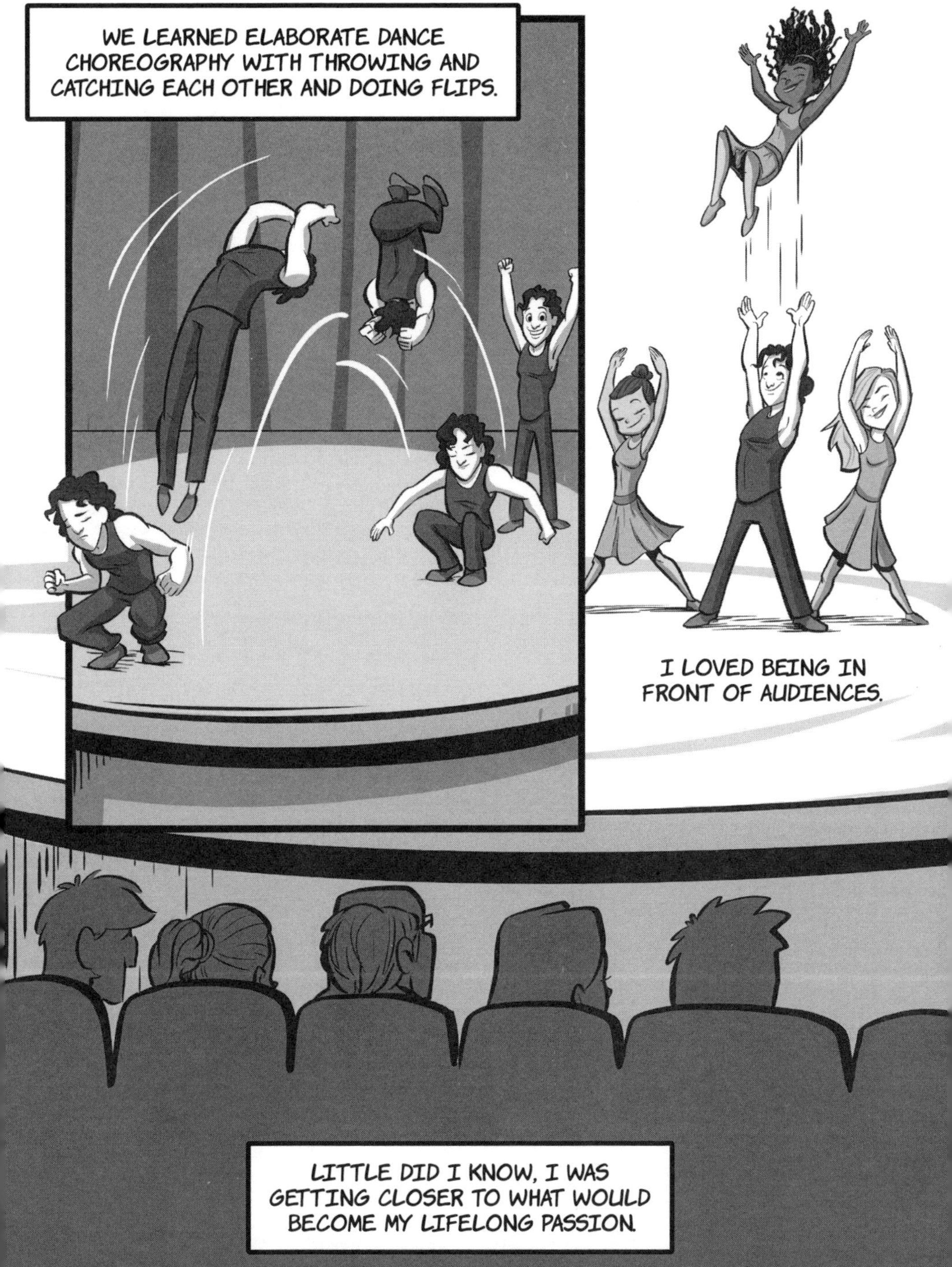
WE LEARNED ELABORATE DANCE CHOREOGRAPHY WITH THROWING AND CATCHING EACH OTHER AND DOING FLIPS.
I LOVED BEING IN FRONT OF AUDIENCES.
LITTLE DID I KNOW, I WAS GETTING CLOSER TO WHAT WOULD BECOME MY LIFELONG PASSION.

CHAPTER TWO

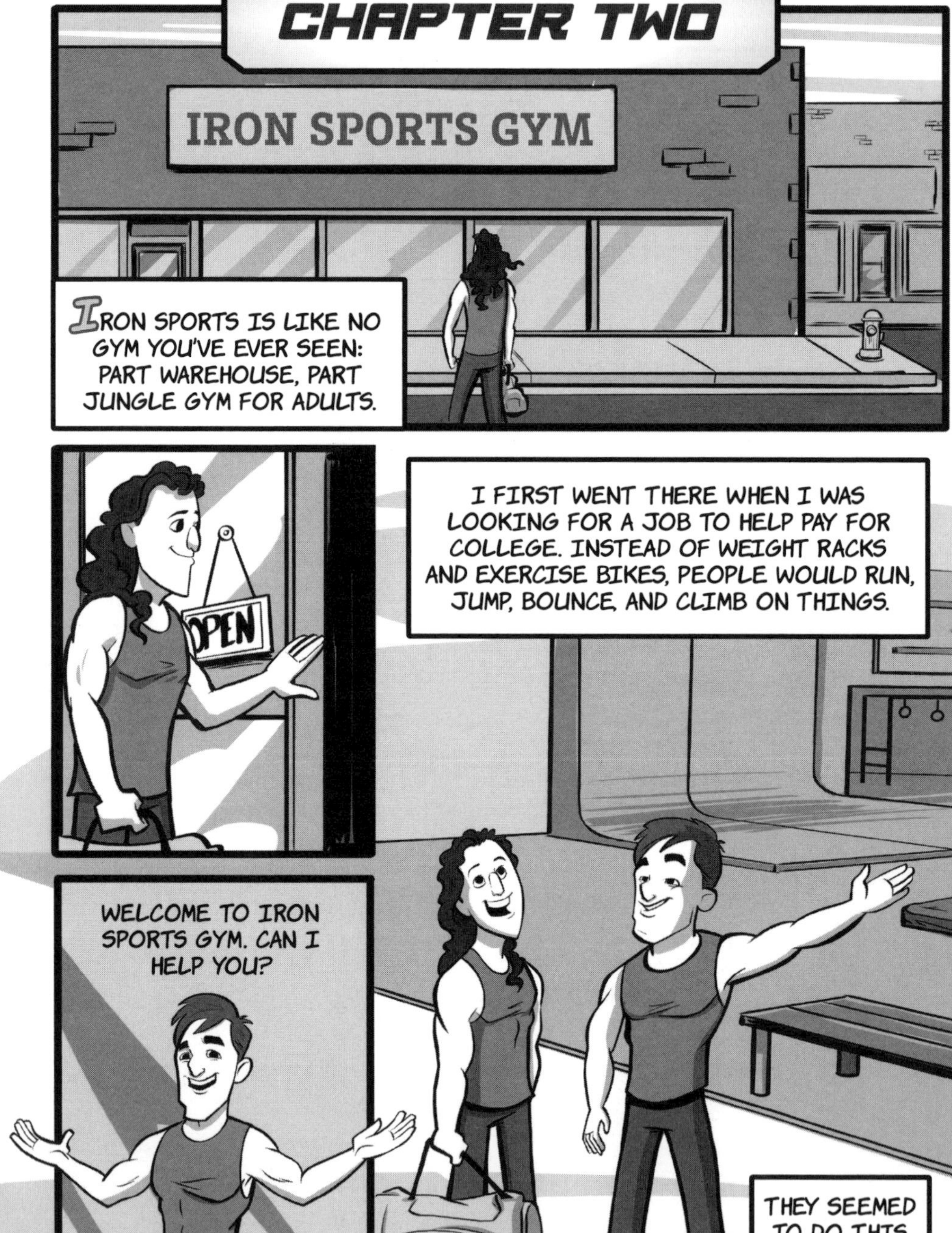
IRON SPORTS GYM
IRON SPORTS IS LIKE NO GYM YOU'VE EVER SEEN: PART WAREHOUSE, PART JUNGLE GYM FOR ADULTS.
OPEN
I FIRST WENT THERE WHEN I WAS LOOKING FOR A JOB TO HELP PAY FOR COLLEGE. INSTEAD OF WEIGHT RACKS AND EXERCISE BIKES, PEOPLE WOULD RUN, JUMP, BOUNCE, AND CLIMB ON THINGS.
WELCOME TO IRON SPORTS GYM. CAN I HELP YOU?
THEY SEEMED TO DO THIS JOYFULLY.

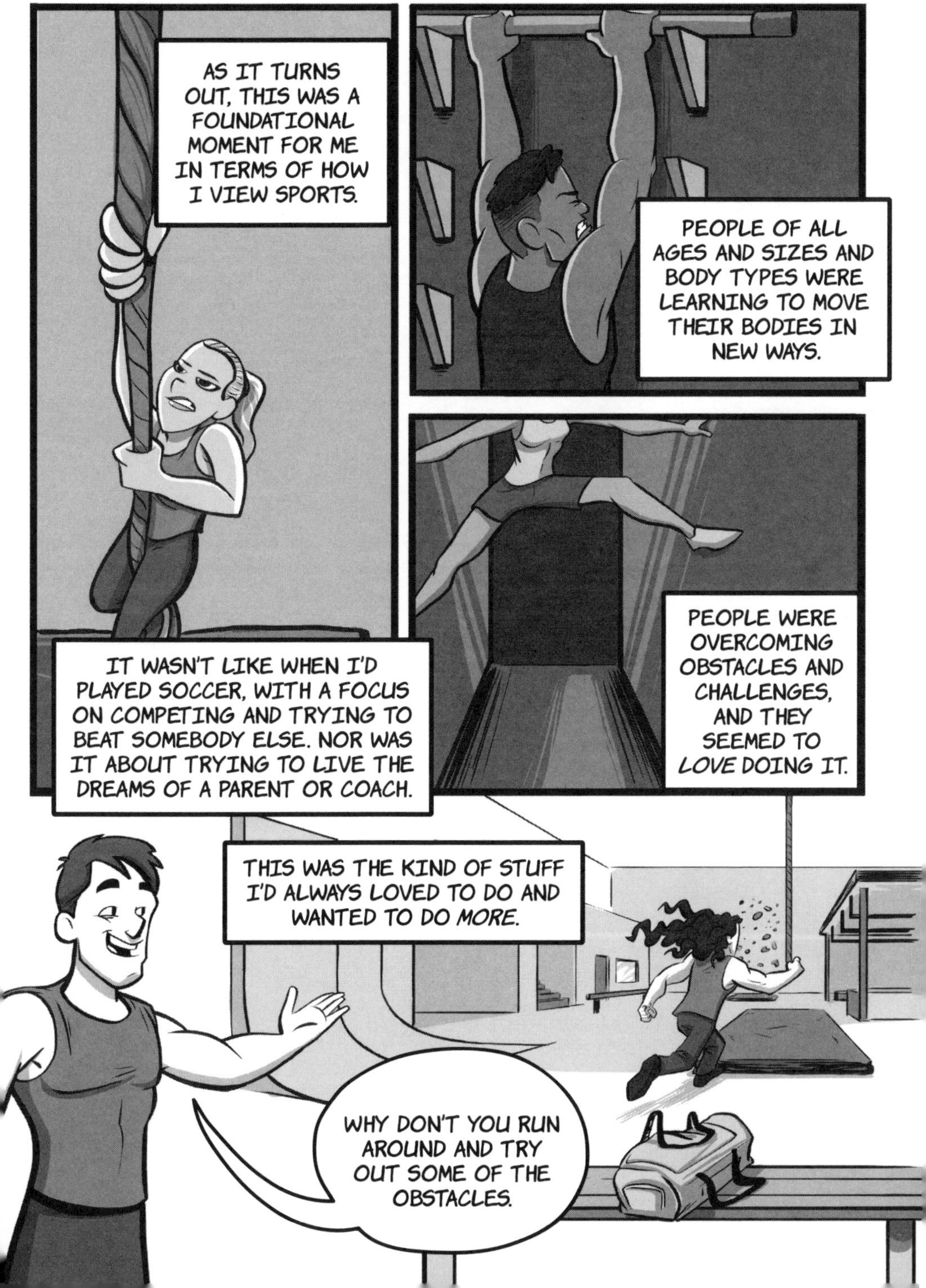
AS IT TURNS OUT, THIS WAS A FOUNDATIONAL MOMENT FOR ME IN TERMS OF HOW I VIEW SPORTS.
PEOPLE OF ALL AGES AND SIZES AND BODY TYPES WERE LEARNING TO MOVE THEIR BODIES IN NEW WAYS.
IT WASN'T LIKE WHEN I'D PLAYED SOCCER, WITH A FOCUS ON COMPETING AND TRYING TO BEAT SOMEBODY ELSE. NOR WAS IT ABOUT TRYING TO LIVE THE DREAMS OF A PARENT OR COACH.
PEOPLE WERE OVERCOMING OBSTACLES AND CHALLENGES, AND THEY SEEMED TO *LOVE* DOING IT.
THIS WAS THE KIND OF STUFF I'D ALWAYS LOVED TO DO AND WANTED TO DO *MORE*.
WHY DON'T YOU RUN AROUND AND TRY OUT SOME OF THE OBSTACLES.

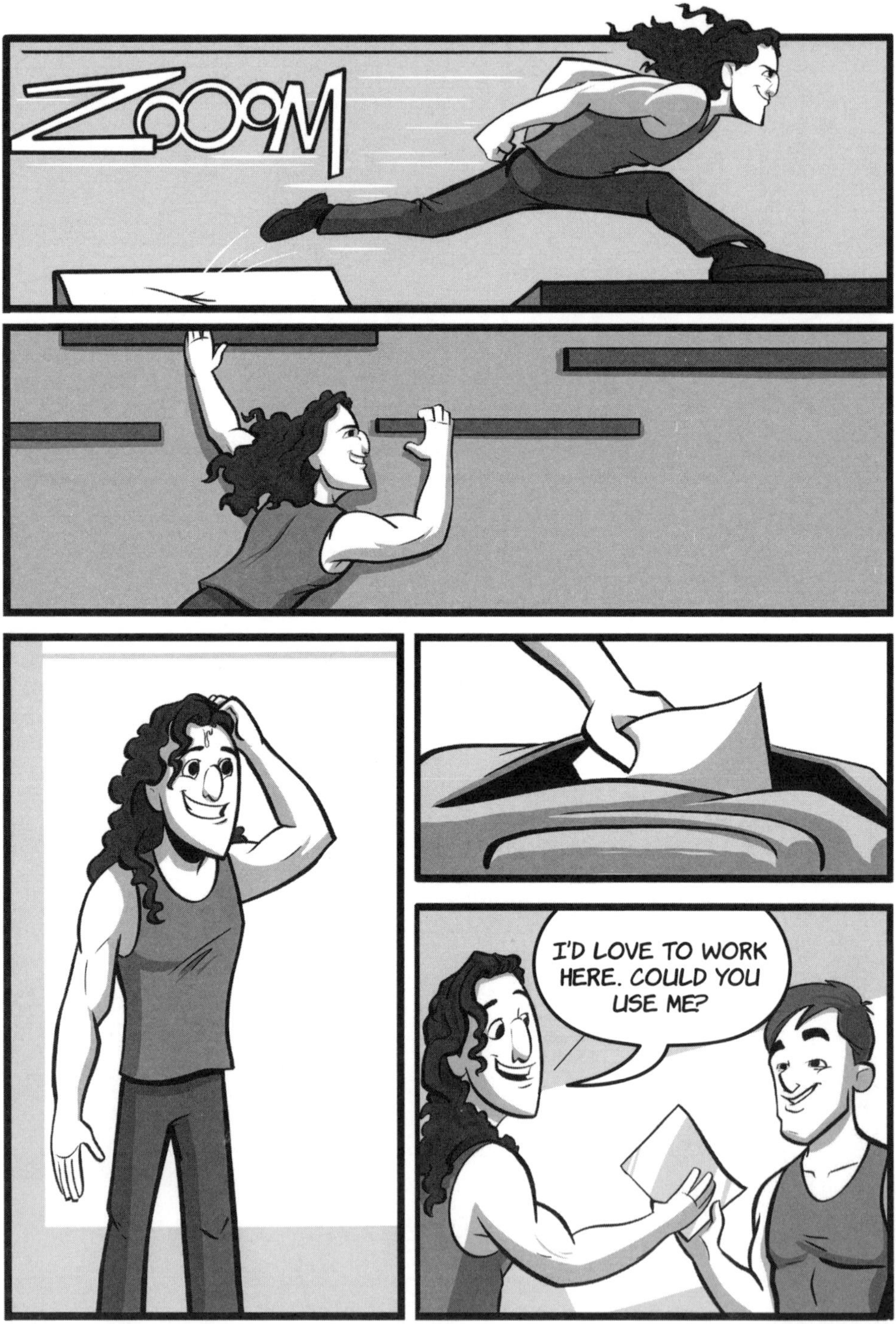
ZOOOM
I'D LOVE TO WORK HERE. COULD YOU USE ME?

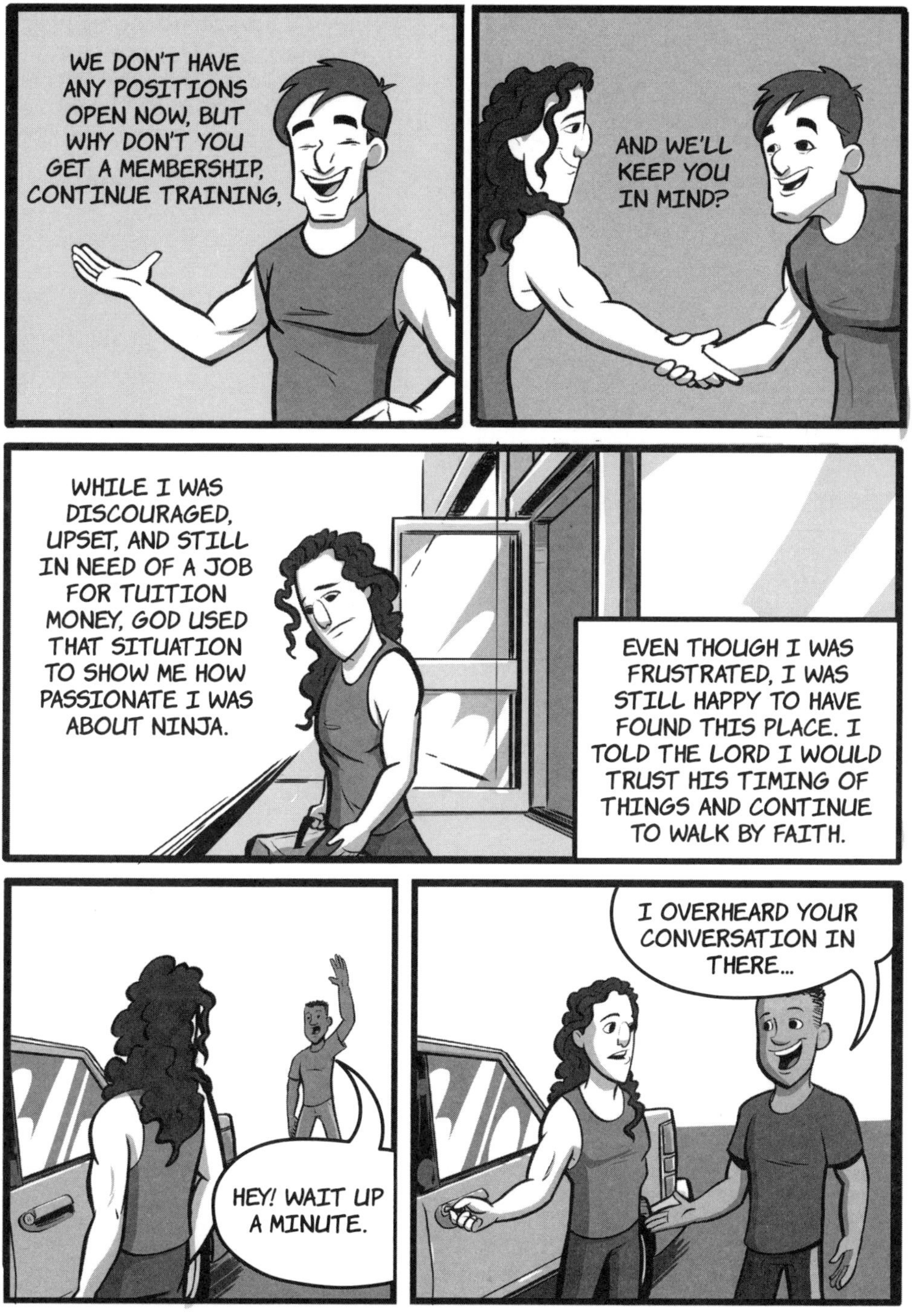
WE DON'T HAVE ANY POSITIONS OPEN NOW, BUT WHY DON'T YOU GET A MEMBERSHIP, CONTINUE TRAINING,
AND WE'LL KEEP YOU IN MIND?
WHILE I WAS DISCOURAGED, UPSET, AND STILL IN NEED OF A JOB FOR TUITION MONEY, GOD USED THAT SITUATION TO SHOW ME HOW PASSIONATE I WAS ABOUT NINJA.
EVEN THOUGH I WAS FRUSTRATED, I WAS STILL HAPPY TO HAVE FOUND THIS PLACE. I TOLD THE LORD I WOULD TRUST HIS TIMING OF THINGS AND CONTINUE TO WALK BY FAITH.
HEY! WAIT UP A MINUTE.
I OVERHEARD YOUR CONVERSATION IN THERE...

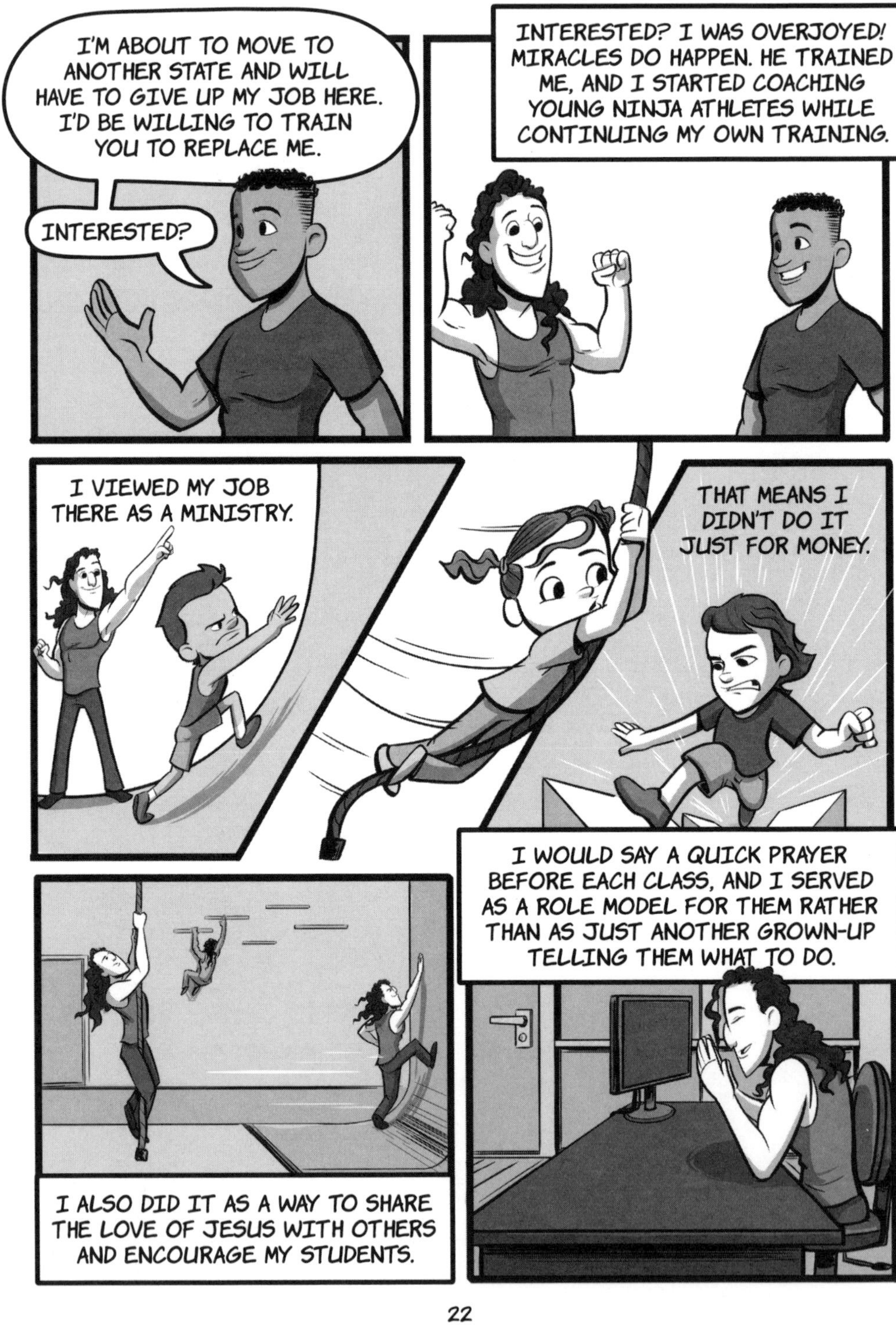
I'M ABOUT TO MOVE TO ANOTHER STATE AND WILL HAVE TO GIVE UP MY JOB HERE. I'D BE WILLING TO TRAIN YOU TO REPLACE ME.
INTERESTED?
INTERESTED? I WAS OVERJOYED! MIRACLES DO HAPPEN. HE TRAINED ME, AND I STARTED COACHING YOUNG NINJA ATHLETES WHILE CONTINUING MY OWN TRAINING.
I VIEWED MY JOB THERE AS A MINISTRY.
THAT MEANS I DIDN'T DO IT JUST FOR MONEY.
I WOULD SAY A QUICK PRAYER BEFORE EACH CLASS, AND I SERVED AS A ROLE MODEL FOR THEM RATHER THAN AS JUST ANOTHER GROWN-UP TELLING THEM WHAT TO DO.
I ALSO DID IT AS A WAY TO SHARE THE LOVE OF JESUS WITH OTHERS AND ENCOURAGE MY STUDENTS.

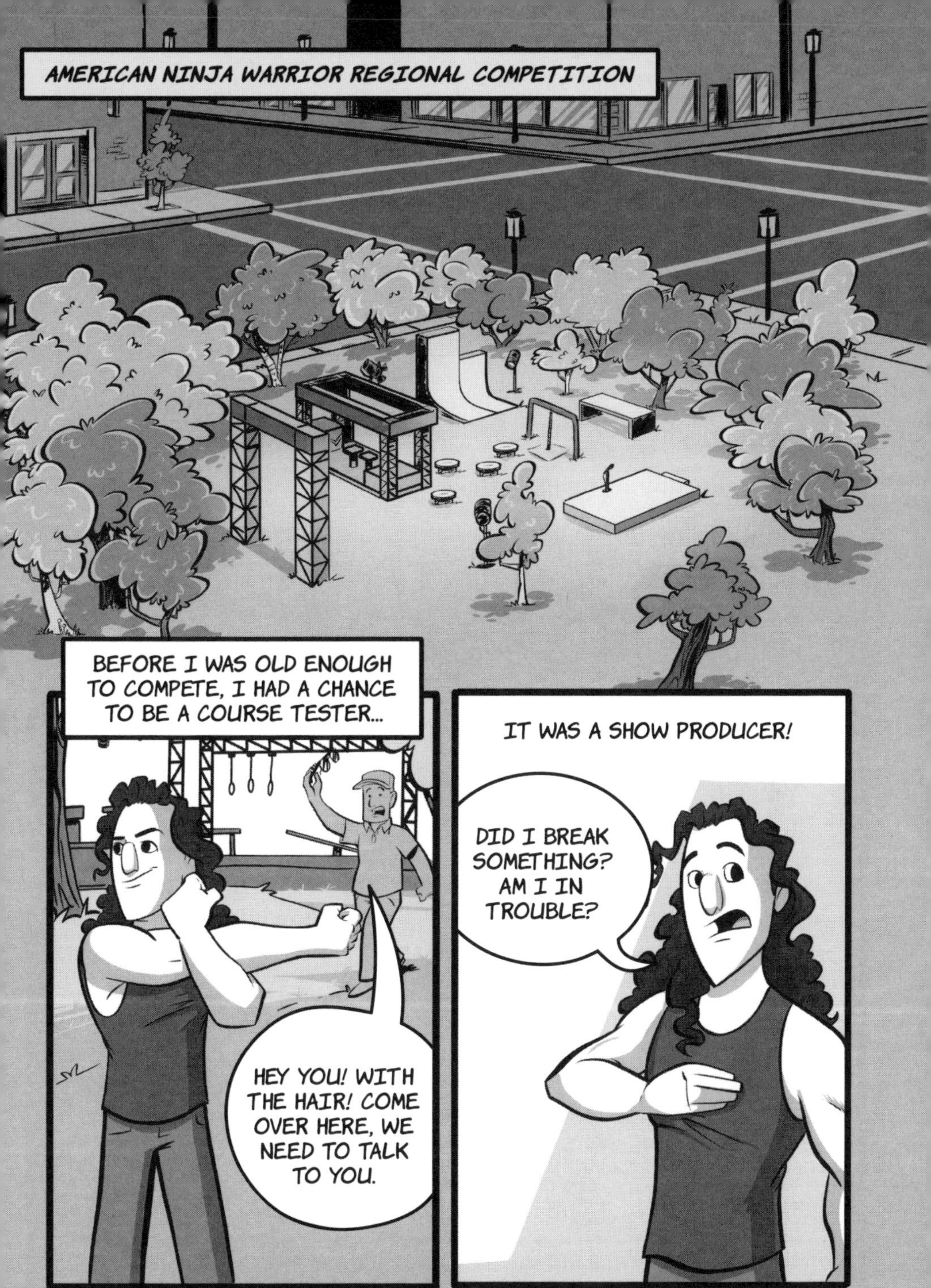
AMERICAN NINJA WARRIOR REGIONAL COMPETITION
BEFORE I WAS OLD ENOUGH TO COMPETE, I HAD A CHANCE TO BE A COURSE TESTER...
HEY YOU! WITH THE HAIR! COME OVER HERE, WE NEED TO TALK TO YOU.
IT WAS A SHOW PRODUCER!
DID I BREAK SOMETHING? AM I IN TROUBLE?

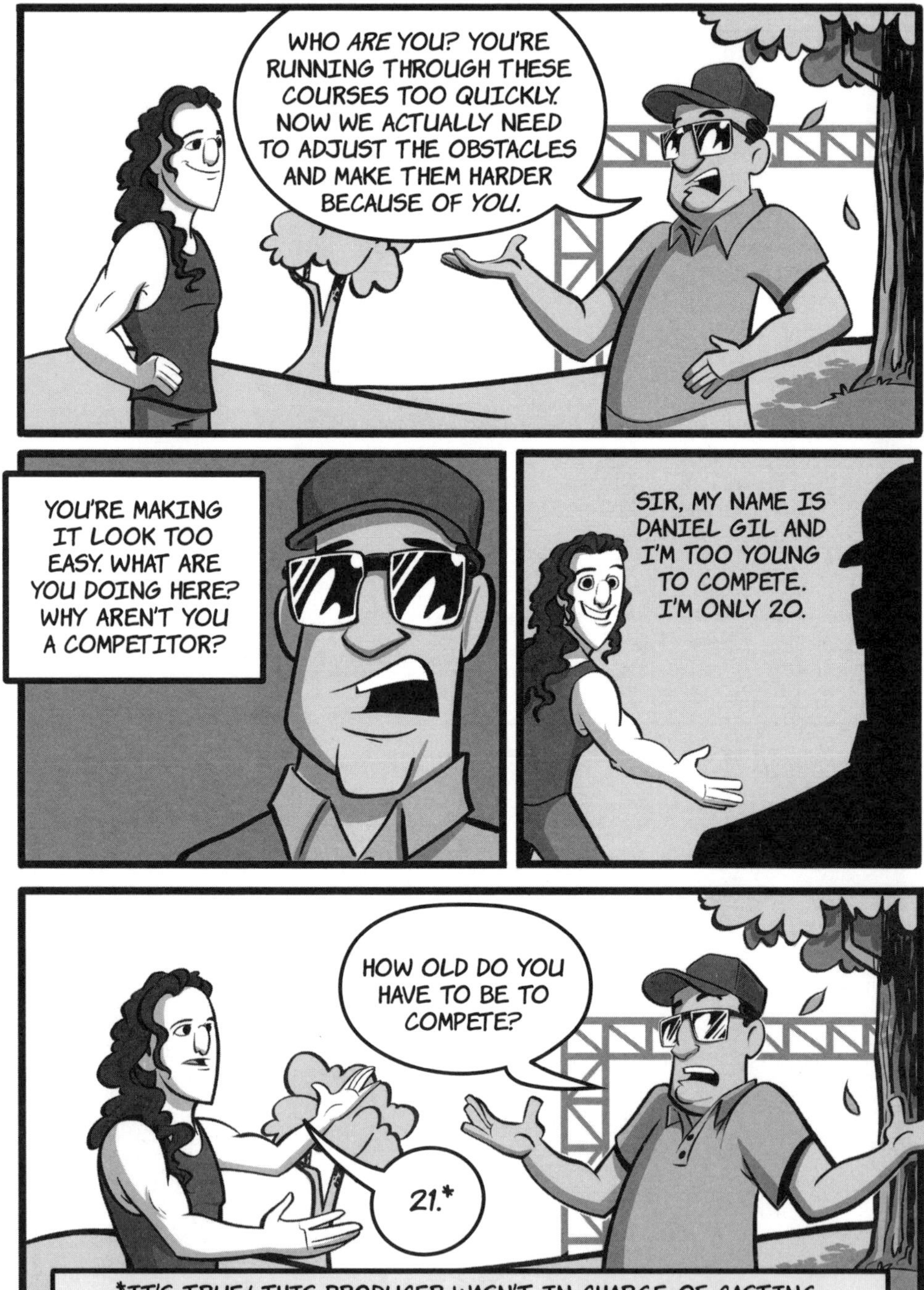
WHO *ARE YOU*? YOU'RE RUNNING THROUGH THESE COURSES TOO QUICKLY. NOW WE ACTUALLY NEED TO ADJUST THE OBSTACLES AND MAKE THEM HARDER BECAUSE OF *YOU*.
YOU'RE MAKING IT LOOK TOO EASY. WHAT ARE YOU DOING HERE? WHY AREN'T YOU A COMPETITOR?
SIR, MY NAME IS DANIEL GIL AND I'M TOO YOUNG TO COMPETE. I'M ONLY 20.
HOW OLD DO YOU HAVE TO BE TO COMPETE?
21.*
*IT'S TRUE! THIS PRODUCER WASN'T IN CHARGE OF CASTING, SO HE DIDN'T KNOW THE AGE. BUT NOW THE MINIMUM AGE IS 15!

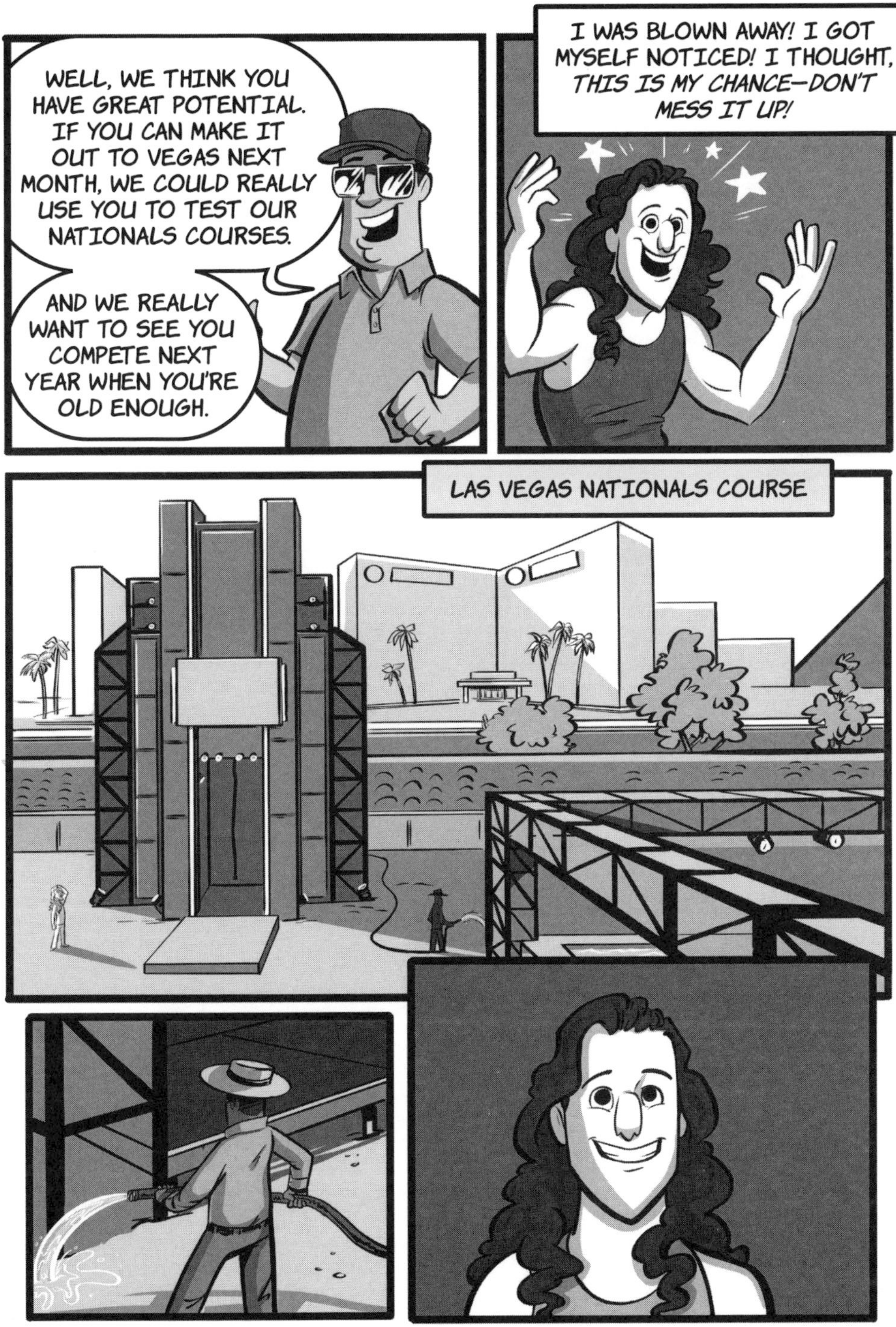
WELL, WE THINK YOU HAVE GREAT POTENTIAL. IF YOU CAN MAKE IT OUT TO VEGAS NEXT MONTH, WE COULD REALLY USE YOU TO TEST OUR NATIONALS COURSES.
AND WE REALLY WANT TO SEE YOU COMPETE NEXT YEAR WHEN YOU'RE OLD ENOUGH.
I WAS BLOWN AWAY! I GOT MYSELF NOTICED! I THOUGHT, *THIS IS MY CHANCE—DON'T MESS IT UP!*
LAS VEGAS NATIONALS COURSE

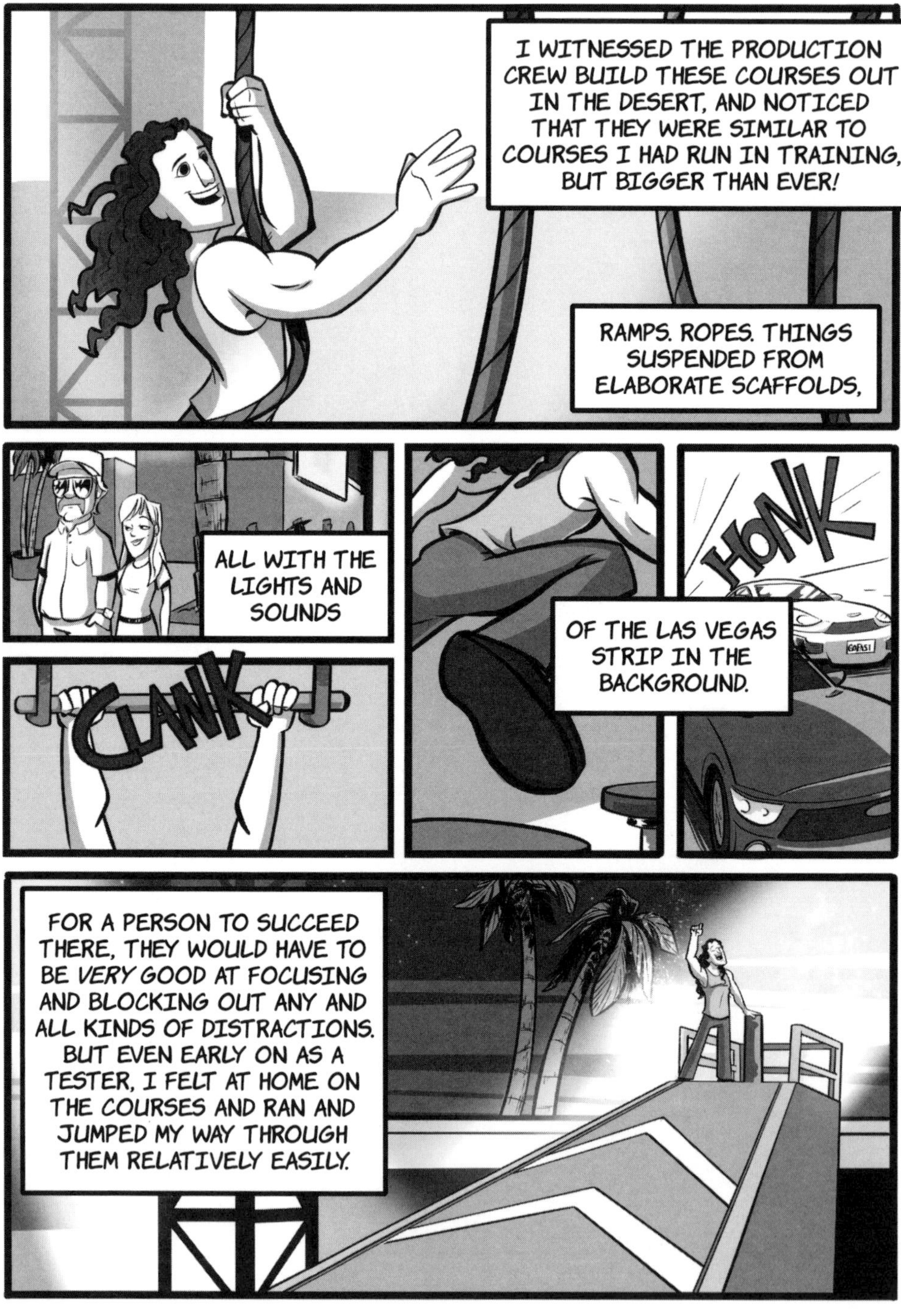

I WITNESSED THE PRODUCTION CREW BUILD THESE COURSES OUT IN THE DESERT, AND NOTICED THAT THEY WERE SIMILAR TO COURSES I HAD RUN IN TRAINING, BUT BIGGER THAN EVER!
RAMPS. ROPES. THINGS SUSPENDED FROM ELABORATE SCAFFOLDS,
ALL WITH THE LIGHTS AND SOUNDS
CLANK
OF THE LAS VEGAS STRIP IN THE BACKGROUND.
HONK
FOR A PERSON TO SUCCEED THERE, THEY WOULD HAVE TO BE *VERY* GOOD AT FOCUSING AND BLOCKING OUT ANY AND ALL KINDS OF DISTRACTIONS. BUT EVEN EARLY ON AS A TESTER, I FELT AT HOME ON THE COURSES AND RAN AND JUMPED MY WAY THROUGH THEM RELATIVELY EASILY.

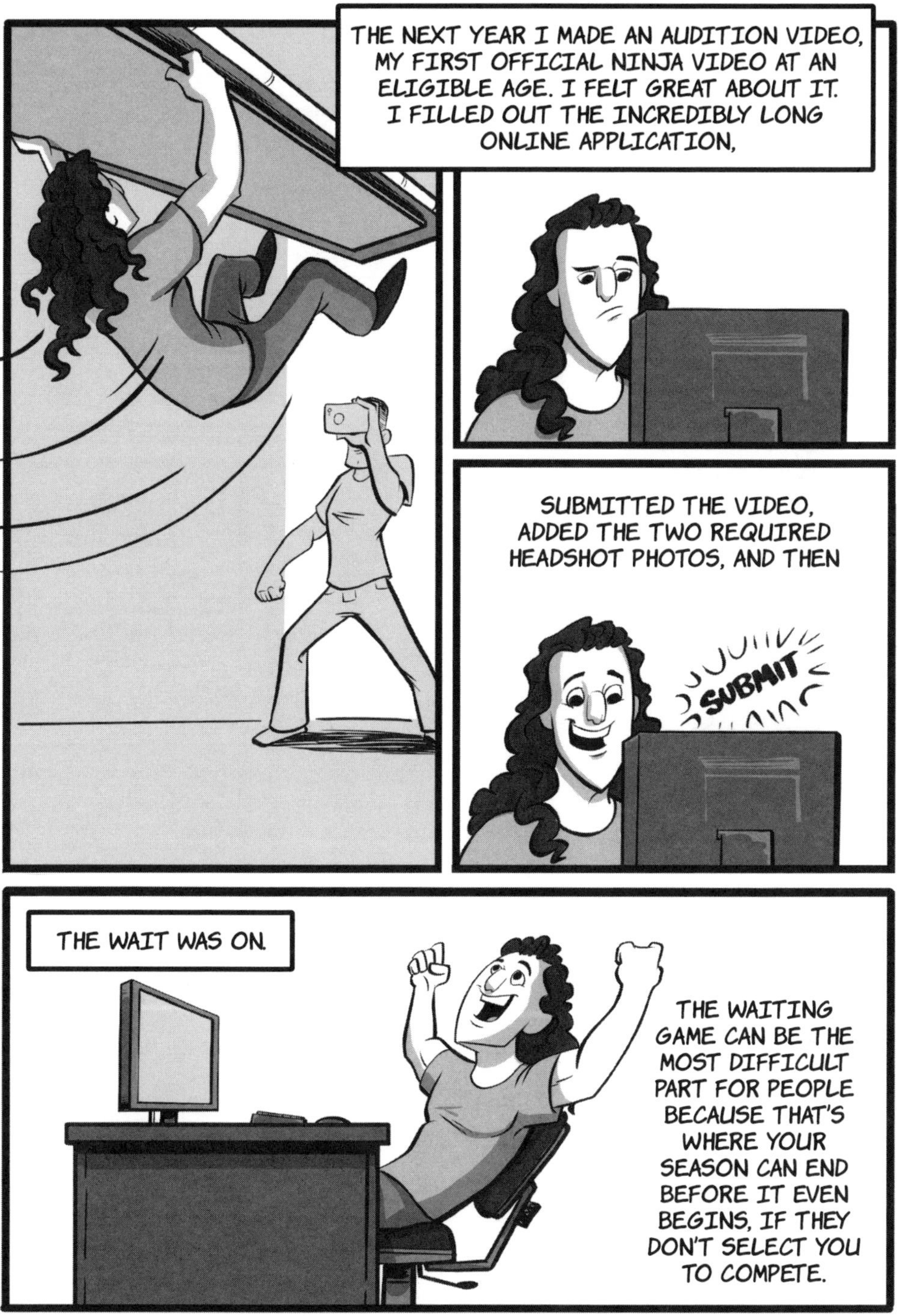
THE NEXT YEAR I MADE AN AUDITION VIDEO, MY FIRST OFFICIAL NINJA VIDEO AT AN ELIGIBLE AGE. I FELT GREAT ABOUT IT. I FILLED OUT THE INCREDIBLY LONG ONLINE APPLICATION,
SUBMITTED THE VIDEO, ADDED THE TWO REQUIRED HEADSHOT PHOTOS, AND THEN
SUBMIT
THE WAIT WAS ON.
THE WAITING GAME CAN BE THE MOST DIFFICULT PART FOR PEOPLE BECAUSE THAT'S WHERE YOUR SEASON CAN END BEFORE IT EVEN BEGINS, IF THEY DON'T SELECT YOU TO COMPETE.

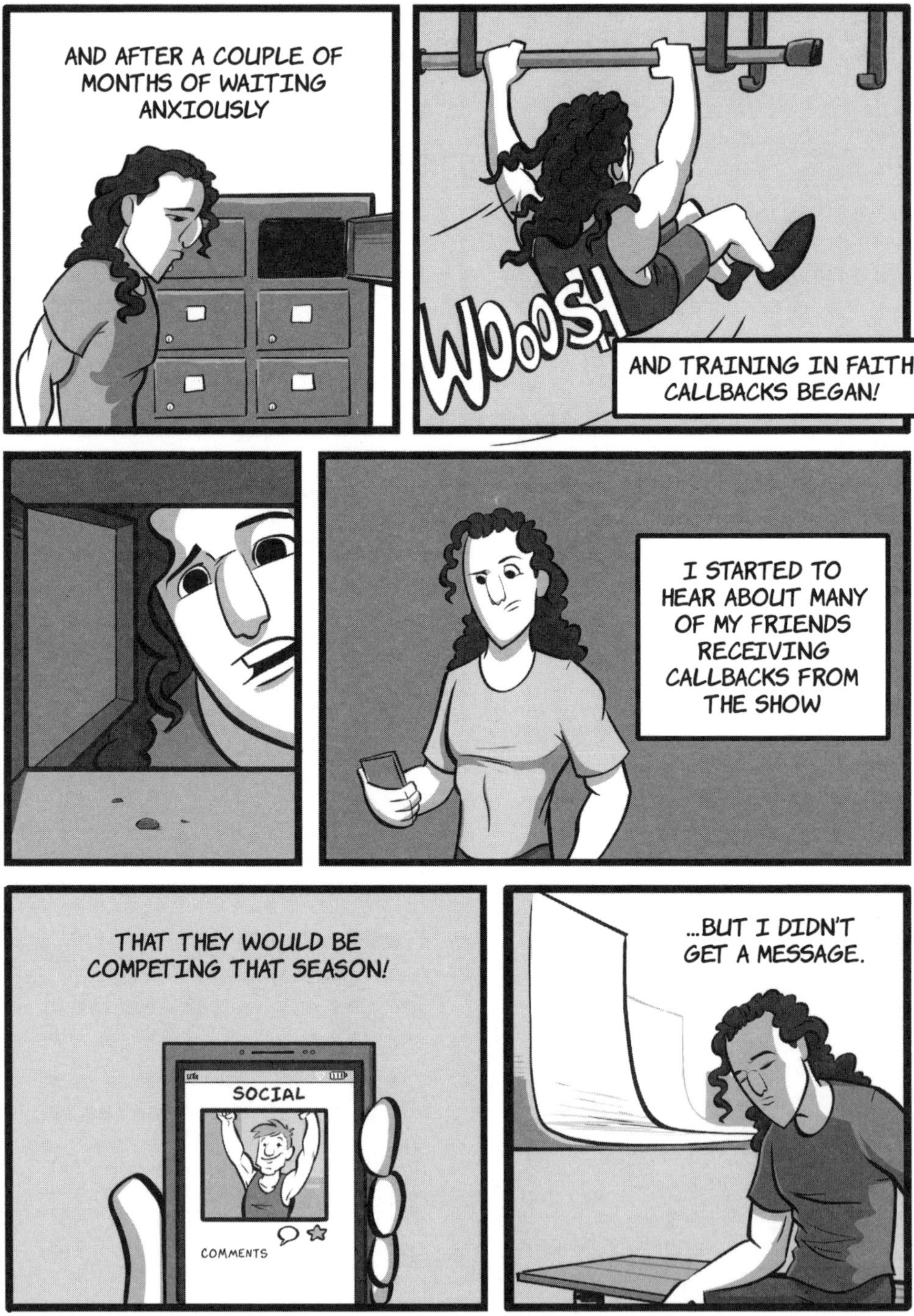

AND AFTER A COUPLE OF MONTHS OF WAITING ANXIOUSLY
WOOOSH
AND TRAINING IN FAITH, CALLBACKS BEGAN!
I STARTED TO HEAR ABOUT MANY OF MY FRIENDS RECEIVING CALLBACKS FROM THE SHOW
THAT THEY WOULD BE COMPETING THAT SEASON!
SOCIAL
COMMENTS
...BUT I DIDN'T GET A MESSAGE.

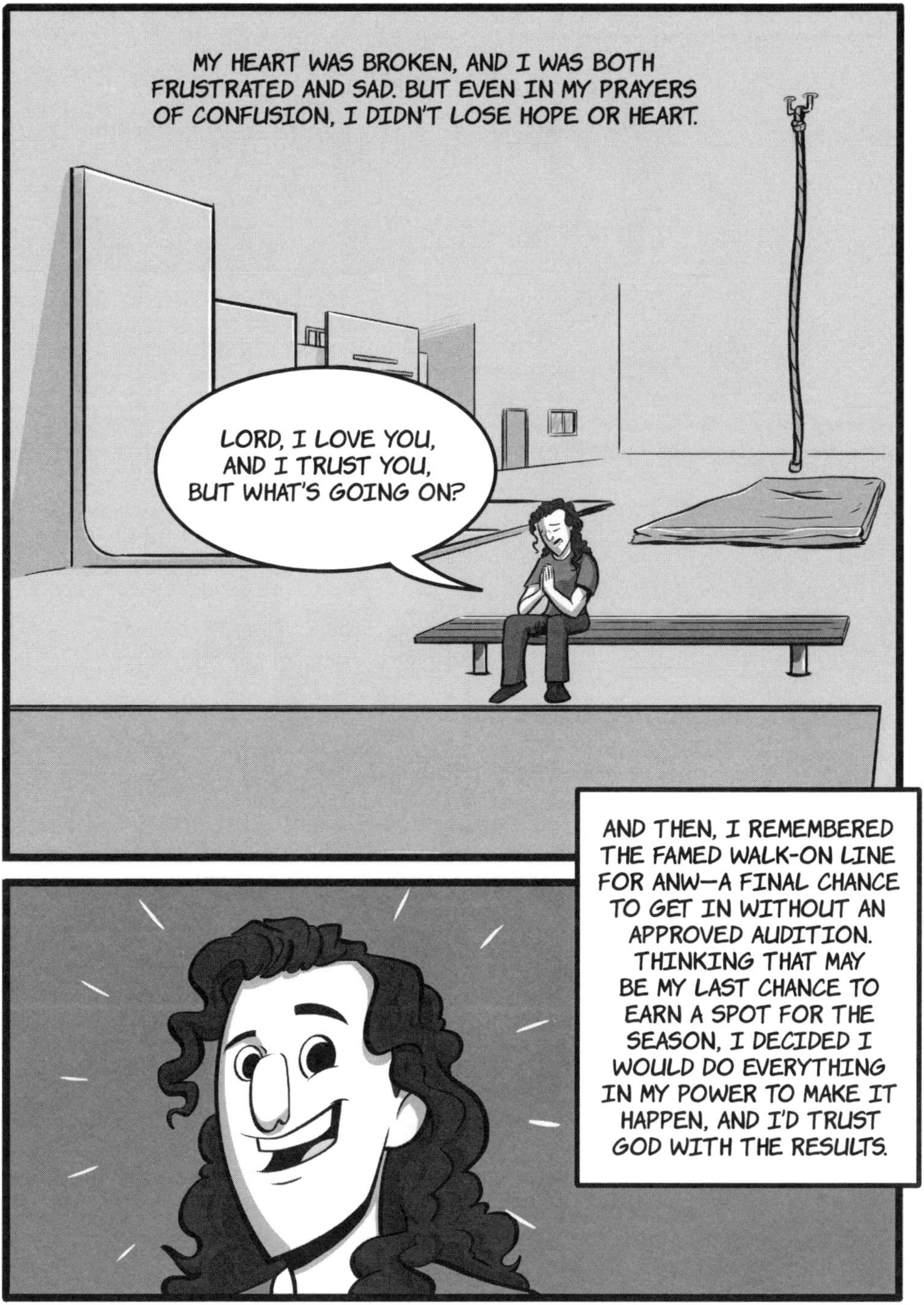
MY HEART WAS BROKEN, AND I WAS BOTH FRUSTRATED AND SAD. BUT EVEN IN MY PRAYERS OF CONFUSION, I DIDN'T LOSE HOPE OR HEART.
LORD, I LOVE YOU, AND I TRUST YOU, BUT WHAT'S GOING ON?
AND THEN, I REMEMBERED THE FAMED WALK-ON LINE FOR ANW—A FINAL CHANCE TO GET IN WITHOUT AN APPROVED AUDITION. THINKING THAT MAY BE MY LAST CHANCE TO EARN A SPOT FOR THE SEASON, I DECIDED I WOULD DO EVERYTHING IN MY POWER TO MAKE IT HAPPEN, AND I'D TRUST GOD WITH THE RESULTS.

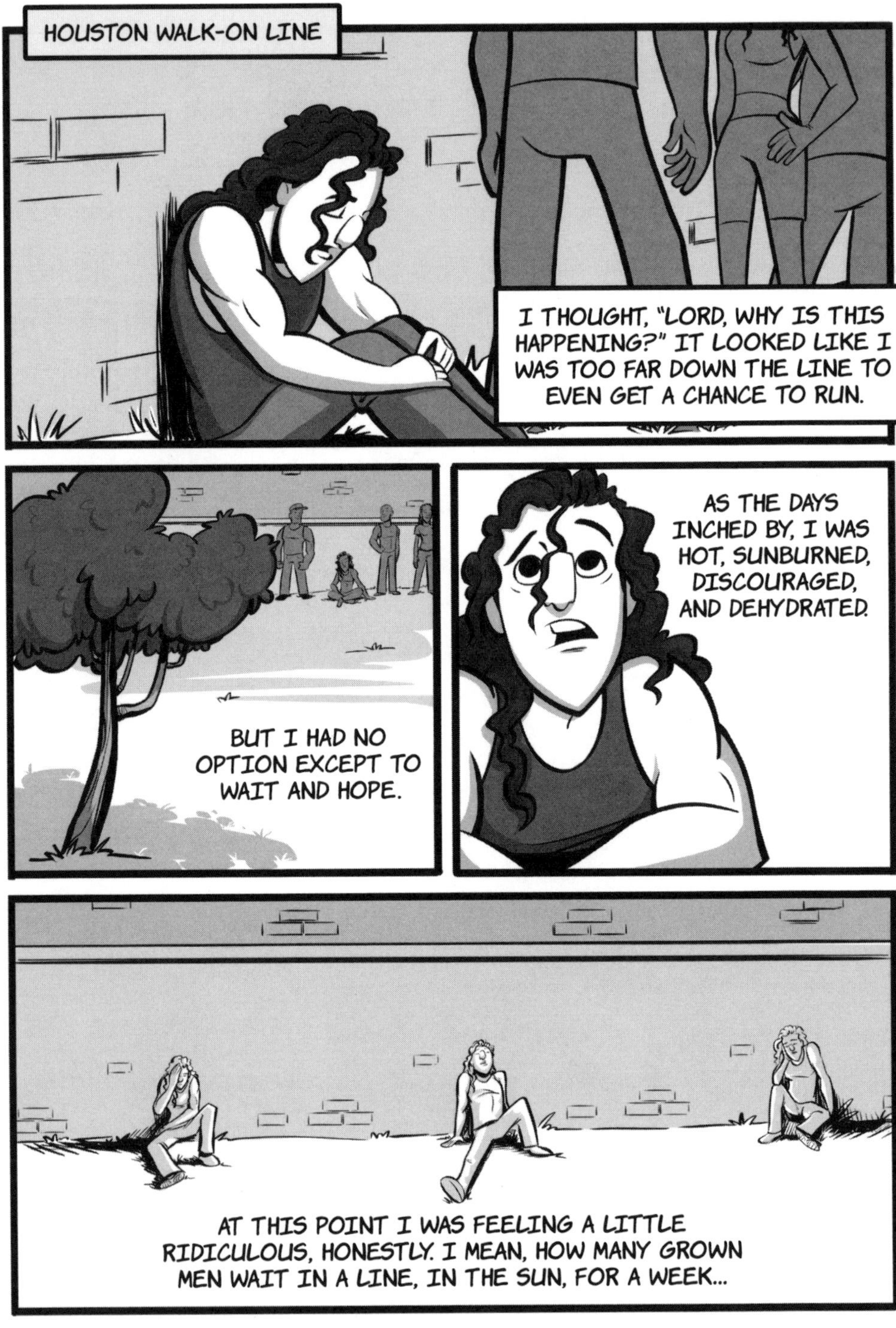
HOUSTON WALK-ON LINE
I THOUGHT, "LORD, WHY IS THIS HAPPENING?" IT LOOKED LIKE I WAS TOO FAR DOWN THE LINE TO EVEN GET A CHANCE TO RUN.
BUT I HAD NO OPTION EXCEPT TO WAIT AND HOPE.
AS THE DAYS INCHED BY, I WAS HOT, SUNBURNED, DISCOURAGED, AND DEHYDRATED.
AT THIS POINT I WAS FEELING A LITTLE RIDICULOUS, HONESTLY. I MEAN, HOW MANY GROWN MEN WAIT IN A LINE, IN THE SUN, FOR A WEEK...

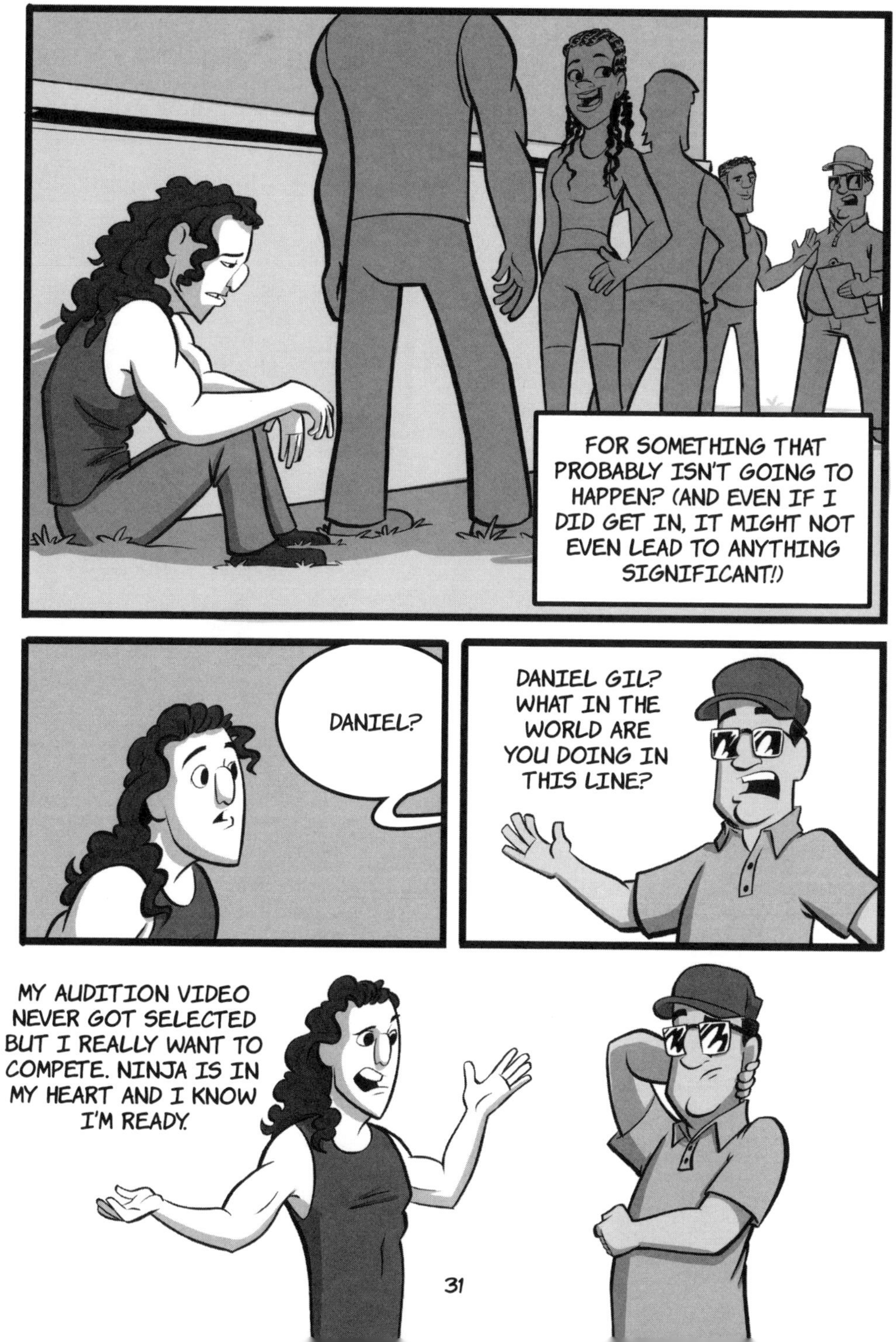

FOR SOMETHING THAT PROBABLY ISN'T GOING TO HAPPEN? (AND EVEN IF I DID GET IN, IT MIGHT NOT EVEN LEAD TO ANYTHING SIGNIFICANT!)
DANIEL?
DANIEL GIL? WHAT IN THE WORLD ARE YOU DOING IN THIS LINE?
MY AUDITION VIDEO NEVER GOT SELECTED BUT I REALLY WANT TO COMPETE. NINJA IS IN MY HEART AND I KNOW I'M READY.

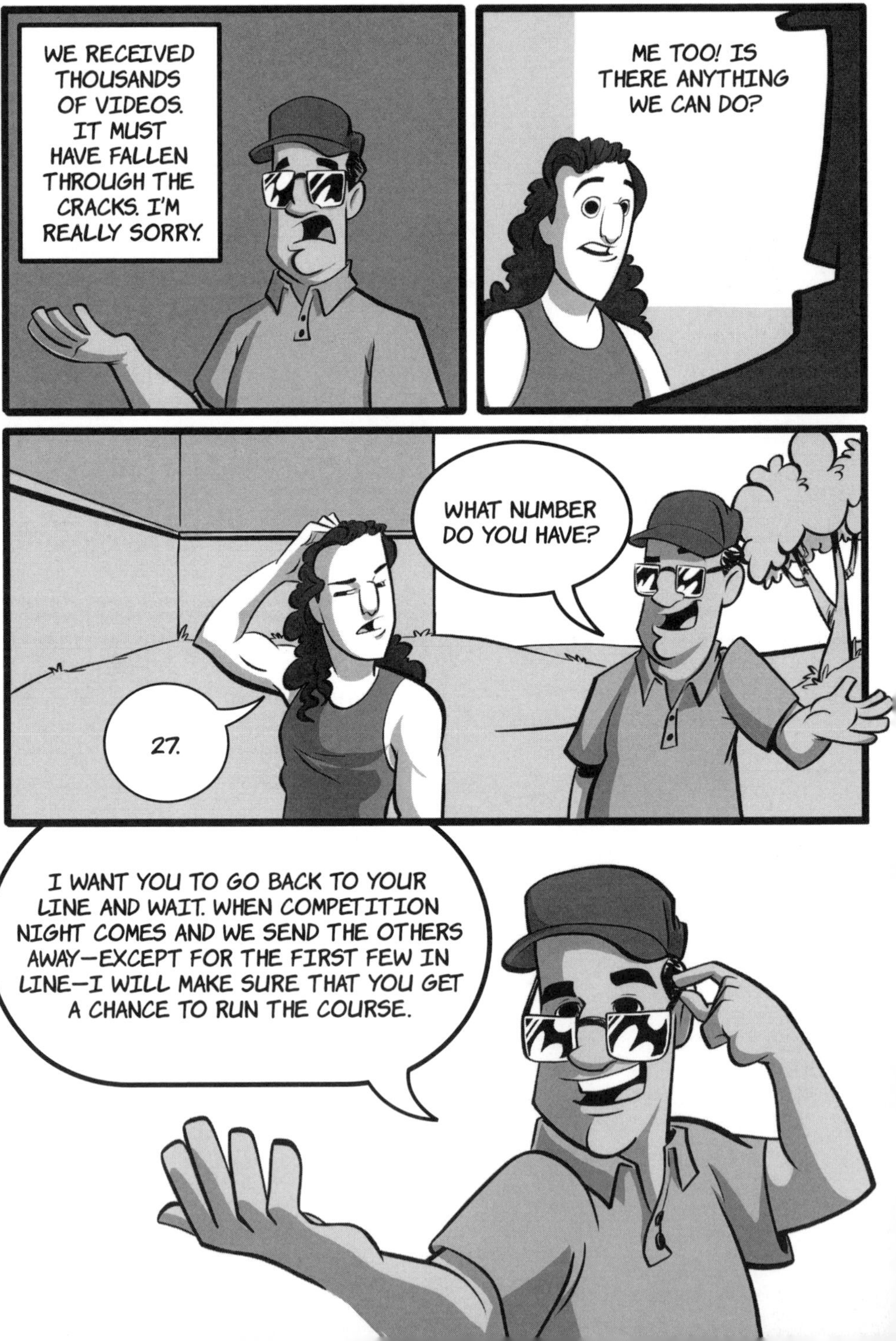
WE RECEIVED THOUSANDS OF VIDEOS. IT MUST HAVE FALLEN THROUGH THE CRACKS. I'M REALLY SORRY.
ME TOO! IS THERE ANYTHING WE CAN DO?
WHAT NUMBER DO YOU HAVE?
27.
I WANT YOU TO GO BACK TO YOUR LINE AND WAIT. WHEN COMPETITION NIGHT COMES AND WE SEND THE OTHERS AWAY—EXCEPT FOR THE FIRST FEW IN LINE—I WILL MAKE SURE THAT YOU GET A CHANCE TO RUN THE COURSE.

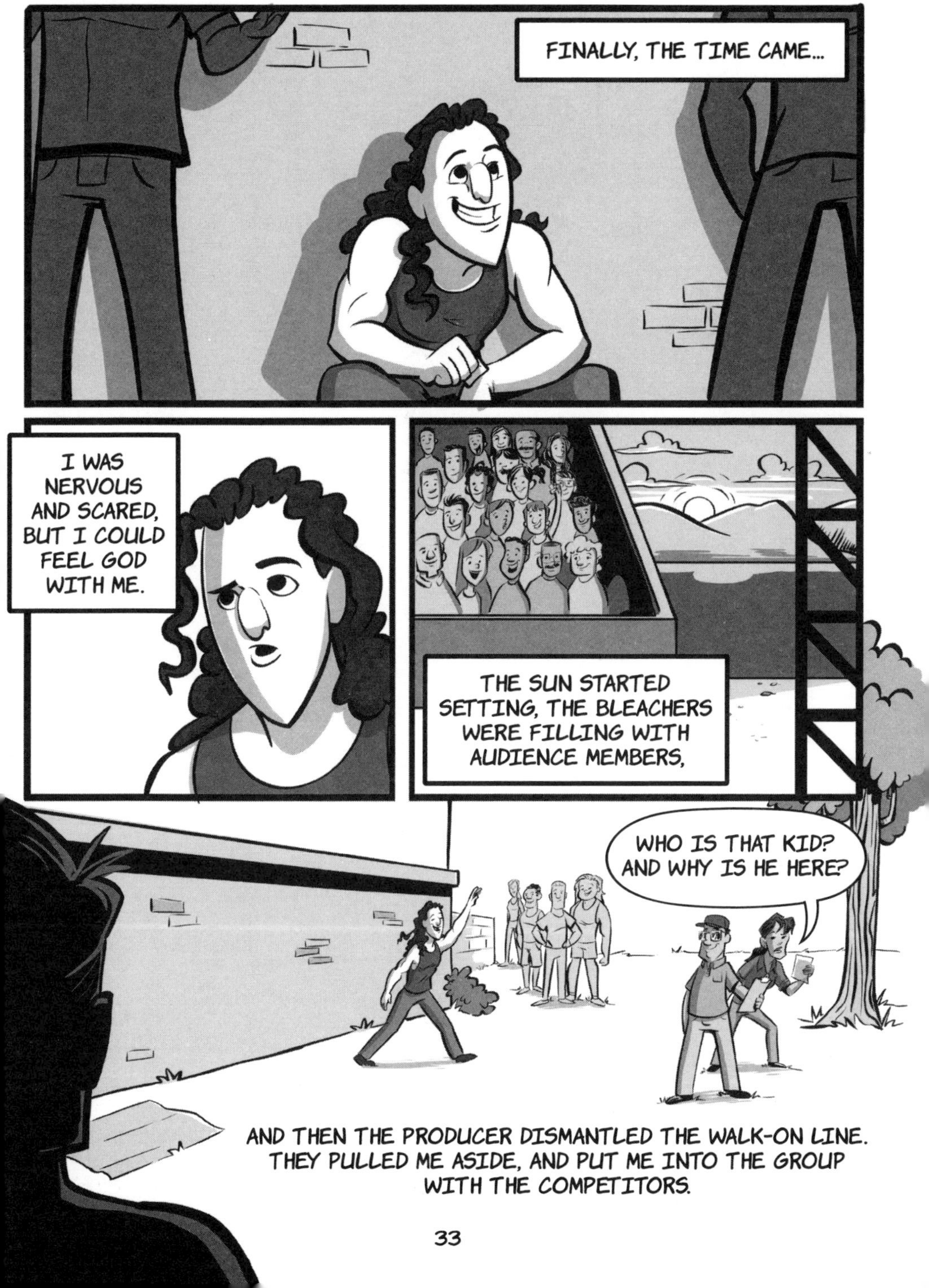

FINALLY, THE TIME CAME...
I WAS NERVOUS AND SCARED, BUT I COULD FEEL GOD WITH ME.
THE SUN STARTED SETTING, THE BLEACHERS WERE FILLING WITH AUDIENCE MEMBERS,
WHO IS THAT KID? AND WHY IS HE HERE?
AND THEN THE PRODUCER DISMANTLED THE WALK-ON LINE. THEY PULLED ME ASIDE, AND PUT ME INTO THE GROUP WITH THE COMPETITORS.

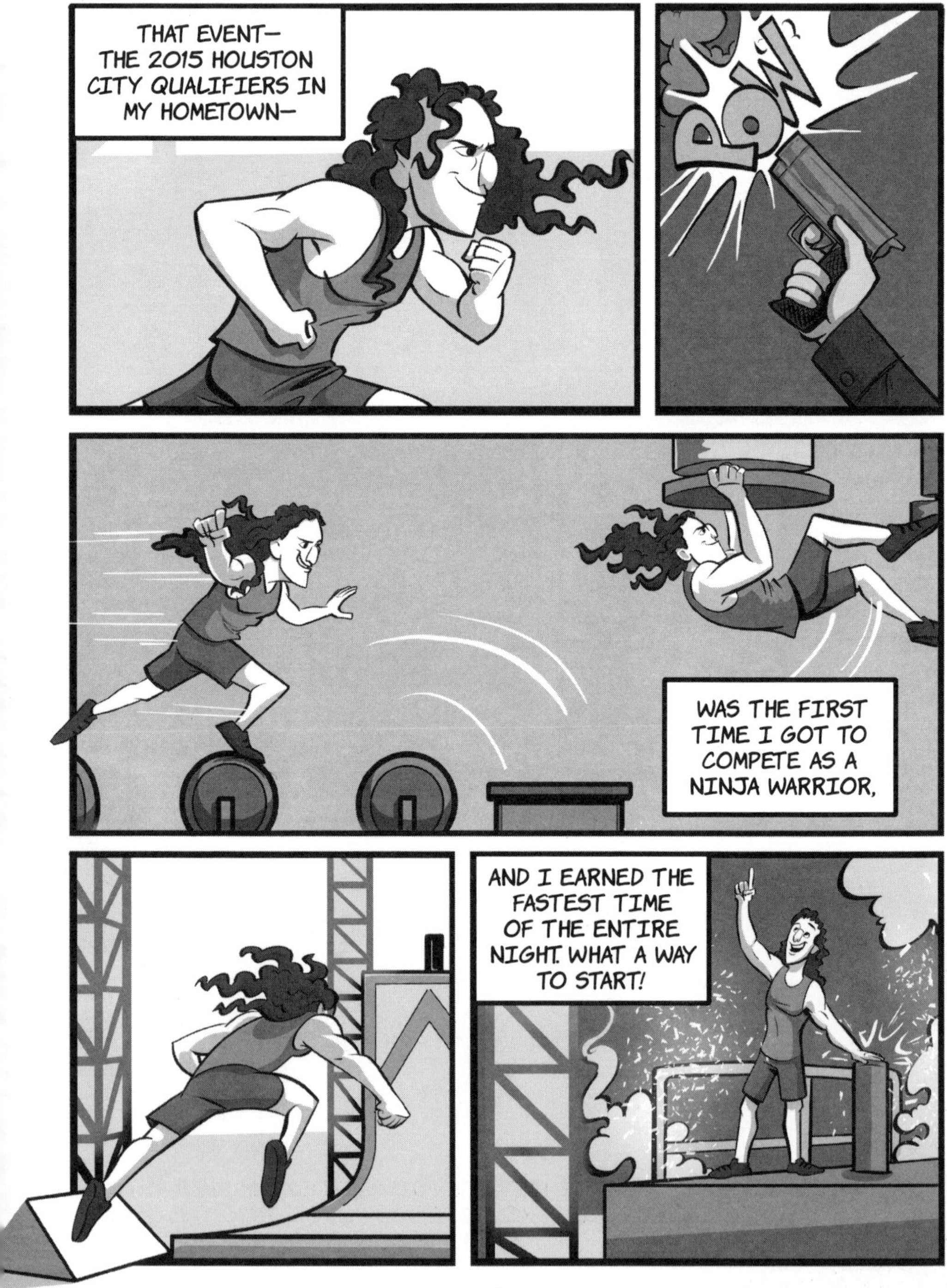
THAT EVENT— THE 2015 HOUSTON CITY QUALIFIERS IN MY HOMETOWN—
POW
WAS THE FIRST TIME I GOT TO COMPETE AS A NINJA WARRIOR,
AND I EARNED THE FASTEST TIME OF THE ENTIRE NIGHT. WHAT A WAY TO START!

LIFE VERSES

JESUS REPLIED, "THE MOST IMPORTANT COMMANDMENT IS THIS: 'LISTEN, O ISRAEL! THE LORD OUR GOD IS THE ONE AND ONLY LORD. AND YOU MUST LOVE THE LORD YOUR GOD WITH ALL YOUR HEART, ALL YOUR SOUL, ALL YOUR MIND, AND ALL YOUR STRENGTH.' THE SECOND IS EQUALLY IMPORTANT: 'LOVE YOUR NEIGHBOR AS YOURSELF.' NO OTHER COMMANDMENT IS GREATER THAN THESE." (MARK 12:29-31)

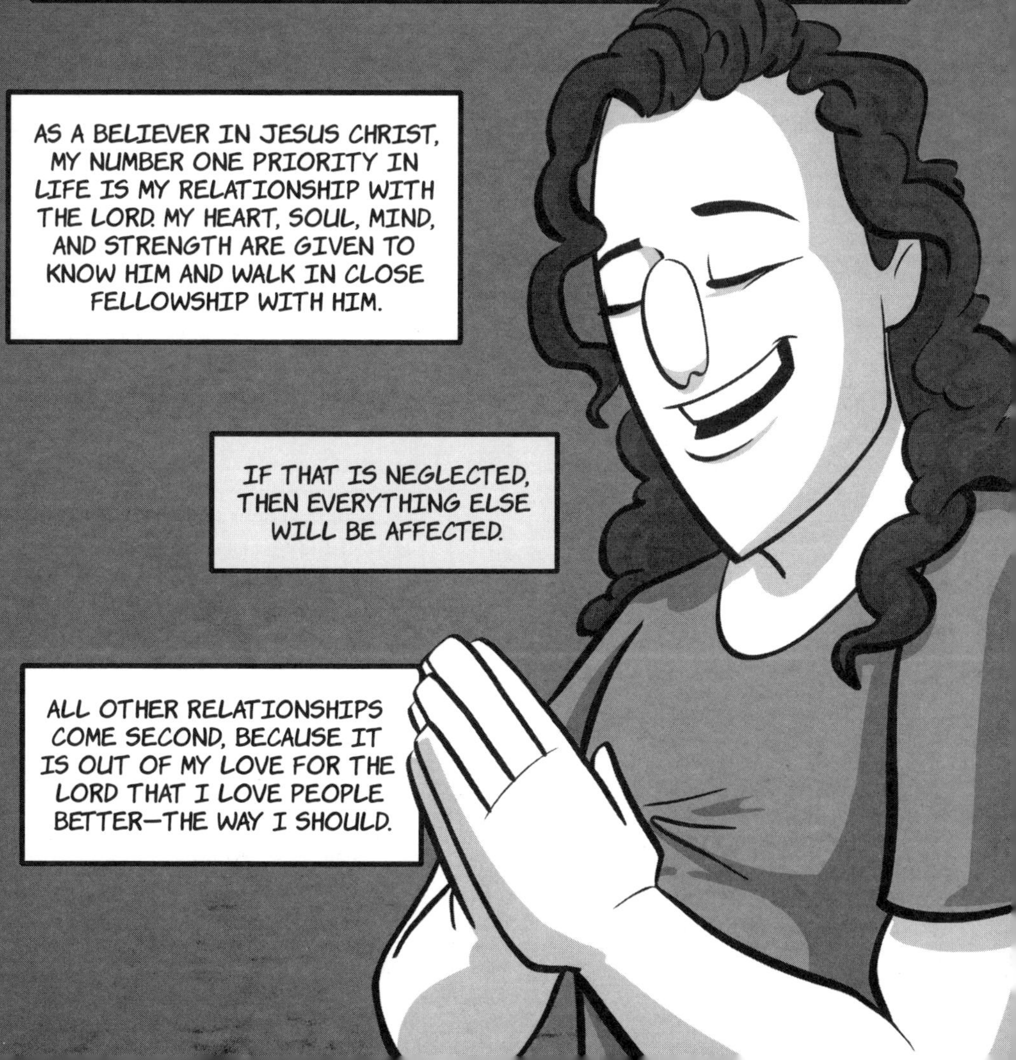
AS A BELIEVER IN JESUS CHRIST, MY NUMBER ONE PRIORITY IN LIFE IS MY RELATIONSHIP WITH THE LORD. MY HEART, SOUL, MIND, AND STRENGTH ARE GIVEN TO KNOW HIM AND WALK IN CLOSE FELLOWSHIP WITH HIM.
IF THAT IS NEGLECTED, THEN EVERYTHING ELSE WILL BE AFFECTED.
ALL OTHER RELATIONSHIPS COME SECOND, BECAUSE IT IS OUT OF MY LOVE FOR THE LORD THAT I LOVE PEOPLE BETTER—THE WAY I SHOULD.

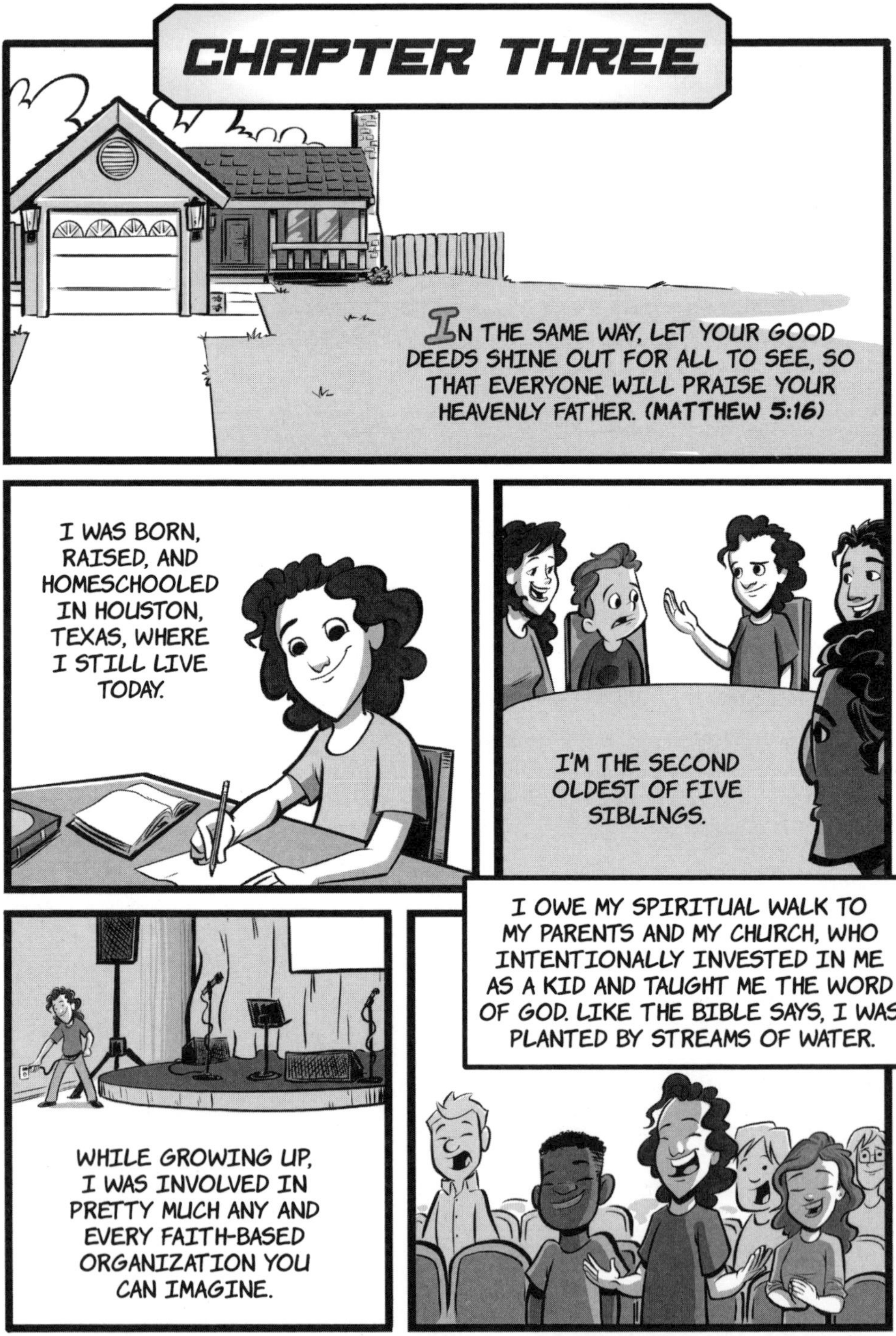
CHAPTER THREE
IN THE SAME WAY, LET YOUR GOOD DEEDS SHINE OUT FOR ALL TO SEE, SO THAT EVERYONE WILL PRAISE YOUR HEAVENLY FATHER. (MATTHEW 5:16)
I WAS BORN, RAISED, AND HOMESCHOOLED IN HOUSTON, TEXAS, WHERE I STILL LIVE TODAY.
I'M THE SECOND OLDEST OF FIVE SIBLINGS.
WHILE GROWING UP, I WAS INVOLVED IN PRETTY MUCH ANY AND EVERY FAITH-BASED ORGANIZATION YOU CAN IMAGINE.
I OWE MY SPIRITUAL WALK TO MY PARENTS AND MY CHURCH, WHO INTENTIONALLY INVESTED IN ME AS A KID AND TAUGHT ME THE WORD OF GOD. LIKE THE BIBLE SAYS, I WAS PLANTED BY STREAMS OF WATER.

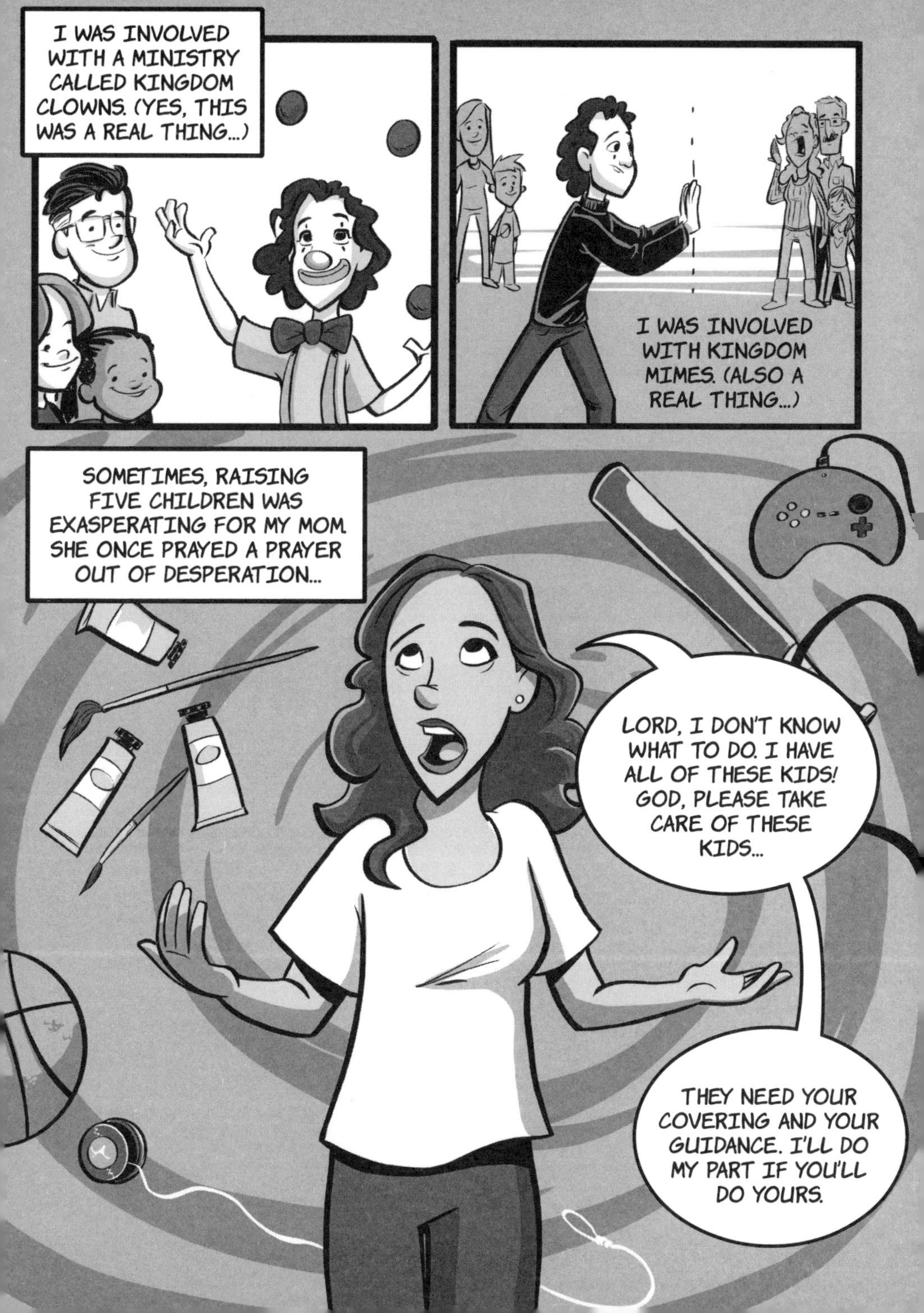

I WAS INVOLVED WITH A MINISTRY CALLED KINGDOM CLOWNS. (YES, THIS WAS A REAL THING...)
I WAS INVOLVED WITH KINGDOM MIMES. (ALSO A REAL THING...)
SOMETIMES, RAISING FIVE CHILDREN WAS EXASPERATING FOR MY MOM. SHE ONCE PRAYED A PRAYER OUT OF DESPERATION...
LORD, I DON'T KNOW WHAT TO DO. I HAVE ALL OF THESE KIDS! GOD, PLEASE TAKE CARE OF THESE KIDS...
THEY NEED YOUR COVERING AND YOUR GUIDANCE. I'LL DO MY PART IF YOU'LL DO YOURS.

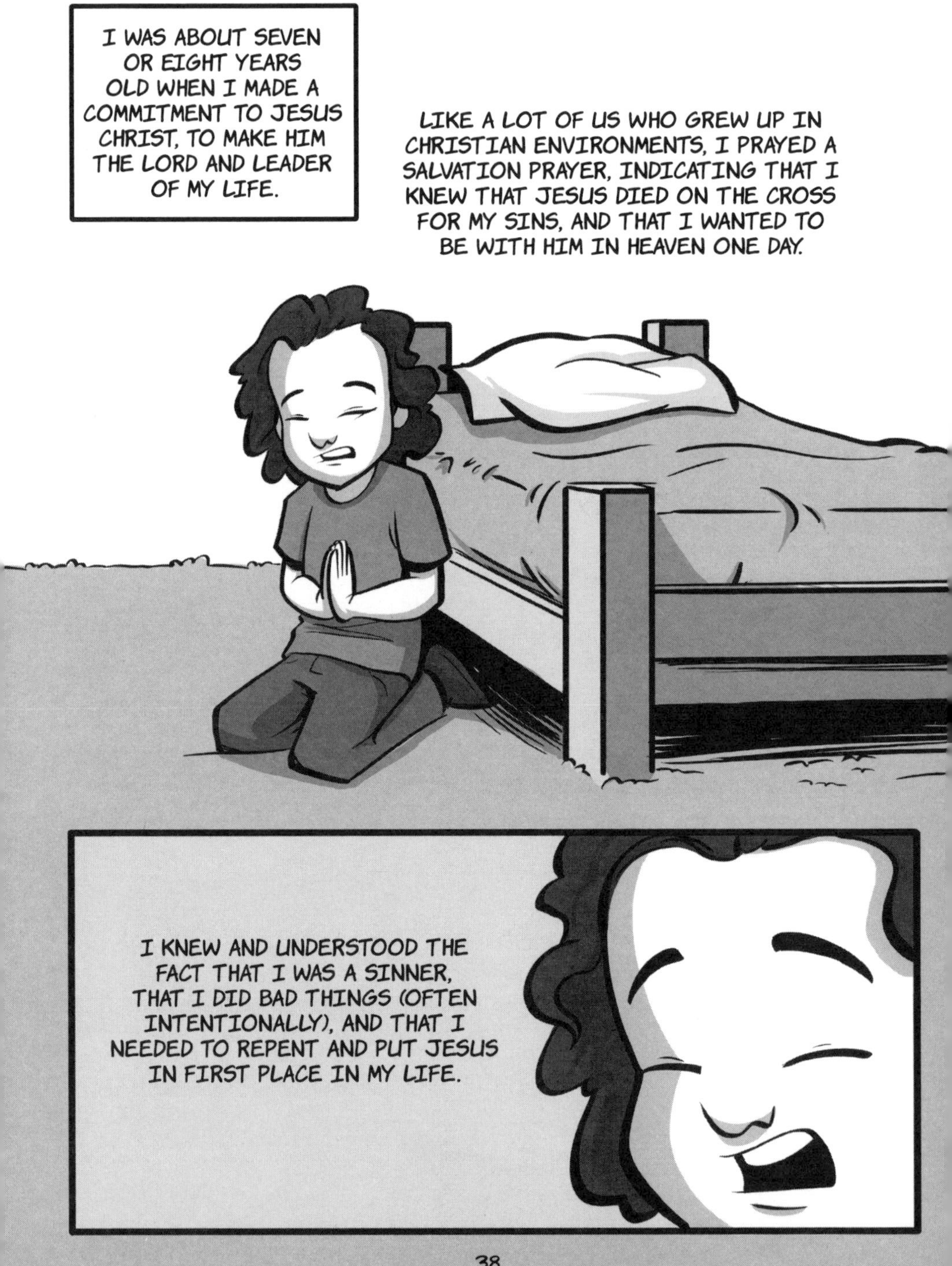
I WAS ABOUT SEVEN OR EIGHT YEARS OLD WHEN I MADE A COMMITMENT TO JESUS CHRIST, TO MAKE HIM THE LORD AND LEADER OF MY LIFE.
LIKE A LOT OF US WHO GREW UP IN CHRISTIAN ENVIRONMENTS, I PRAYED A SALVATION PRAYER, INDICATING THAT I KNEW THAT JESUS DIED ON THE CROSS FOR MY SINS, AND THAT I WANTED TO BE WITH HIM IN HEAVEN ONE DAY.
I KNEW AND UNDERSTOOD THE FACT THAT I WAS A SINNER, THAT I DID BAD THINGS (OFTEN INTENTIONALLY), AND THAT I NEEDED TO REPENT AND PUT JESUS IN FIRST PLACE IN MY LIFE.

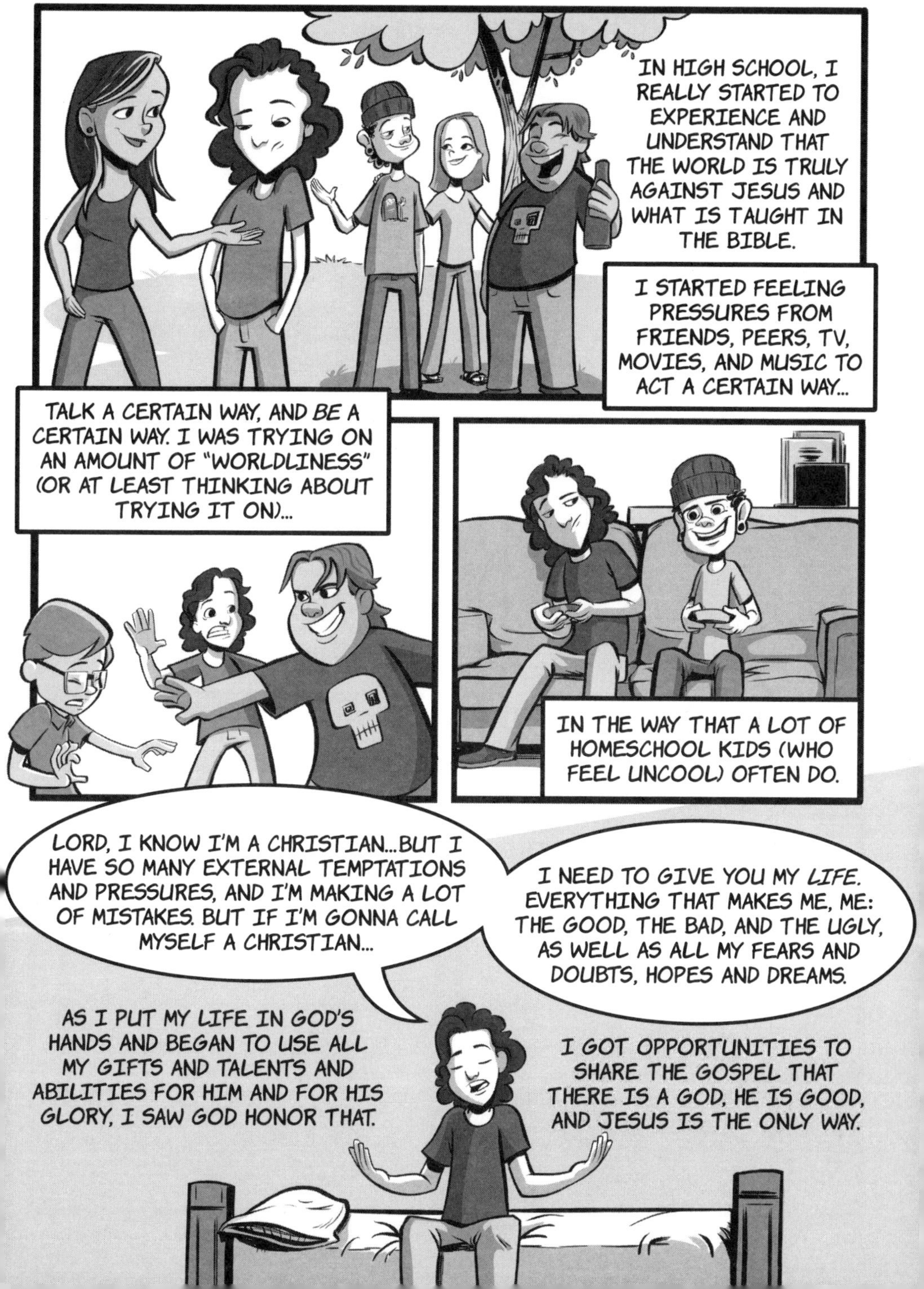
IN HIGH SCHOOL, I REALLY STARTED TO EXPERIENCE AND UNDERSTAND THAT THE WORLD IS TRULY AGAINST JESUS AND WHAT IS TAUGHT IN THE BIBLE.
I STARTED FEELING PRESSURES FROM FRIENDS, PEERS, TV, MOVIES, AND MUSIC TO ACT A CERTAIN WAY...
TALK A CERTAIN WAY, AND *BE* A CERTAIN WAY. I WAS TRYING ON AN AMOUNT OF "WORLDLINESS" (OR AT LEAST THINKING ABOUT TRYING IT ON)...
IN THE WAY THAT A LOT OF HOMESCHOOL KIDS (WHO FEEL UNCOOL) OFTEN DO.
LORD, I KNOW I'M A CHRISTIAN...BUT I HAVE SO MANY EXTERNAL TEMPTATIONS AND PRESSURES, AND I'M MAKING A LOT OF MISTAKES. BUT IF I'M GONNA CALL MYSELF A CHRISTIAN...
I NEED TO GIVE YOU MY *LIFE*. EVERYTHING THAT MAKES ME, ME: THE GOOD, THE BAD, AND THE UGLY, AS WELL AS ALL MY FEARS AND DOUBTS, HOPES AND DREAMS.
AS I PUT MY LIFE IN GOD'S HANDS AND BEGAN TO USE ALL MY GIFTS AND TALENTS AND ABILITIES FOR HIM AND FOR HIS GLORY, I SAW GOD HONOR THAT.
I GOT OPPORTUNITIES TO SHARE THE GOSPEL THAT THERE IS A GOD, HE IS GOOD, AND JESUS IS THE ONLY WAY.

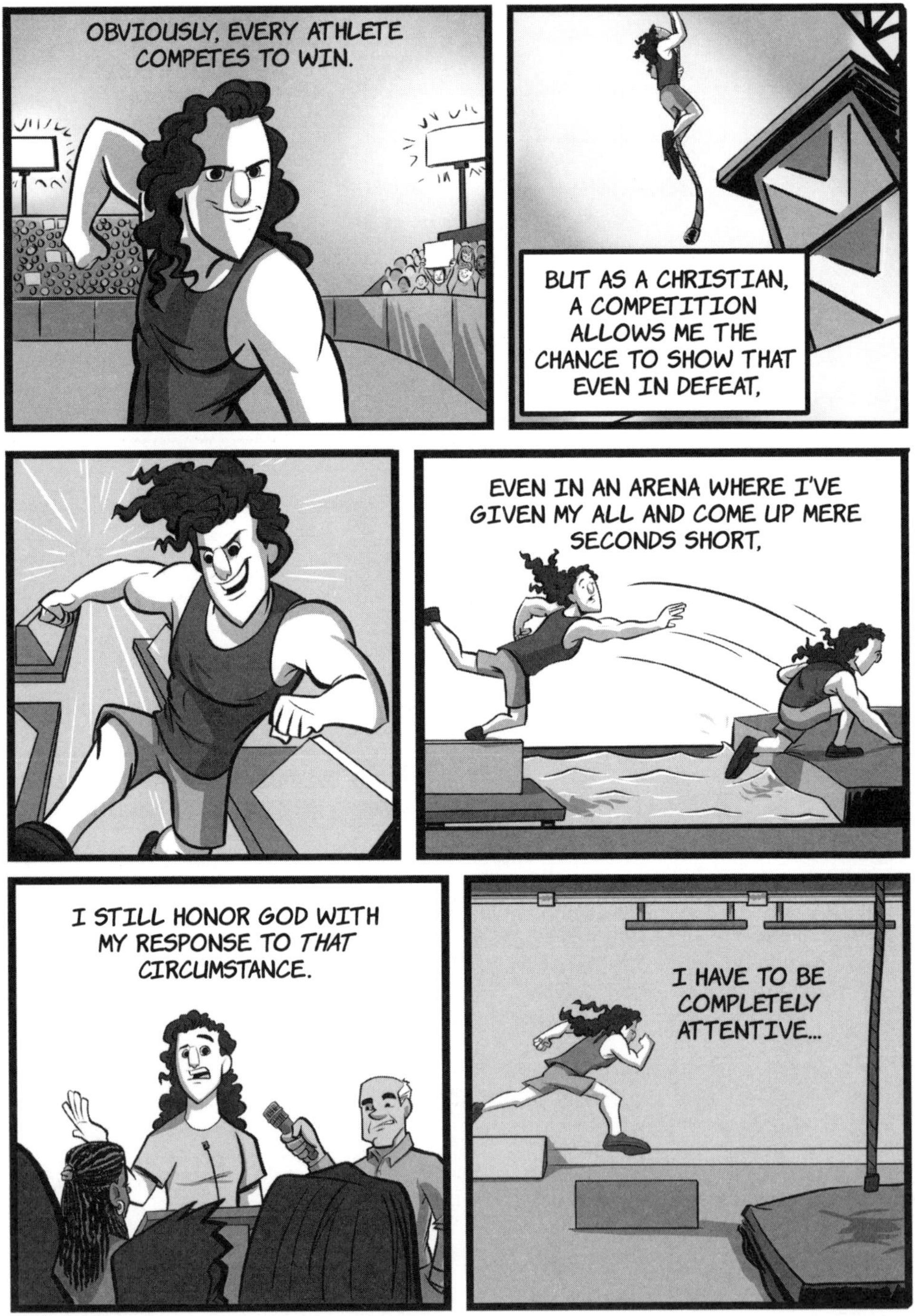
OBVIOUSLY, EVERY ATHLETE COMPETES TO WIN.
BUT AS A CHRISTIAN, A COMPETITION ALLOWS ME THE CHANCE TO SHOW THAT EVEN IN DEFEAT,
EVEN IN AN ARENA WHERE I'VE GIVEN MY ALL AND COME UP MERE SECONDS SHORT,
I STILL HONOR GOD WITH MY RESPONSE TO *THAT* CIRCUMSTANCE.
I HAVE TO BE COMPLETELY ATTENTIVE...

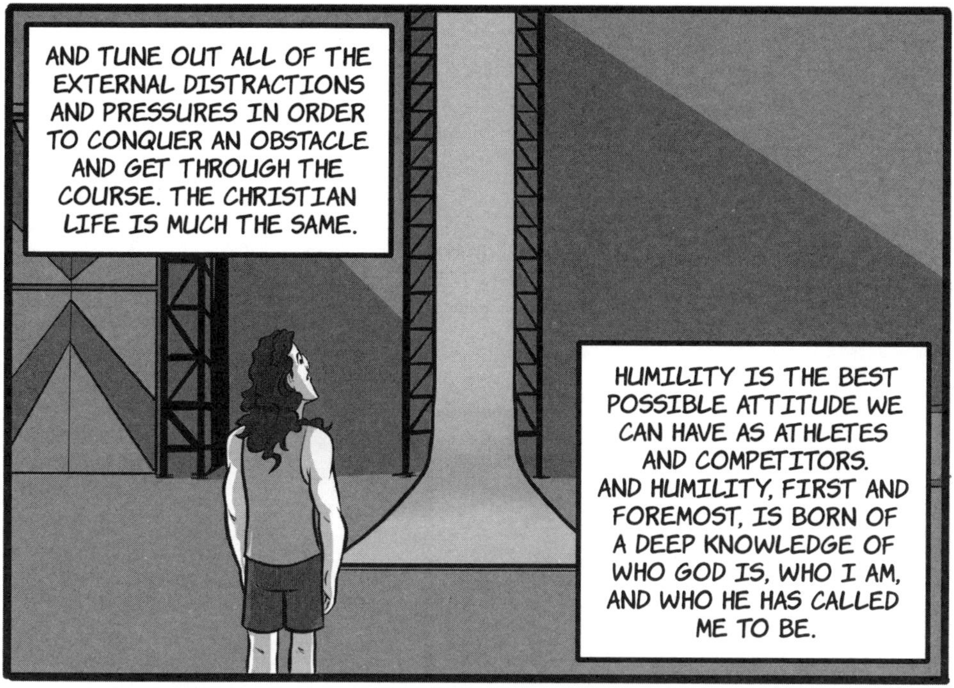
AND TUNE OUT ALL OF THE EXTERNAL DISTRACTIONS AND PRESSURES IN ORDER TO CONQUER AN OBSTACLE AND GET THROUGH THE COURSE. THE CHRISTIAN LIFE IS MUCH THE SAME.
HUMILITY IS THE BEST POSSIBLE ATTITUDE WE CAN HAVE AS ATHLETES AND COMPETITORS. AND HUMILITY, FIRST AND FOREMOST, IS BORN OF A DEEP KNOWLEDGE OF WHO GOD IS, WHO I AM, AND WHO HE HAS CALLED ME TO BE.

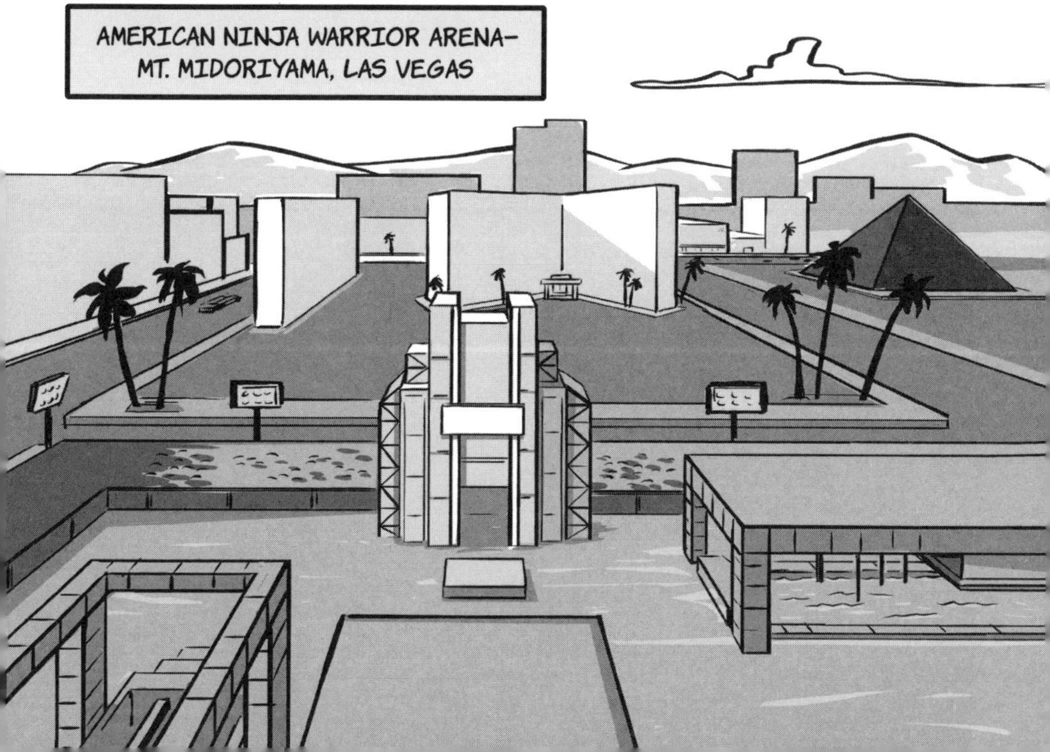
AMERICAN NINJA WARRIOR ARENA–
MT. MIDORIYAMA, LAS VEGAS

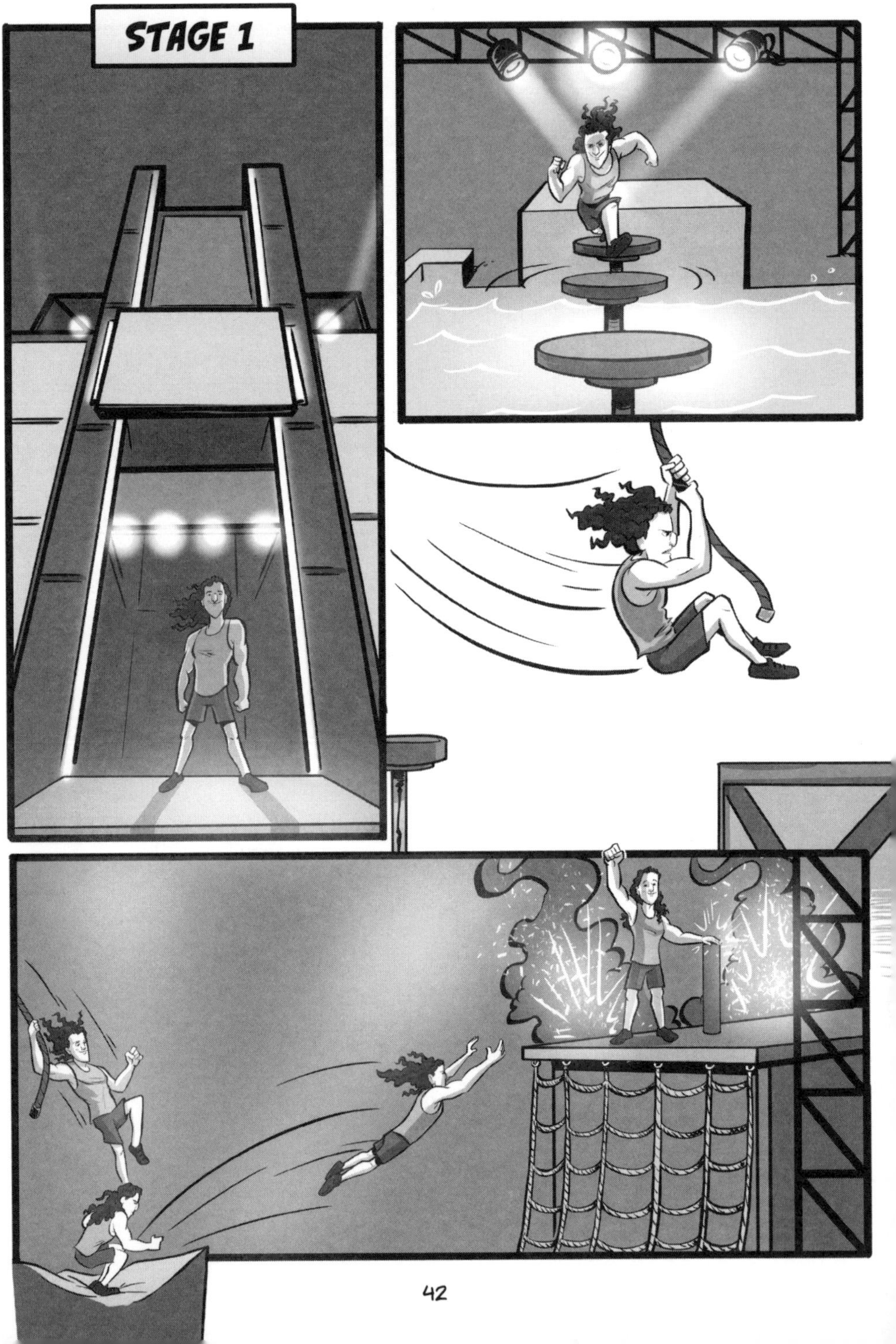
STAGE 1

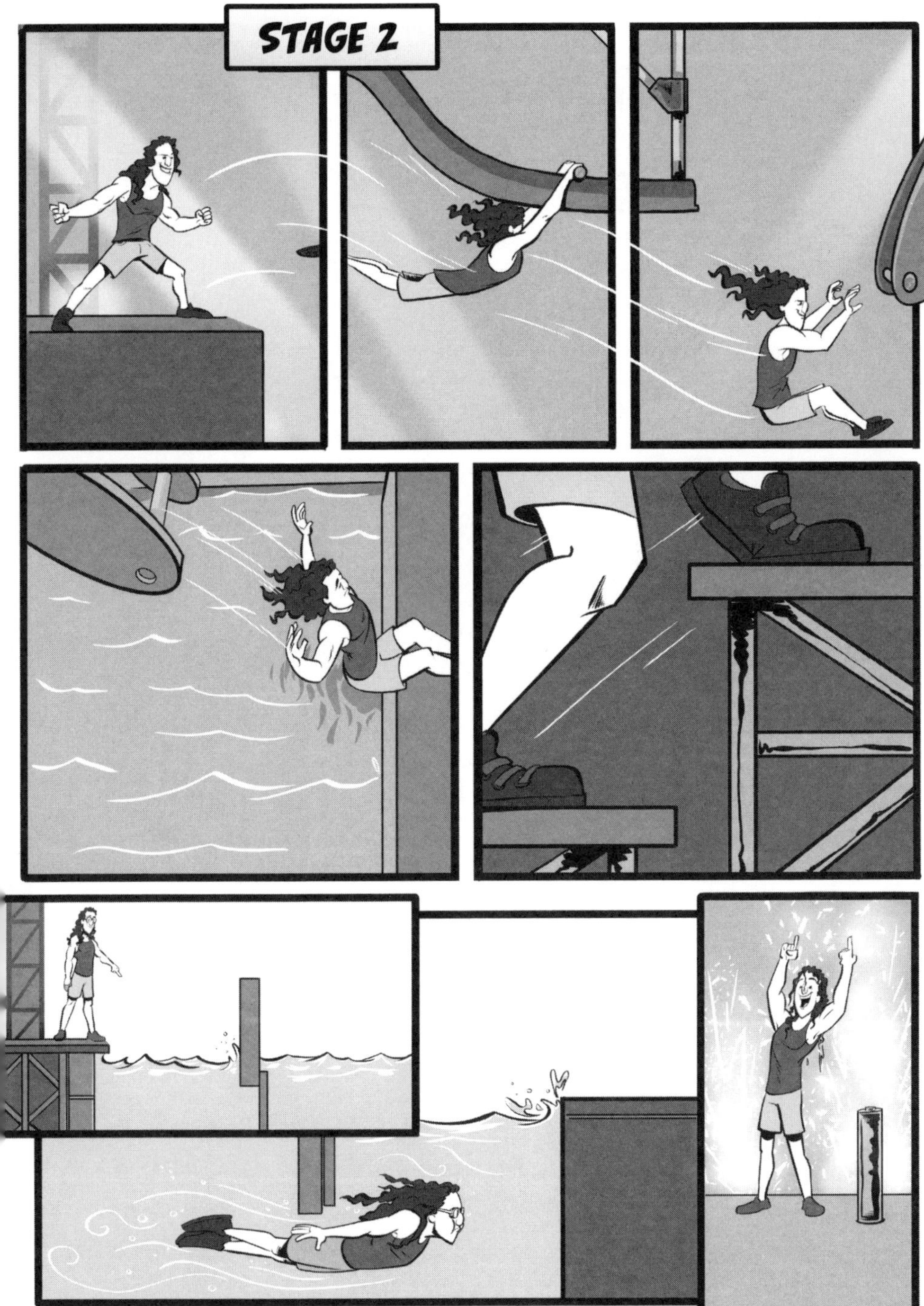
STAGE 2

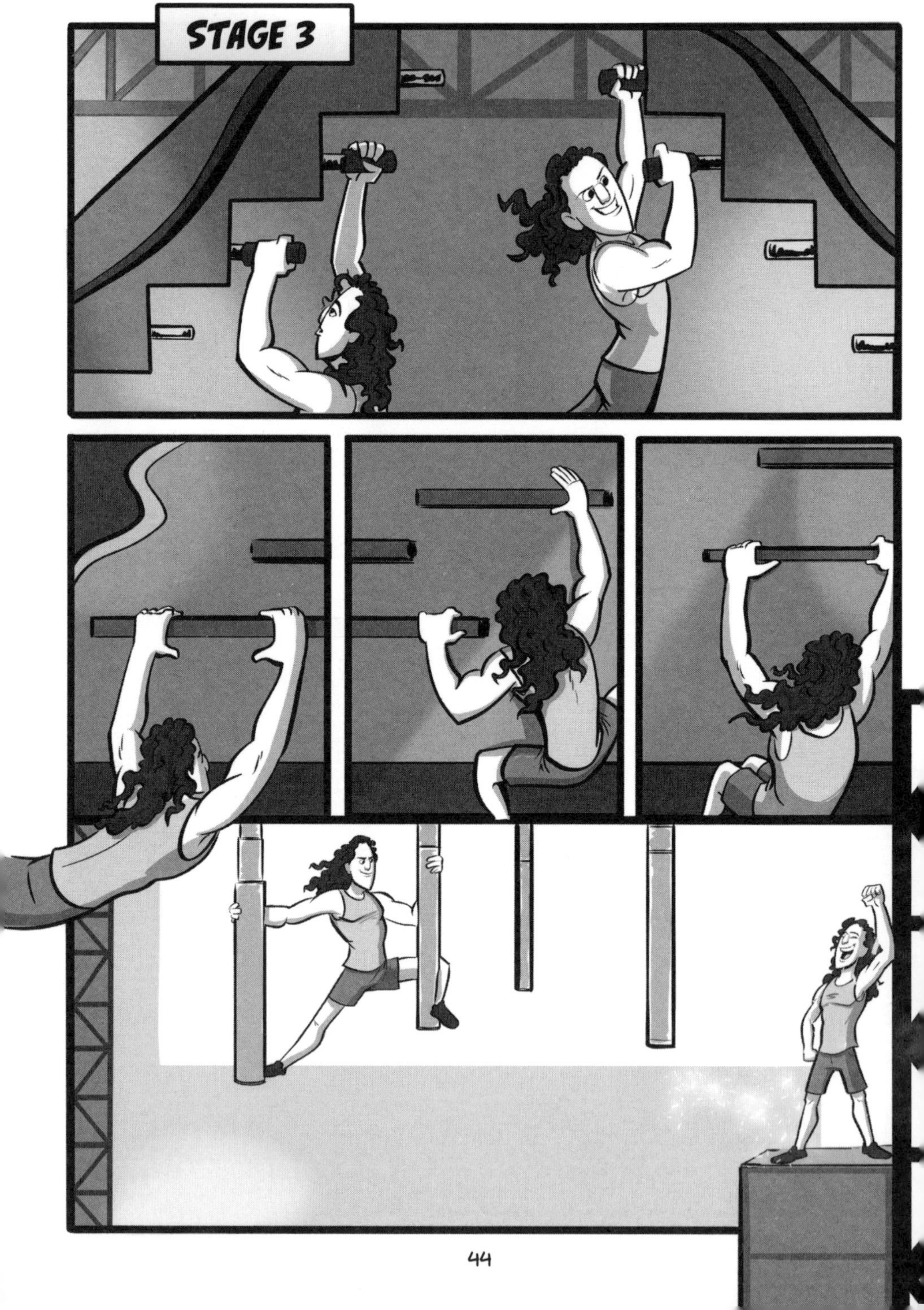
STAGE 3

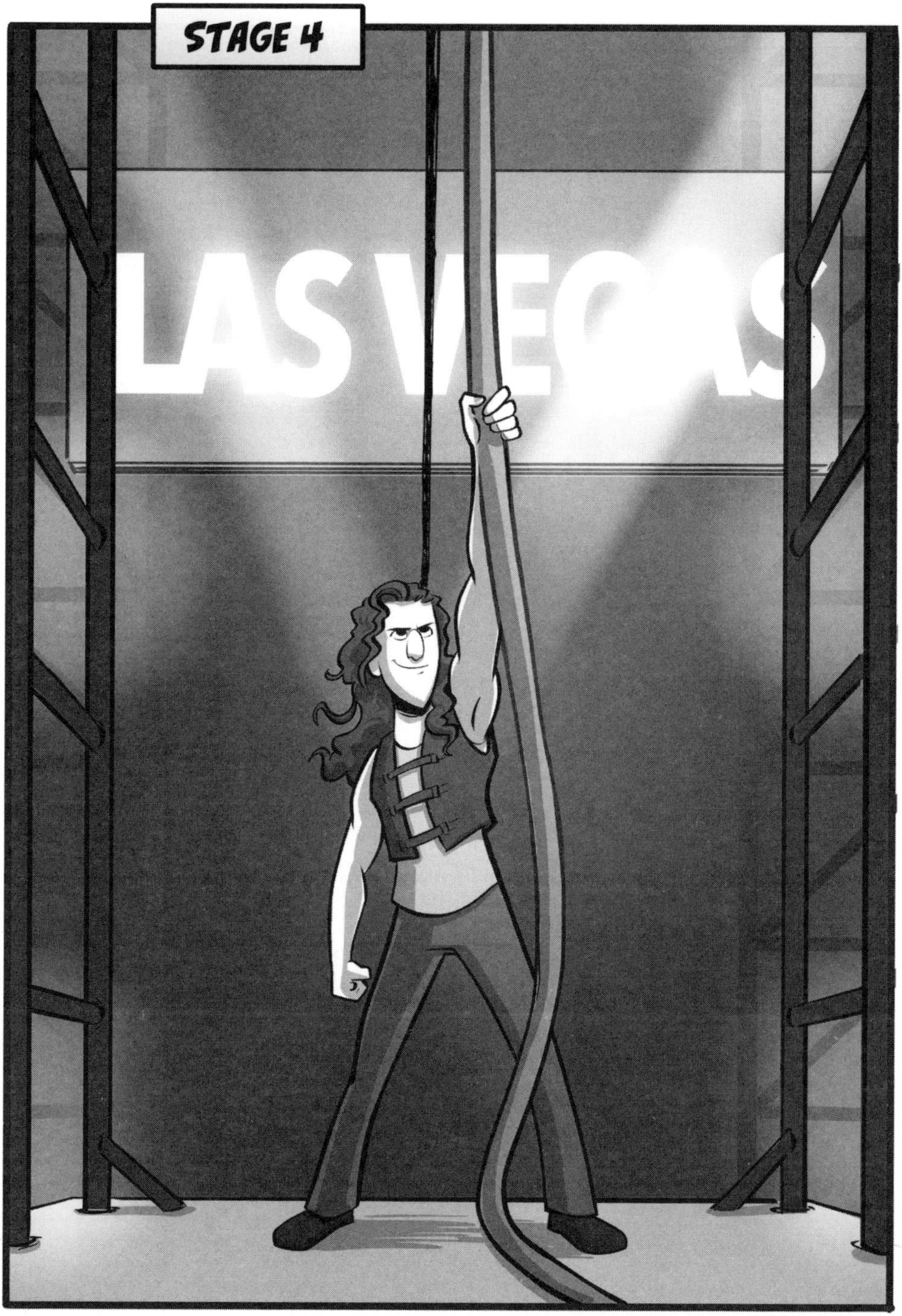
STAGE 4
LAS VEGAS

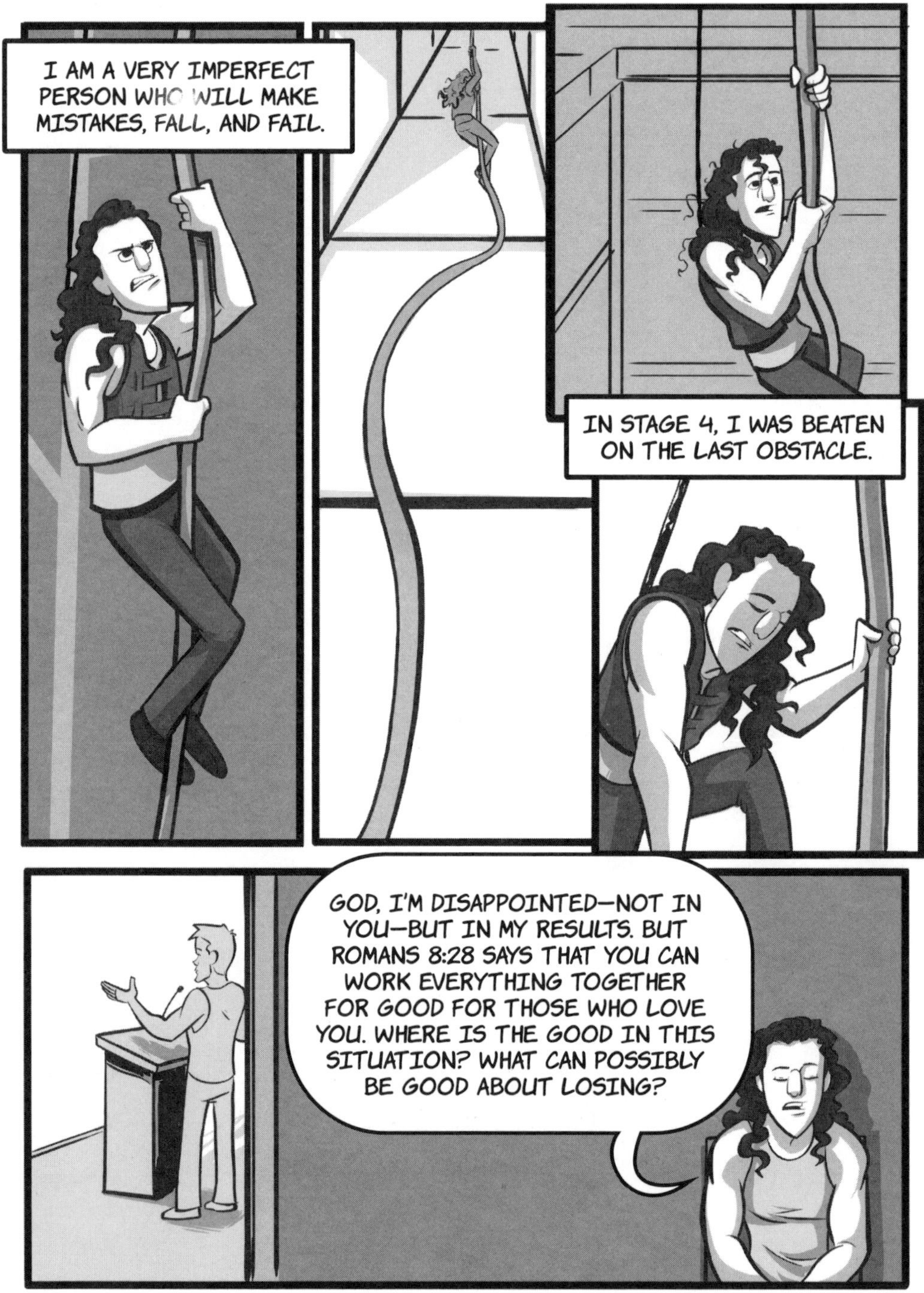
I AM A VERY IMPERFECT PERSON WHO WILL MAKE MISTAKES, FALL, AND FAIL.
IN STAGE 4, I WAS BEATEN ON THE LAST OBSTACLE.
GOD, I'M DISAPPOINTED—NOT IN YOU—BUT IN MY RESULTS. BUT ROMANS 8:28 SAYS THAT YOU CAN WORK EVERYTHING TOGETHER FOR GOOD FOR THOSE WHO LOVE YOU. WHERE IS THE GOOD IN THIS SITUATION? WHAT CAN POSSIBLY BE GOOD ABOUT LOSING?

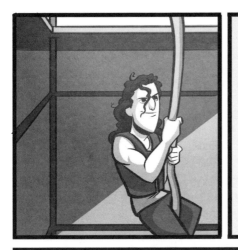

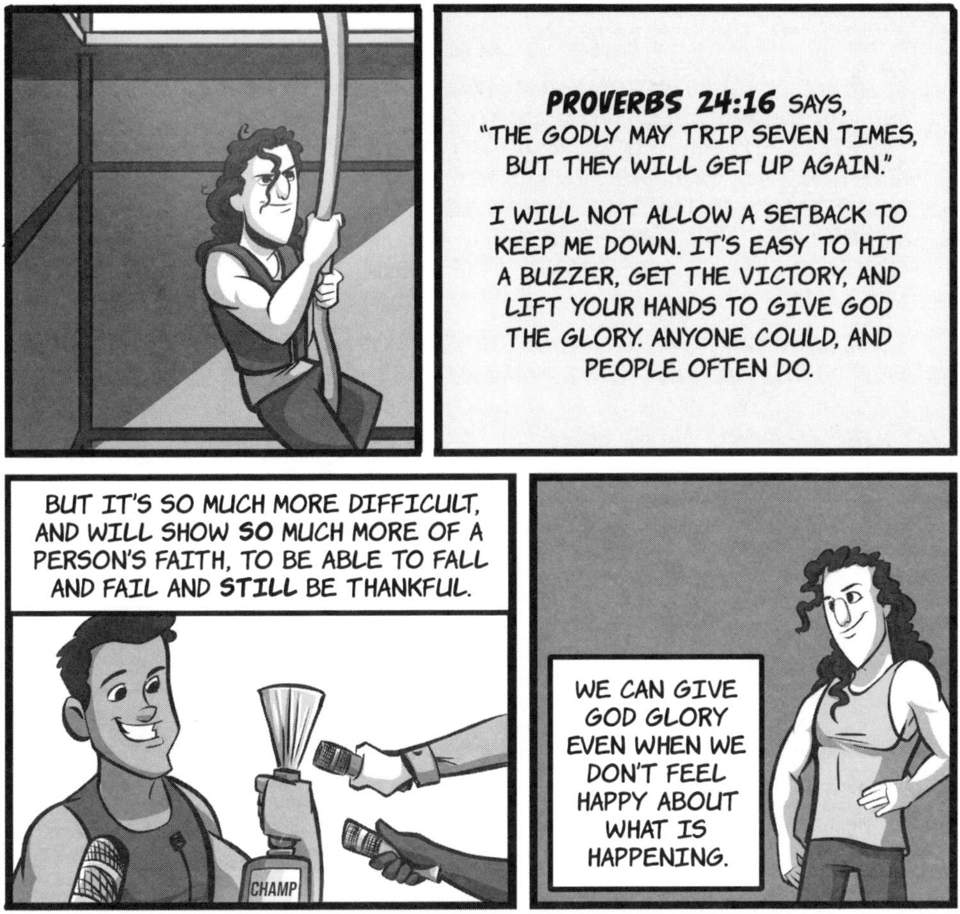
PROVERBS 24:16 SAYS,
"THE GODLY MAY TRIP SEVEN TIMES, BUT THEY WILL GET UP AGAIN."
I WILL NOT ALLOW A SETBACK TO KEEP ME DOWN. IT'S EASY TO HIT A BUZZER, GET THE VICTORY, AND LIFT YOUR HANDS TO GIVE GOD THE GLORY. ANYONE COULD, AND PEOPLE OFTEN DO.
BUT IT'S SO MUCH MORE DIFFICULT, AND WILL SHOW SO MUCH MORE OF A PERSON'S FAITH, TO BE ABLE TO FALL AND FAIL AND STILL BE THANKFUL.
CHAMP
WE CAN GIVE GOD GLORY EVEN WHEN WE DON'T FEEL HAPPY ABOUT WHAT IS HAPPENING.
WE CAN'T LET OUR FAILURES—EITHER IN SIN OR COMPETITION—DEFINE US.

LIFE VERSES

*C*AN ALL YOUR WORRIES ADD A SINGLE MOMENT TO YOUR LIFE? AND WHY WORRY ABOUT YOUR CLOTHING? LOOK AT THE LILIES OF THE FIELD AND HOW THEY GROW. THEY DON'T WORK OR MAKE THEIR CLOTHING, YET SOLOMON IN ALL HIS GLORY WAS NOT DRESSED AS BEAUTIFULLY AS THEY ARE. AND IF GOD CARES SO WONDERFULLY FOR WILDFLOWERS THAT ARE HERE TODAY AND THROWN INTO THE FIRE TOMORROW, HE WILL CERTAINLY CARE FOR YOU. WHY DO YOU HAVE SO LITTLE FAITH?

SO DON'T WORRY ABOUT THESE THINGS, SAYING, "WHAT WILL WE EAT? WHAT WILL WE DRINK? WHAT WILL WE WEAR?" THESE THINGS DOMINATE THE THOUGHTS OF UNBELIEVERS, BUT YOUR HEAVENLY FATHER ALREADY KNOWS ALL YOUR NEEDS. SEEK THE KINGDOM OF GOD ABOVE ALL ELSE, AND LIVE RIGHTEOUSLY, AND HE WILL GIVE YOU EVERYTHING YOU NEED. (MATTHEW 6:27-33)

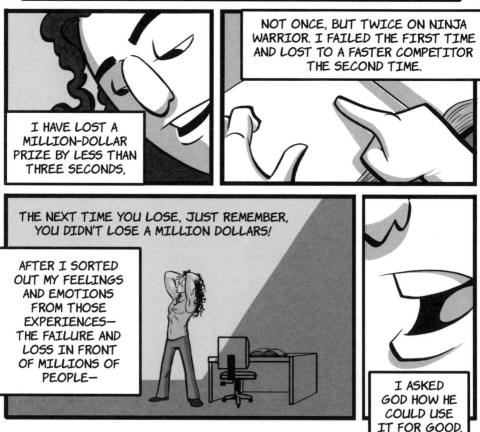

I HAVE LOST A MILLION-DOLLAR PRIZE BY LESS THAN THREE SECONDS,

NOT ONCE, BUT TWICE ON NINJA WARRIOR. I FAILED THE FIRST TIME AND LOST TO A FASTER COMPETITOR THE SECOND TIME.

THE NEXT TIME YOU LOSE, JUST REMEMBER, YOU DIDN'T LOSE A MILLION DOLLARS!

AFTER I SORTED OUT MY FEELINGS AND EMOTIONS FROM THOSE EXPERIENCES— THE FAILURE AND LOSS IN FRONT OF MILLIONS OF PEOPLE—

I ASKED GOD HOW HE COULD USE IT FOR GOOD.

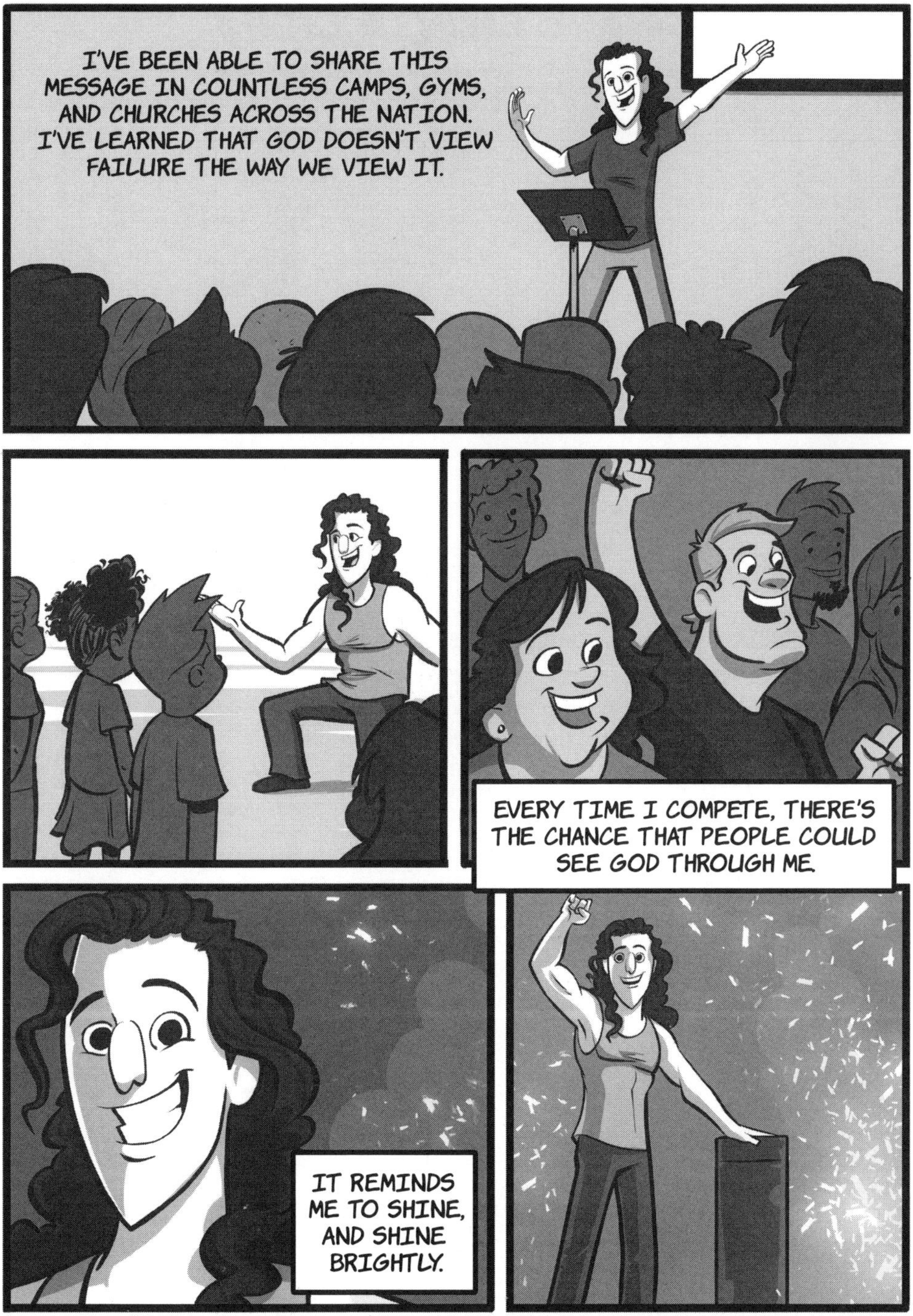
I'VE BEEN ABLE TO SHARE THIS MESSAGE IN COUNTLESS CAMPS, GYMS, AND CHURCHES ACROSS THE NATION. I'VE LEARNED THAT GOD DOESN'T VIEW FAILURE THE WAY WE VIEW IT.
EVERY TIME I COMPETE, THERE'S THE CHANCE THAT PEOPLE COULD SEE GOD THROUGH ME.
IT REMINDS ME TO SHINE, AND SHINE BRIGHTLY.

CHAPTER FOUR

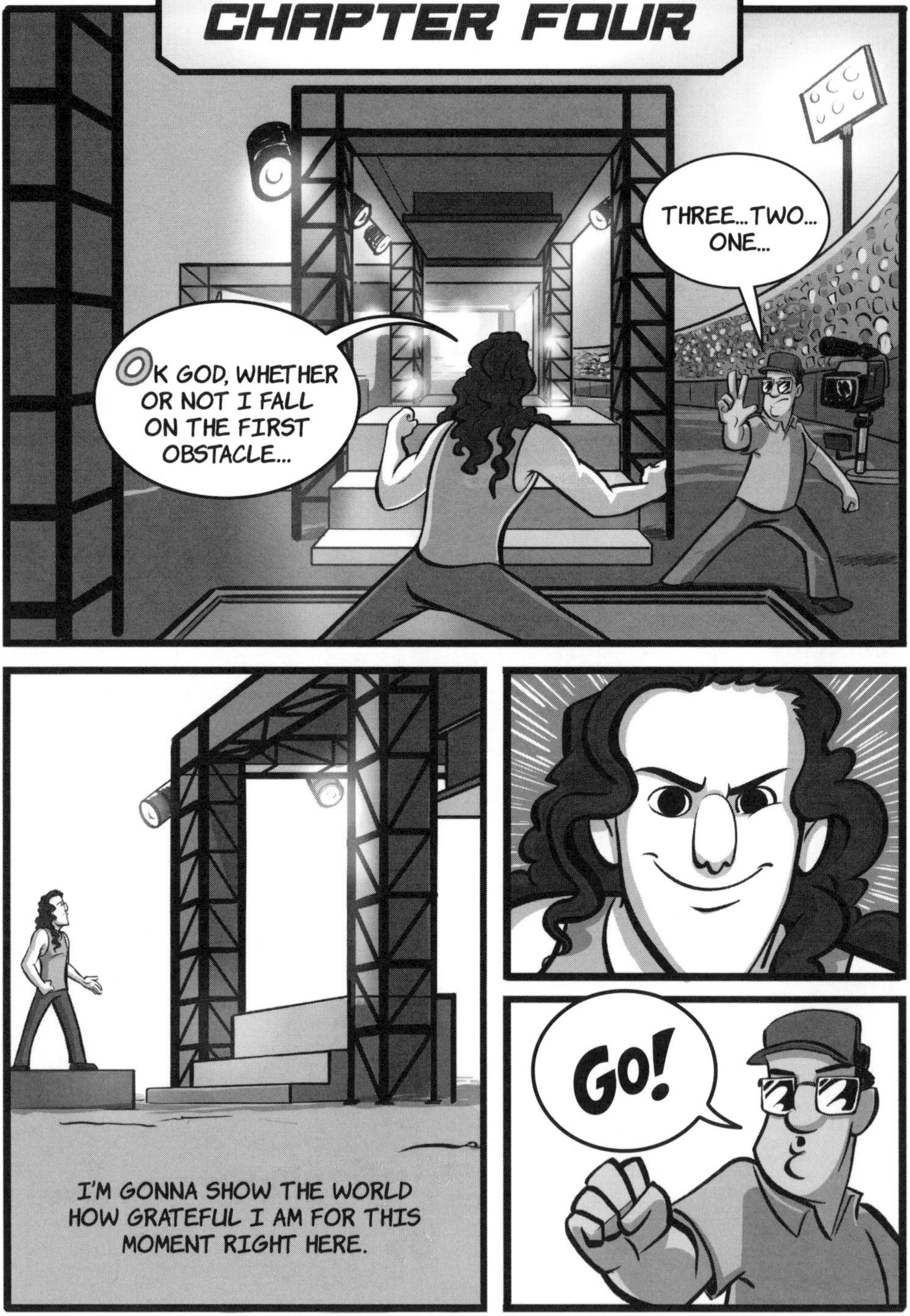

THREE...TWO... ONE...
OK GOD, WHETHER OR NOT I FALL ON THE FIRST OBSTACLE...
I'M GONNA SHOW THE WORLD HOW GRATEFUL I AM FOR THIS MOMENT RIGHT HERE.
GO!

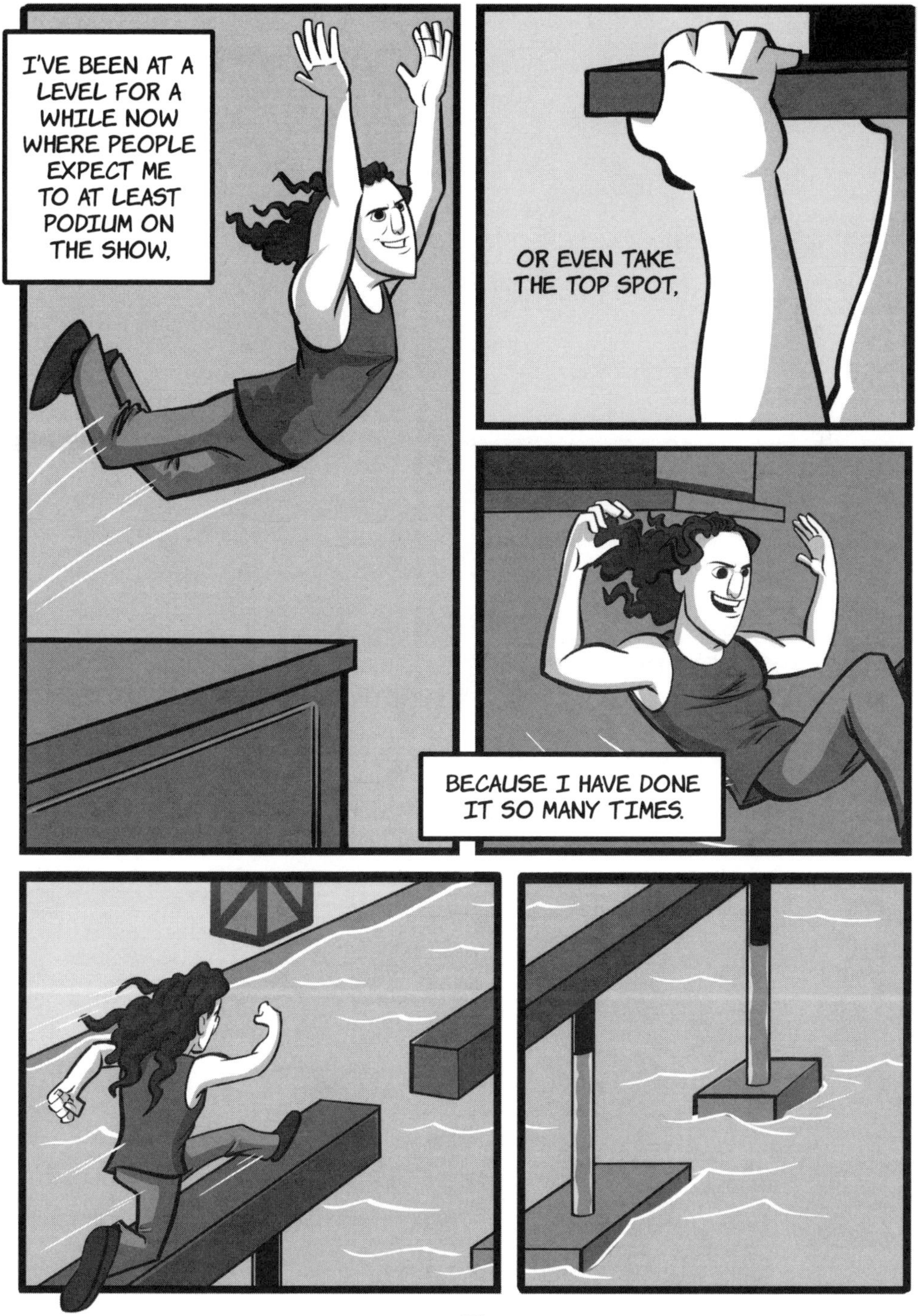
I'VE BEEN AT A LEVEL FOR A WHILE NOW WHERE PEOPLE EXPECT ME TO AT LEAST PODIUM ON THE SHOW,
OR EVEN TAKE THE TOP SPOT,
BECAUSE I HAVE DONE IT SO MANY TIMES.

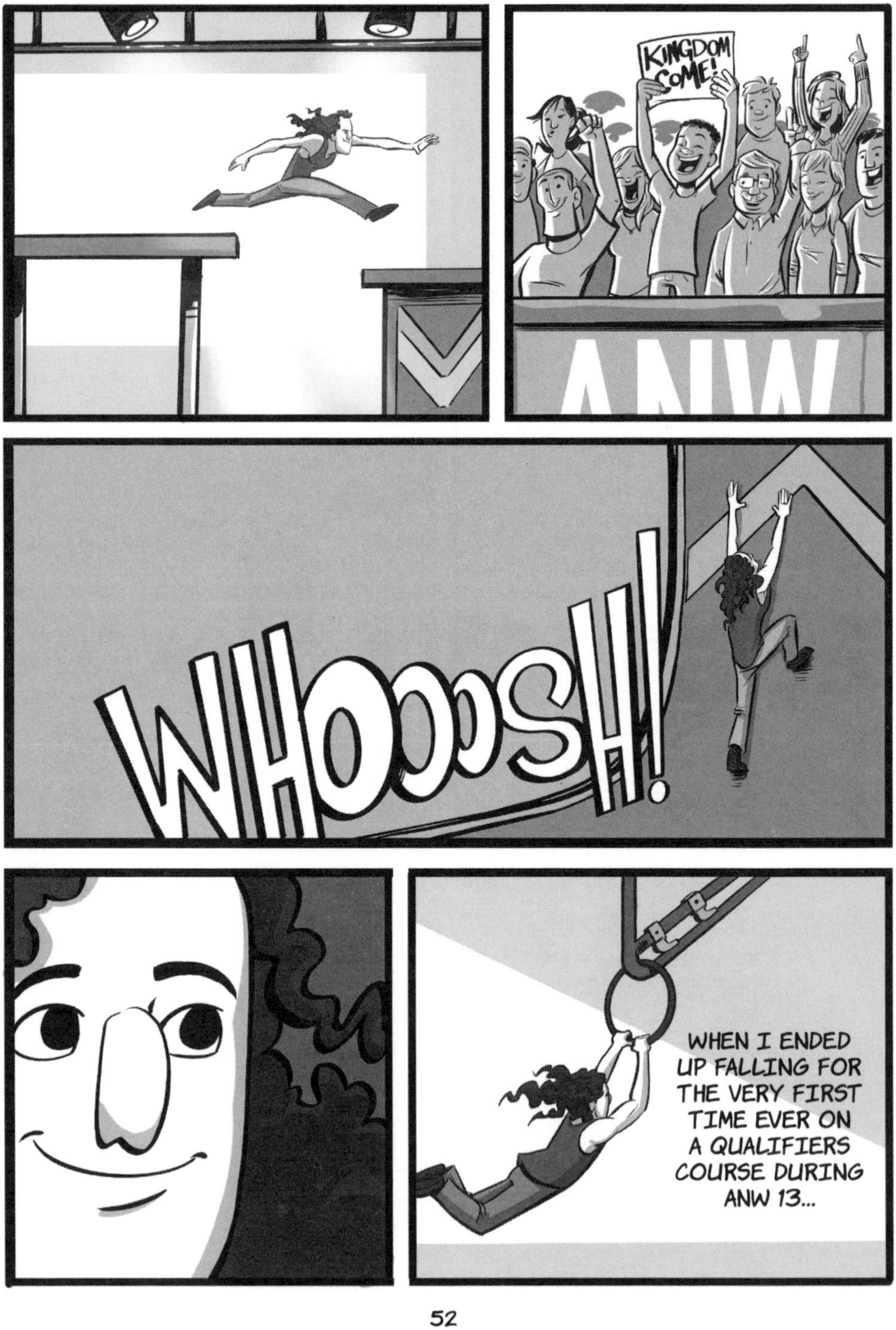
KINGDOM COME!
ANW
WHOOOSH!
WHEN I ENDED UP FALLING FOR THE VERY FIRST TIME EVER ON A QUALIFIERS COURSE DURING ANW 13...

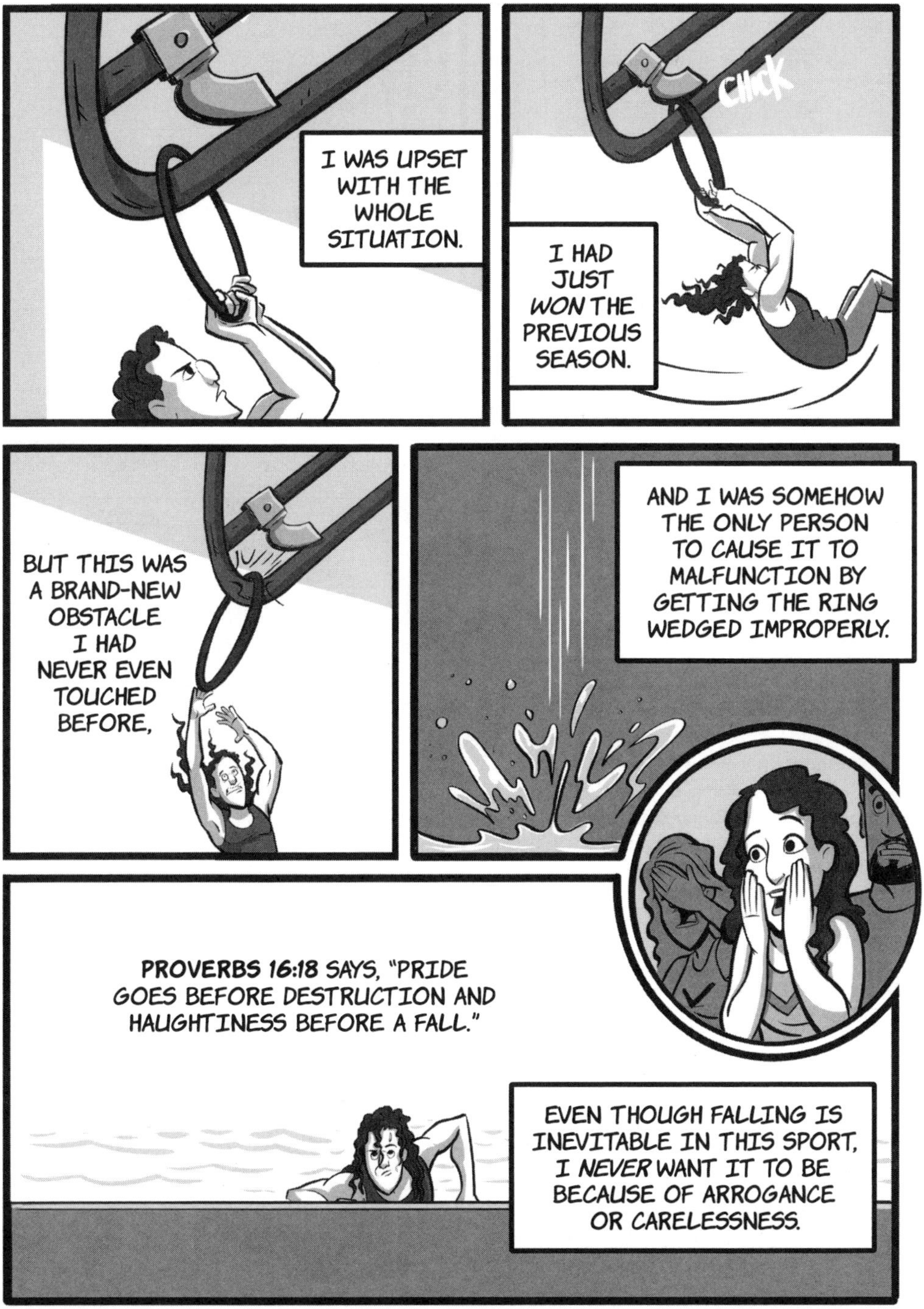
I WAS UPSET WITH THE WHOLE SITUATION.
CLICK
I HAD JUST *WON* THE PREVIOUS SEASON.
BUT THIS WAS A BRAND-NEW OBSTACLE I HAD NEVER EVEN TOUCHED BEFORE,
AND I WAS SOMEHOW THE ONLY PERSON TO CAUSE IT TO MALFUNCTION BY GETTING THE RING WEDGED IMPROPERLY.
PROVERBS 16:18 SAYS, "PRIDE GOES BEFORE DESTRUCTION AND HAUGHTINESS BEFORE A FALL."
EVEN THOUGH FALLING IS INEVITABLE IN THIS SPORT, I *NEVER* WANT IT TO BE BECAUSE OF ARROGANCE OR CARELESSNESS.

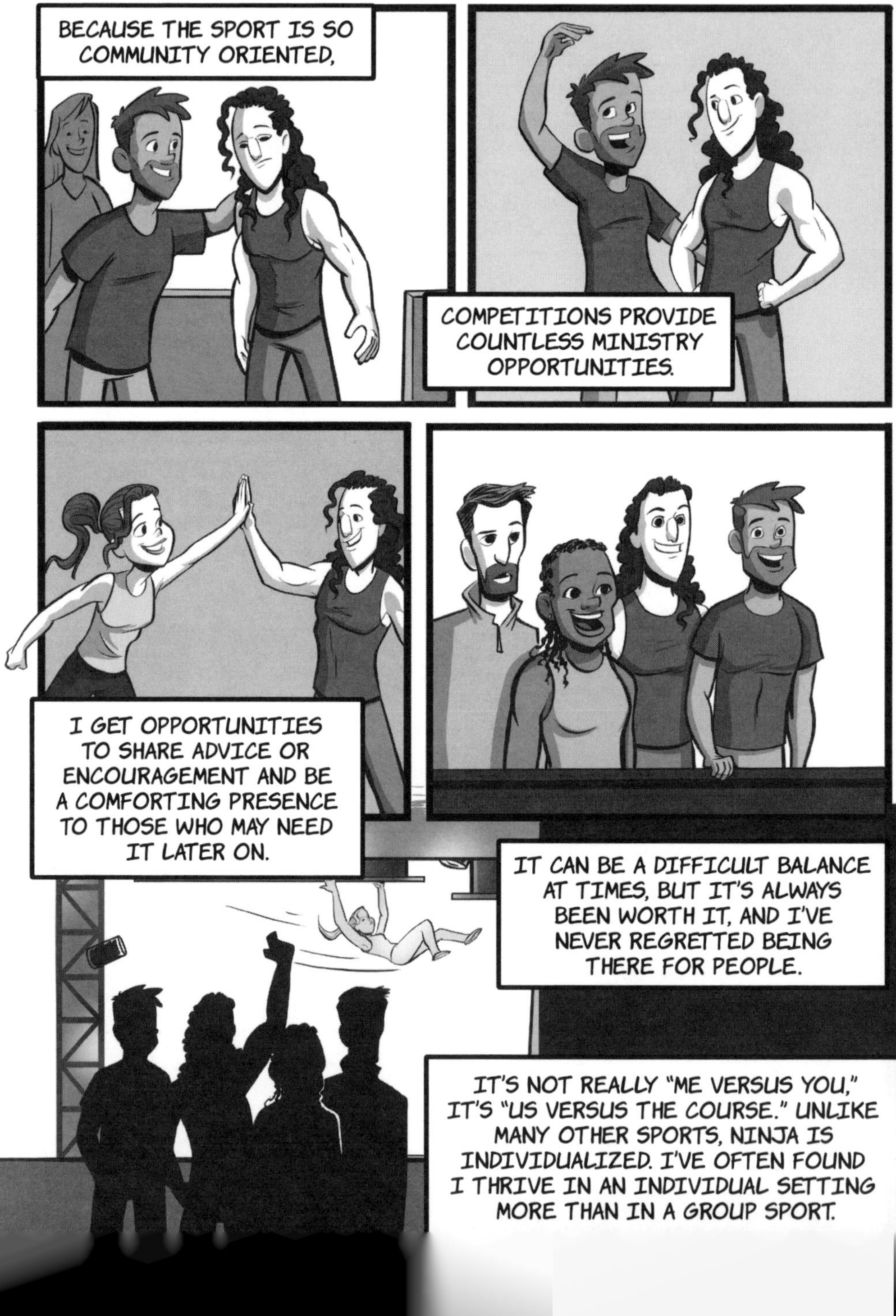
BECAUSE THE SPORT IS SO COMMUNITY ORIENTED,
COMPETITIONS PROVIDE COUNTLESS MINISTRY OPPORTUNITIES.
I GET OPPORTUNITIES TO SHARE ADVICE OR ENCOURAGEMENT AND BE A COMFORTING PRESENCE TO THOSE WHO MAY NEED IT LATER ON.
IT CAN BE A DIFFICULT BALANCE AT TIMES, BUT IT'S ALWAYS BEEN WORTH IT, AND I'VE NEVER REGRETTED BEING THERE FOR PEOPLE.
IT'S NOT REALLY "ME VERSUS YOU," IT'S "US VERSUS THE COURSE." UNLIKE MANY OTHER SPORTS, NINJA IS INDIVIDUALIZED. I'VE OFTEN FOUND I THRIVE IN AN INDIVIDUAL SETTING MORE THAN IN A GROUP SPORT.

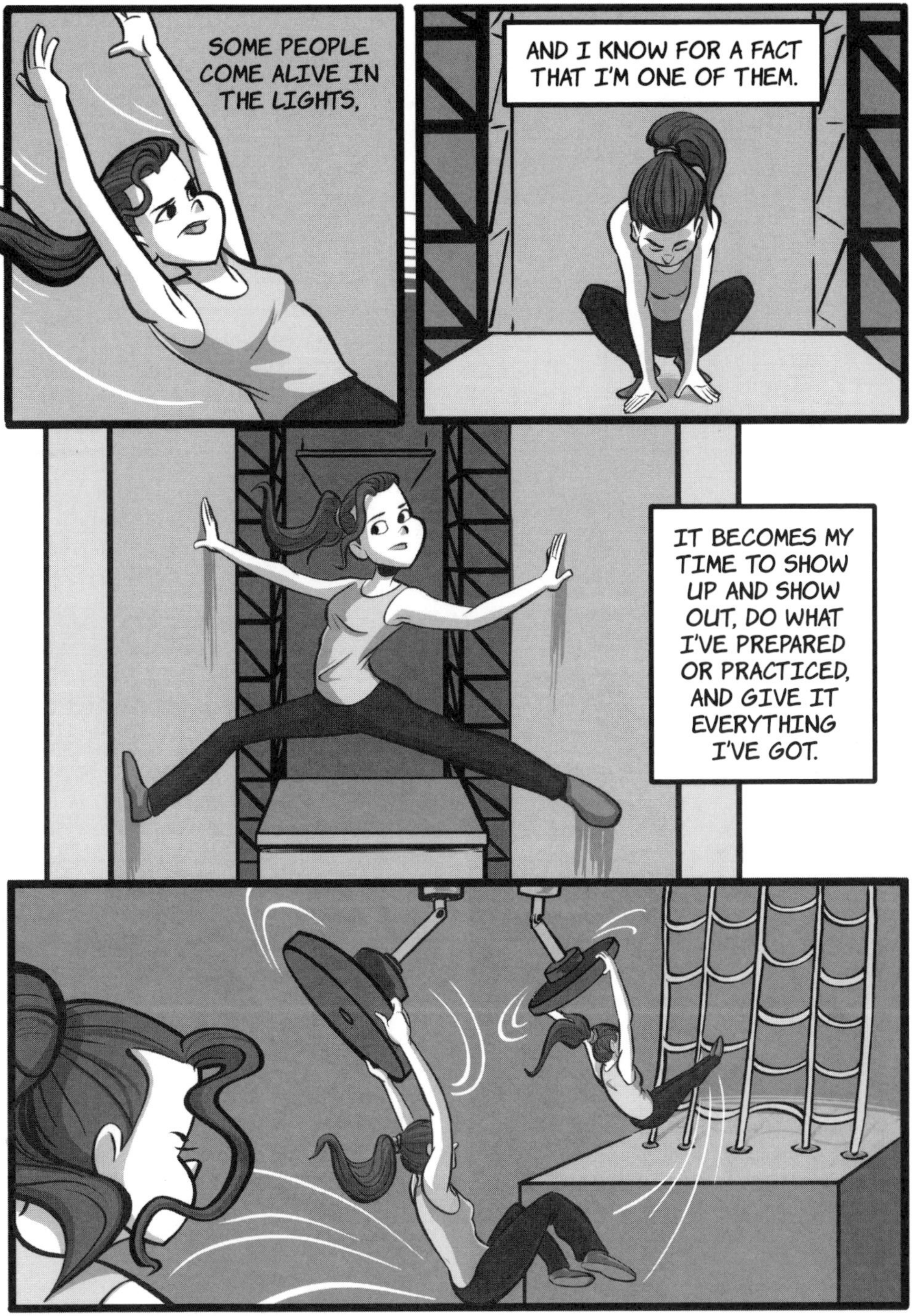
SOME PEOPLE COME ALIVE IN THE LIGHTS,
AND I KNOW FOR A FACT THAT I'M ONE OF THEM.
IT BECOMES MY TIME TO SHOW UP AND SHOW OUT, DO WHAT I'VE PREPARED OR PRACTICED, AND GIVE IT EVERYTHING I'VE GOT.

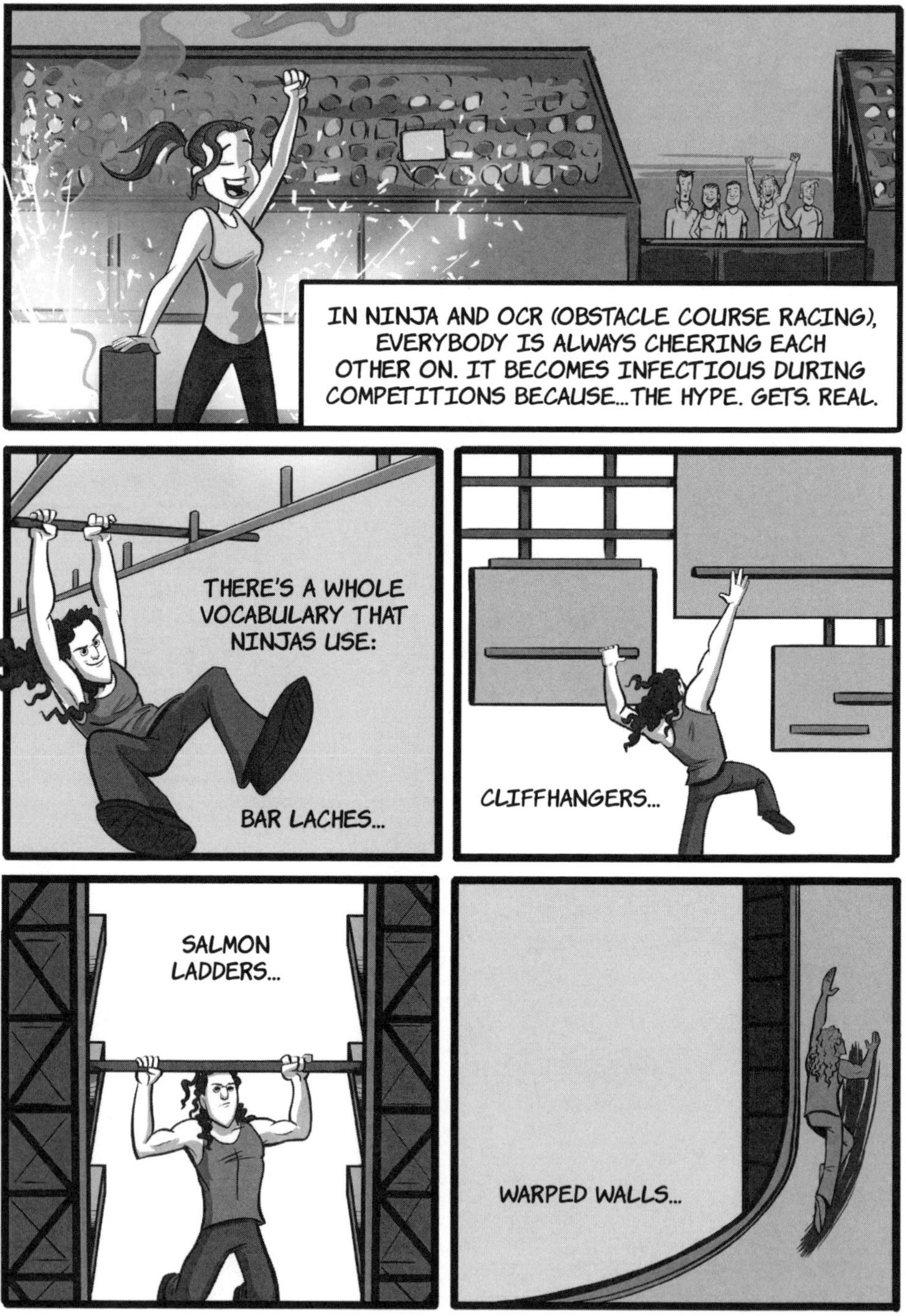
IN NINJA AND OCR (OBSTACLE COURSE RACING), EVERYBODY IS ALWAYS CHEERING EACH OTHER ON. IT BECOMES INFECTIOUS DURING COMPETITIONS BECAUSE...THE HYPE. GETS. REAL.
THERE'S A WHOLE VOCABULARY THAT NINJAS USE:
BAR LACHES...
CLIFFHANGERS...
SALMON LADDERS...
WARPED WALLS...

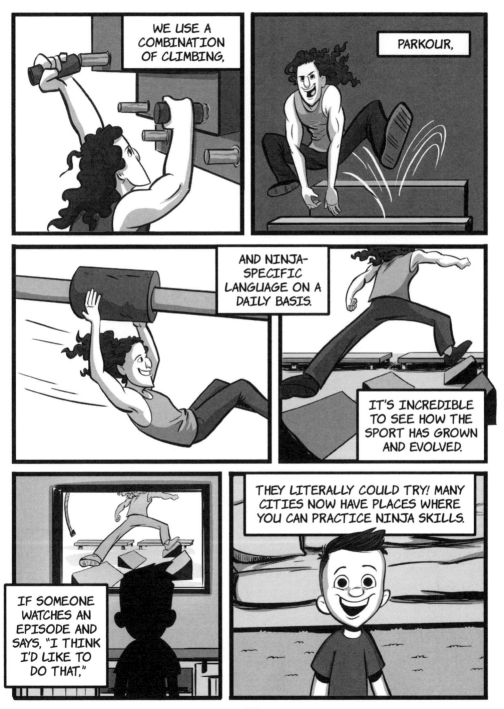

WE USE A COMBINATION OF CLIMBING,

PARKOUR,

AND NINJA-SPECIFIC LANGUAGE ON A DAILY BASIS.

IT'S INCREDIBLE TO SEE HOW THE SPORT HAS GROWN AND EVOLVED.

IF SOMEONE WATCHES AN EPISODE AND SAYS, "I THINK I'D LIKE TO DO THAT,"

THEY LITERALLY COULD TRY! MANY CITIES NOW HAVE PLACES WHERE YOU CAN PRACTICE NINJA SKILLS.

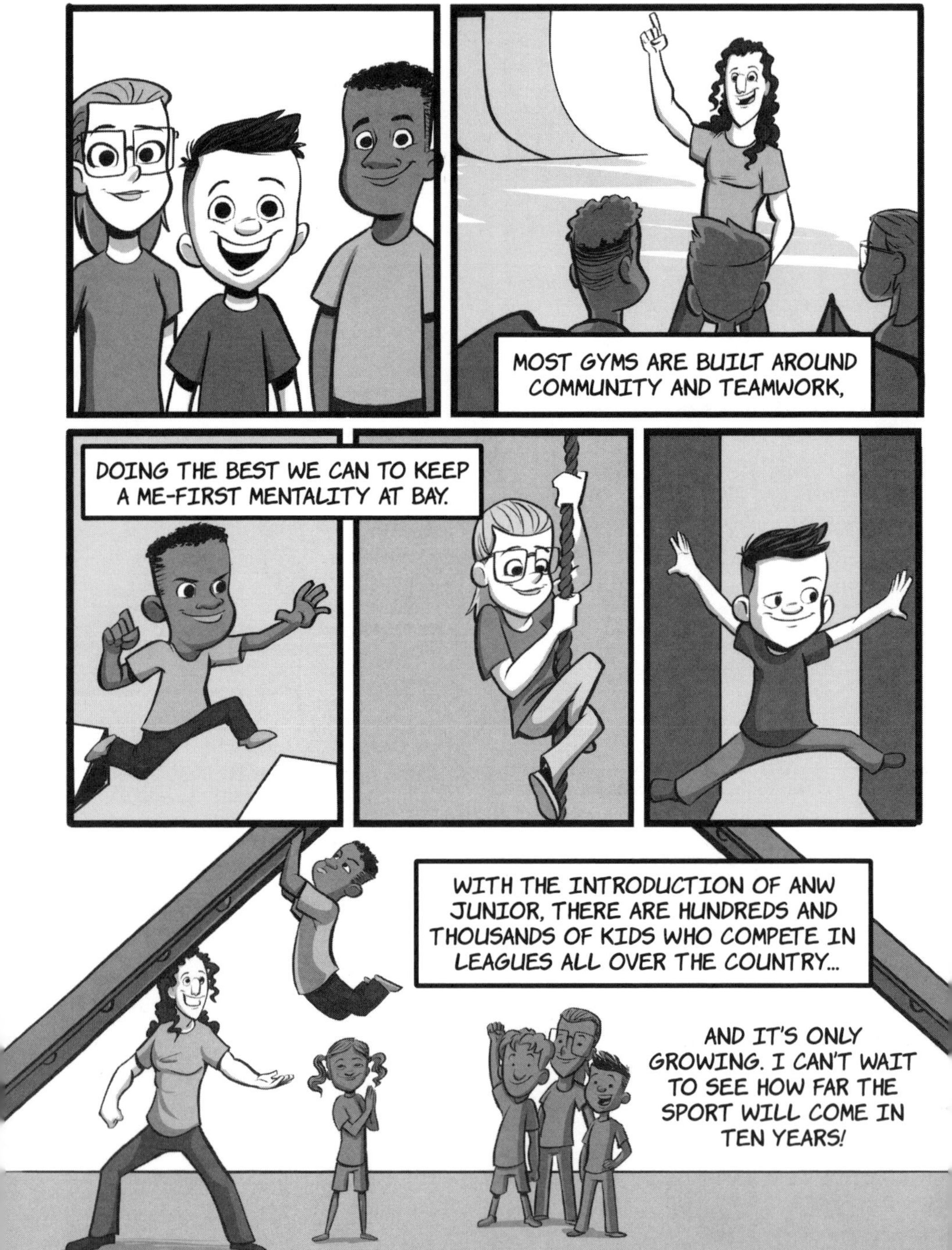
MOST GYMS ARE BUILT AROUND COMMUNITY AND TEAMWORK,
DOING THE BEST WE CAN TO KEEP A ME-FIRST MENTALITY AT BAY.
WITH THE INTRODUCTION OF ANW JUNIOR, THERE ARE HUNDREDS AND THOUSANDS OF KIDS WHO COMPETE IN LEAGUES ALL OVER THE COUNTRY...
AND IT'S ONLY GROWING. I CAN'T WAIT TO SEE HOW FAR THE SPORT WILL COME IN TEN YEARS!

CHAPTER FIVE

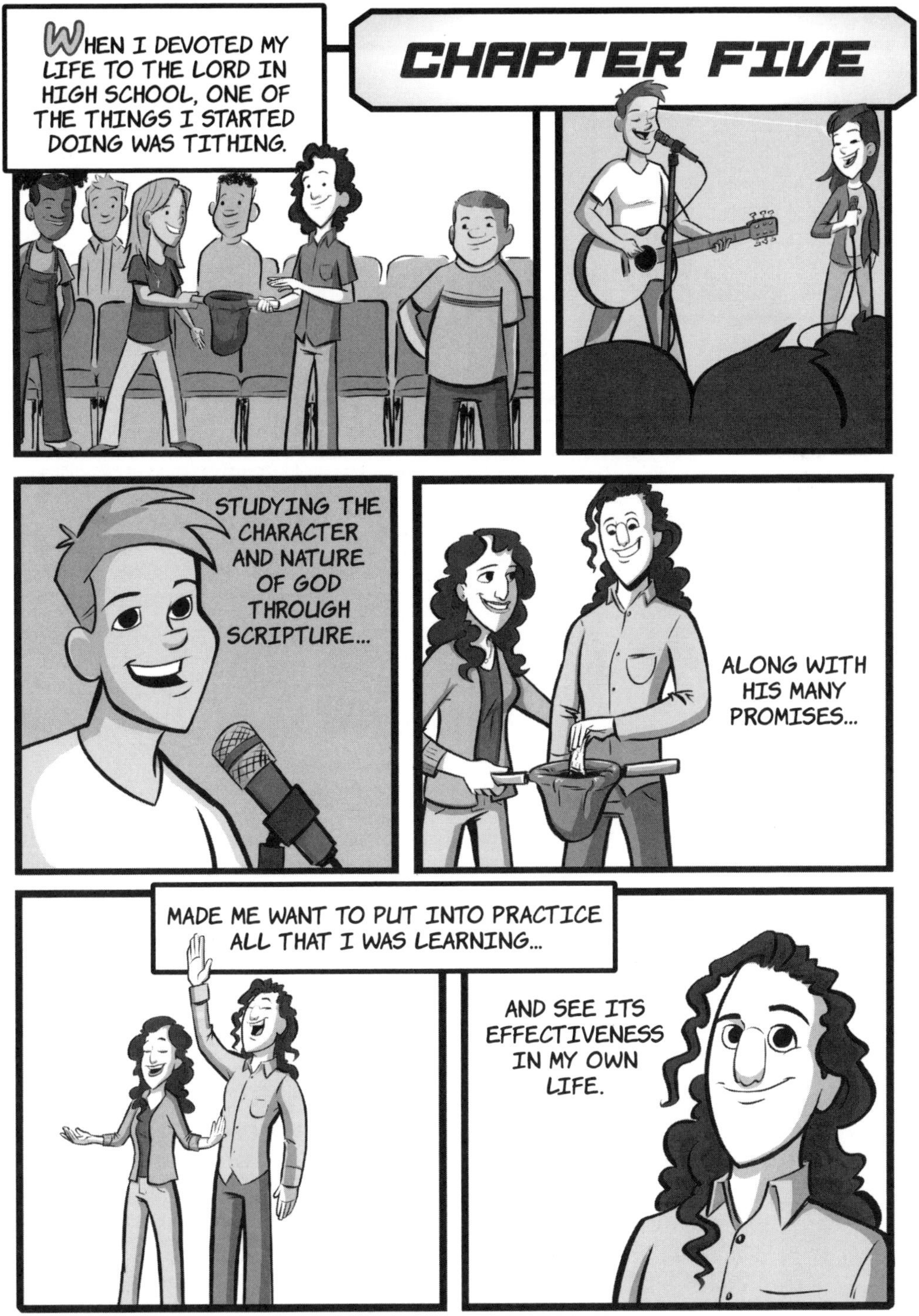
WHEN I DEVOTED MY LIFE TO THE LORD IN HIGH SCHOOL, ONE OF THE THINGS I STARTED DOING WAS TITHING.
STUDYING THE CHARACTER AND NATURE OF GOD THROUGH SCRIPTURE...
ALONG WITH HIS MANY PROMISES...
MADE ME WANT TO PUT INTO PRACTICE ALL THAT I WAS LEARNING...
AND SEE ITS EFFECTIVENESS IN MY OWN LIFE.

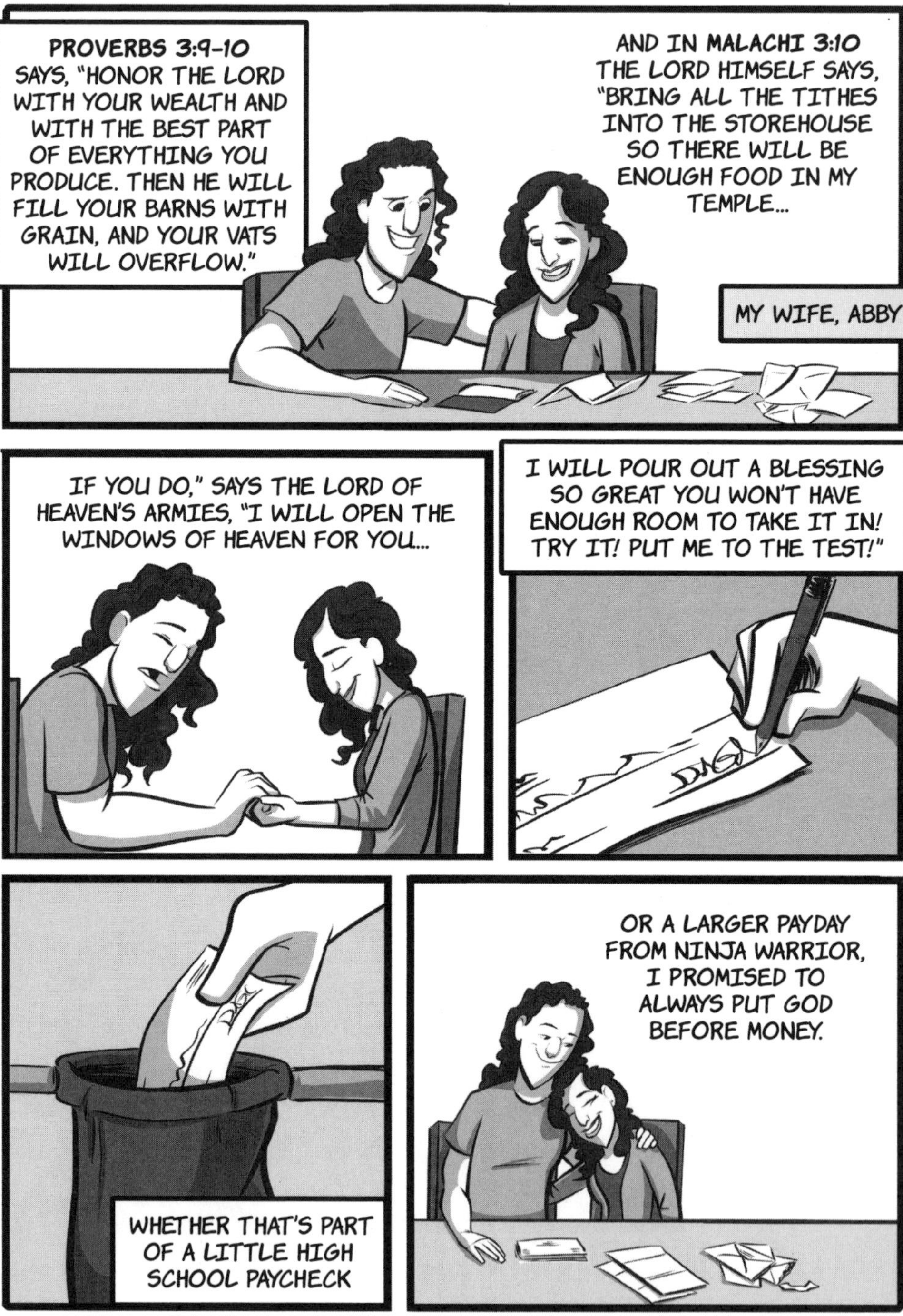
PROVERBS 3:9-10 SAYS, "HONOR THE LORD WITH YOUR WEALTH AND WITH THE BEST PART OF EVERYTHING YOU PRODUCE. THEN HE WILL FILL YOUR BARNS WITH GRAIN, AND YOUR VATS WILL OVERFLOW."
AND IN MALACHI 3:10 THE LORD HIMSELF SAYS, "BRING ALL THE TITHES INTO THE STOREHOUSE SO THERE WILL BE ENOUGH FOOD IN MY TEMPLE...
MY WIFE, ABBY
IF YOU DO," SAYS THE LORD OF HEAVEN'S ARMIES, "I WILL OPEN THE WINDOWS OF HEAVEN FOR YOU...
I WILL POUR OUT A BLESSING SO GREAT YOU WON'T HAVE ENOUGH ROOM TO TAKE IT IN! TRY IT! PUT ME TO THE TEST!"
WHETHER THAT'S PART OF A LITTLE HIGH SCHOOL PAYCHECK
OR A LARGER PAYDAY FROM NINJA WARRIOR, I PROMISED TO ALWAYS PUT GOD BEFORE MONEY.

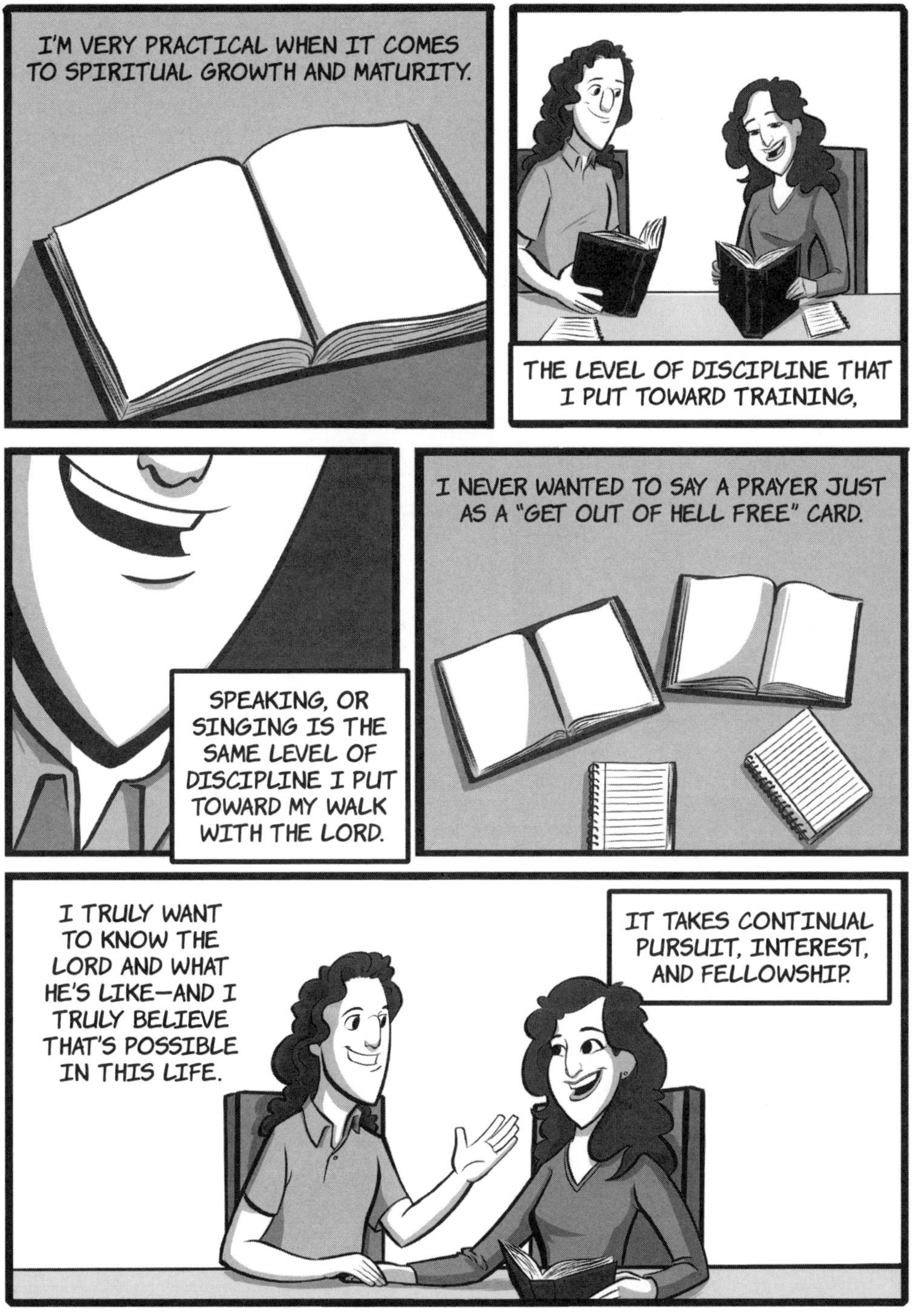
I'M VERY PRACTICAL WHEN IT COMES TO SPIRITUAL GROWTH AND MATURITY.
THE LEVEL OF DISCIPLINE THAT I PUT TOWARD TRAINING,
SPEAKING, OR SINGING IS THE SAME LEVEL OF DISCIPLINE I PUT TOWARD MY WALK WITH THE LORD.
I NEVER WANTED TO SAY A PRAYER JUST AS A "GET OUT OF HELL FREE" CARD.
I TRULY WANT TO KNOW THE LORD AND WHAT HE'S LIKE—AND I TRULY BELIEVE THAT'S POSSIBLE IN THIS LIFE.
IT TAKES CONTINUAL PURSUIT, INTEREST, AND FELLOWSHIP.

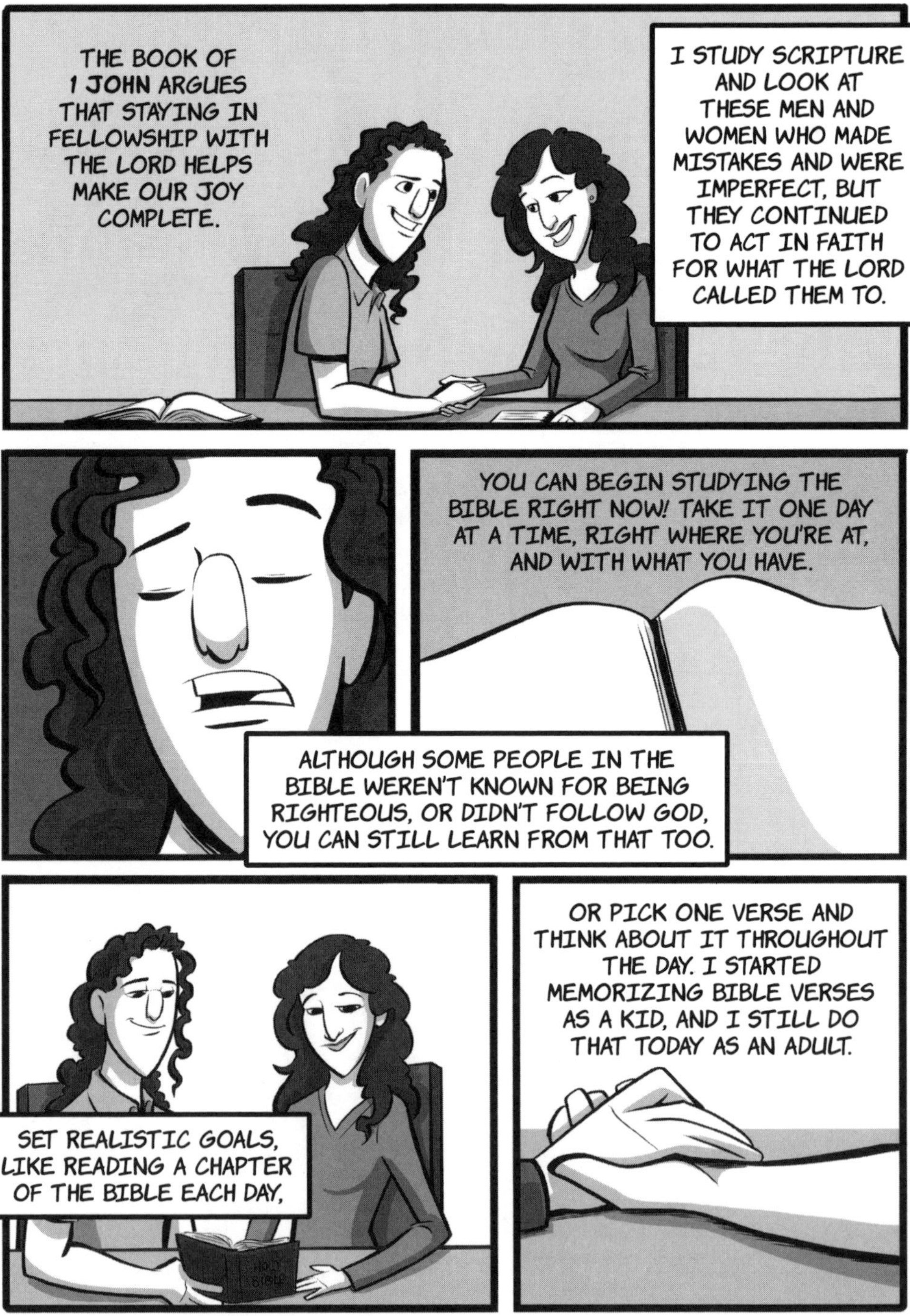
THE BOOK OF 1 JOHN ARGUES THAT STAYING IN FELLOWSHIP WITH THE LORD HELPS MAKE OUR JOY COMPLETE.
I STUDY SCRIPTURE AND LOOK AT THESE MEN AND WOMEN WHO MADE MISTAKES AND WERE IMPERFECT, BUT THEY CONTINUED TO ACT IN FAITH FOR WHAT THE LORD CALLED THEM TO.
YOU CAN BEGIN STUDYING THE BIBLE RIGHT NOW! TAKE IT ONE DAY AT A TIME, RIGHT WHERE YOU'RE AT, AND WITH WHAT YOU HAVE.
ALTHOUGH SOME PEOPLE IN THE BIBLE WEREN'T KNOWN FOR BEING RIGHTEOUS, OR DIDN'T FOLLOW GOD, YOU CAN STILL LEARN FROM THAT TOO.
SET REALISTIC GOALS, LIKE READING A CHAPTER OF THE BIBLE EACH DAY,
HOLY BIBLE
OR PICK ONE VERSE AND THINK ABOUT IT THROUGHOUT THE DAY. I STARTED MEMORIZING BIBLE VERSES AS A KID, AND I STILL DO THAT TODAY AS AN ADULT.

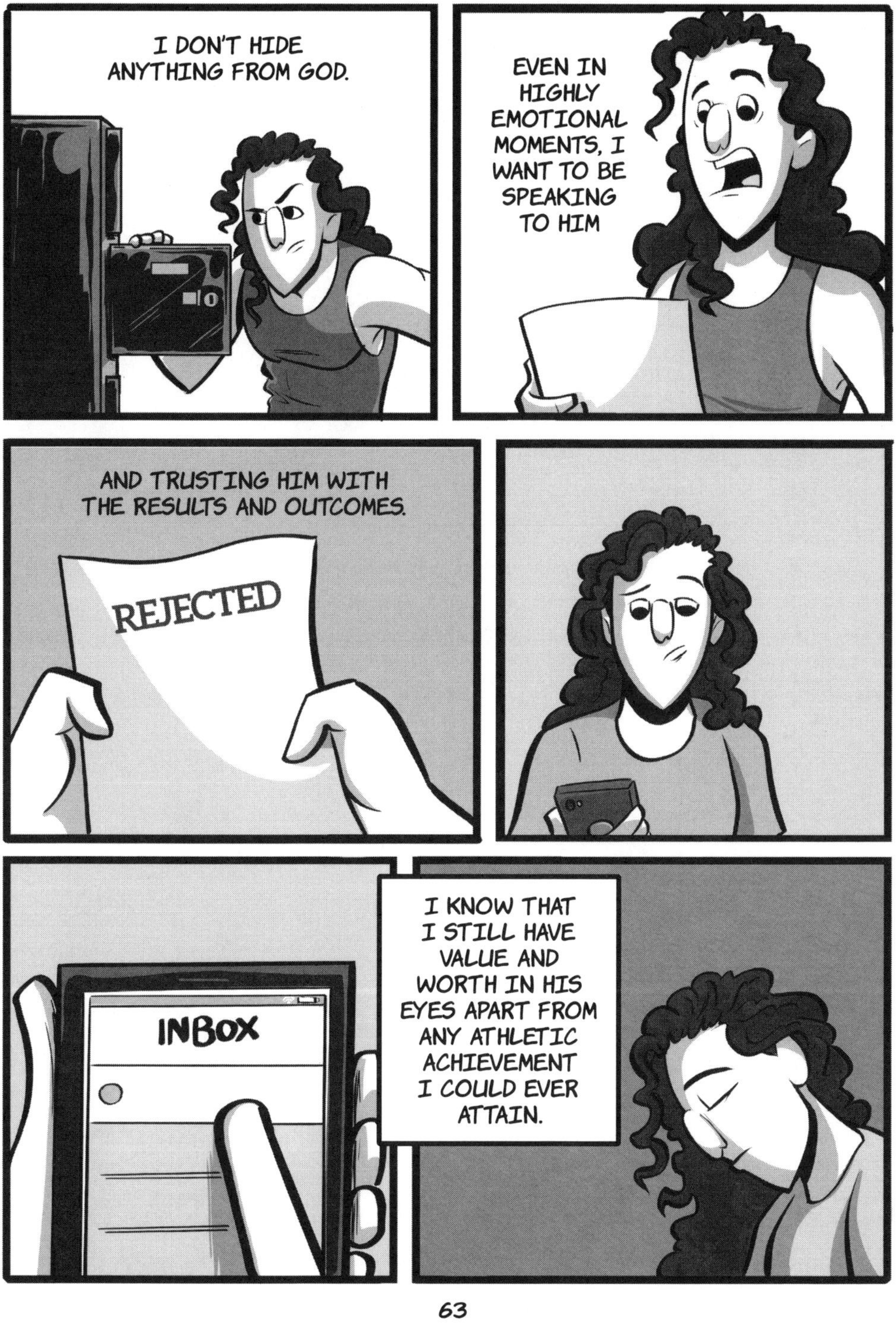
I DON'T HIDE ANYTHING FROM GOD.
EVEN IN HIGHLY EMOTIONAL MOMENTS, I WANT TO BE SPEAKING TO HIM
AND TRUSTING HIM WITH THE RESULTS AND OUTCOMES.
REJECTED
INBOX
I KNOW THAT I STILL HAVE VALUE AND WORTH IN HIS EYES APART FROM ANY ATHLETIC ACHIEVEMENT I COULD EVER ATTAIN.

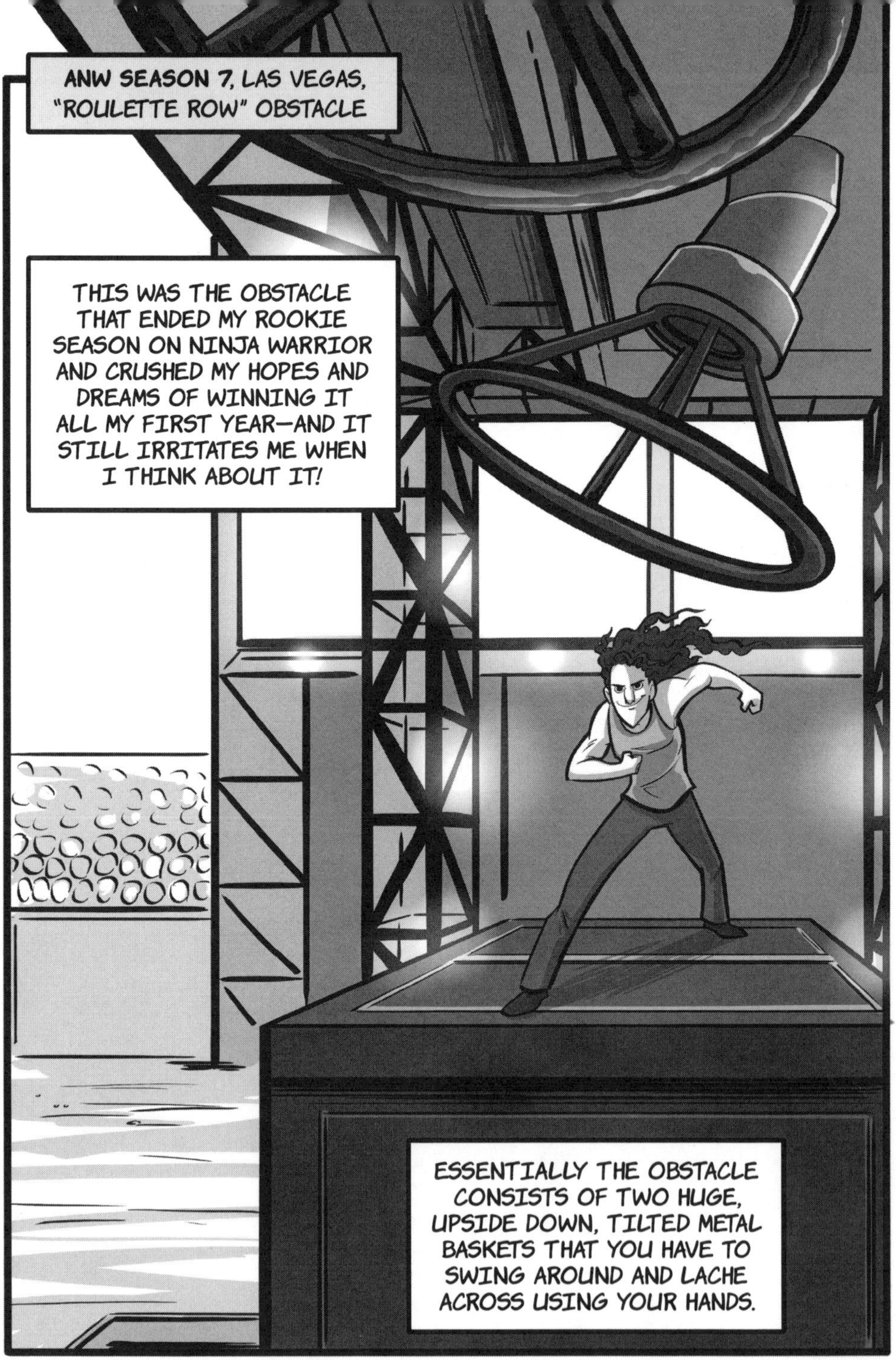
ANW SEASON 7, LAS VEGAS, "ROULETTE ROW" OBSTACLE
THIS WAS THE OBSTACLE THAT ENDED MY ROOKIE SEASON ON NINJA WARRIOR AND CRUSHED MY HOPES AND DREAMS OF WINNING IT ALL MY FIRST YEAR—AND IT STILL IRRITATES ME WHEN I THINK ABOUT IT!
ESSENTIALLY THE OBSTACLE CONSISTS OF TWO HUGE, UPSIDE DOWN, TILTED METAL BASKETS THAT YOU HAVE TO SWING AROUND AND LACHE ACROSS USING YOUR HANDS.

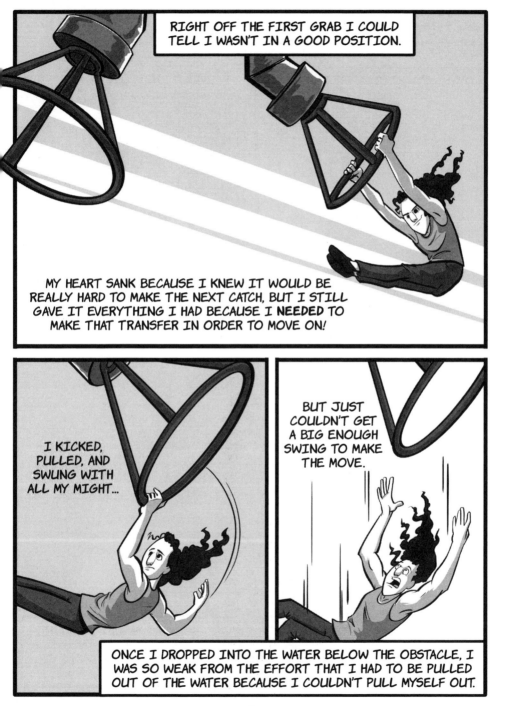

RIGHT OFF THE FIRST GRAB I COULD TELL I WASN'T IN A GOOD POSITION.

MY HEART SANK BECAUSE I KNEW IT WOULD BE REALLY HARD TO MAKE THE NEXT CATCH, BUT I STILL GAVE IT EVERYTHING I HAD BECAUSE I **NEEDED** TO MAKE THAT TRANSFER IN ORDER TO MOVE ON!

I KICKED, PULLED, AND SWUNG WITH ALL MY MIGHT...

BUT JUST COULDN'T GET A BIG ENOUGH SWING TO MAKE THE MOVE.

ONCE I DROPPED INTO THE WATER BELOW THE OBSTACLE, I WAS SO WEAK FROM THE EFFORT THAT I HAD TO BE PULLED OUT OF THE WATER BECAUSE I COULDN'T PULL MYSELF OUT.

WHEN I THINK ABOUT NEAR LOSSES LIKE THIS, I STILL FEEL THE STING OF THAT DISAPPOINTMENT, BUT MY TRUST AND MY FAITH ARE UNWAVERING.

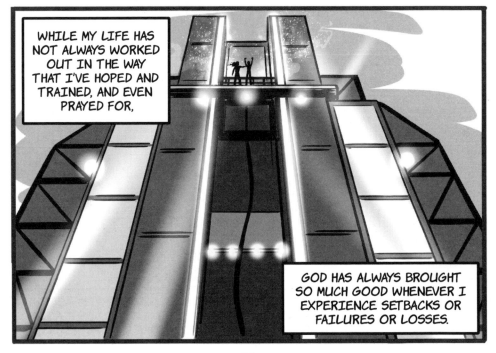

WHILE MY LIFE HAS NOT ALWAYS WORKED OUT IN THE WAY THAT I'VE HOPED AND TRAINED, AND EVEN PRAYED FOR,

GOD HAS ALWAYS BROUGHT SO MUCH GOOD WHENEVER I EXPERIENCE SETBACKS OR FAILURES OR LOSSES.

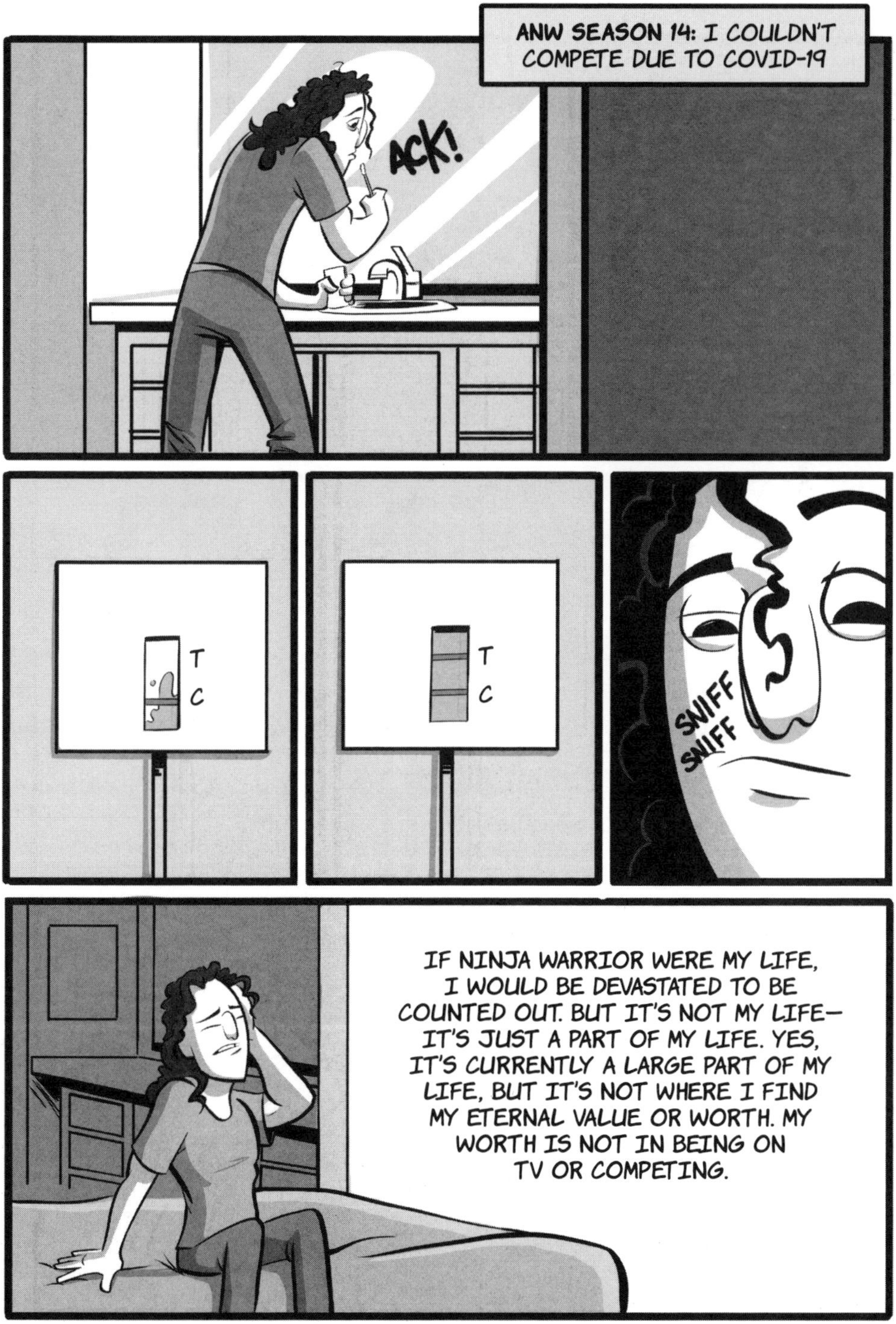
ANW SEASON 14: I COULDN'T COMPETE DUE TO COVID-19
ACK!
T
C
T
C
SNIFF
SNIFF
IF NINJA WARRIOR WERE MY LIFE, I WOULD BE DEVASTATED TO BE COUNTED OUT. BUT IT'S NOT MY LIFE—IT'S JUST A PART OF MY LIFE. YES, IT'S CURRENTLY A LARGE PART OF MY LIFE, BUT IT'S NOT WHERE I FIND MY ETERNAL VALUE OR WORTH. MY WORTH IS NOT IN BEING ON TV OR COMPETING.

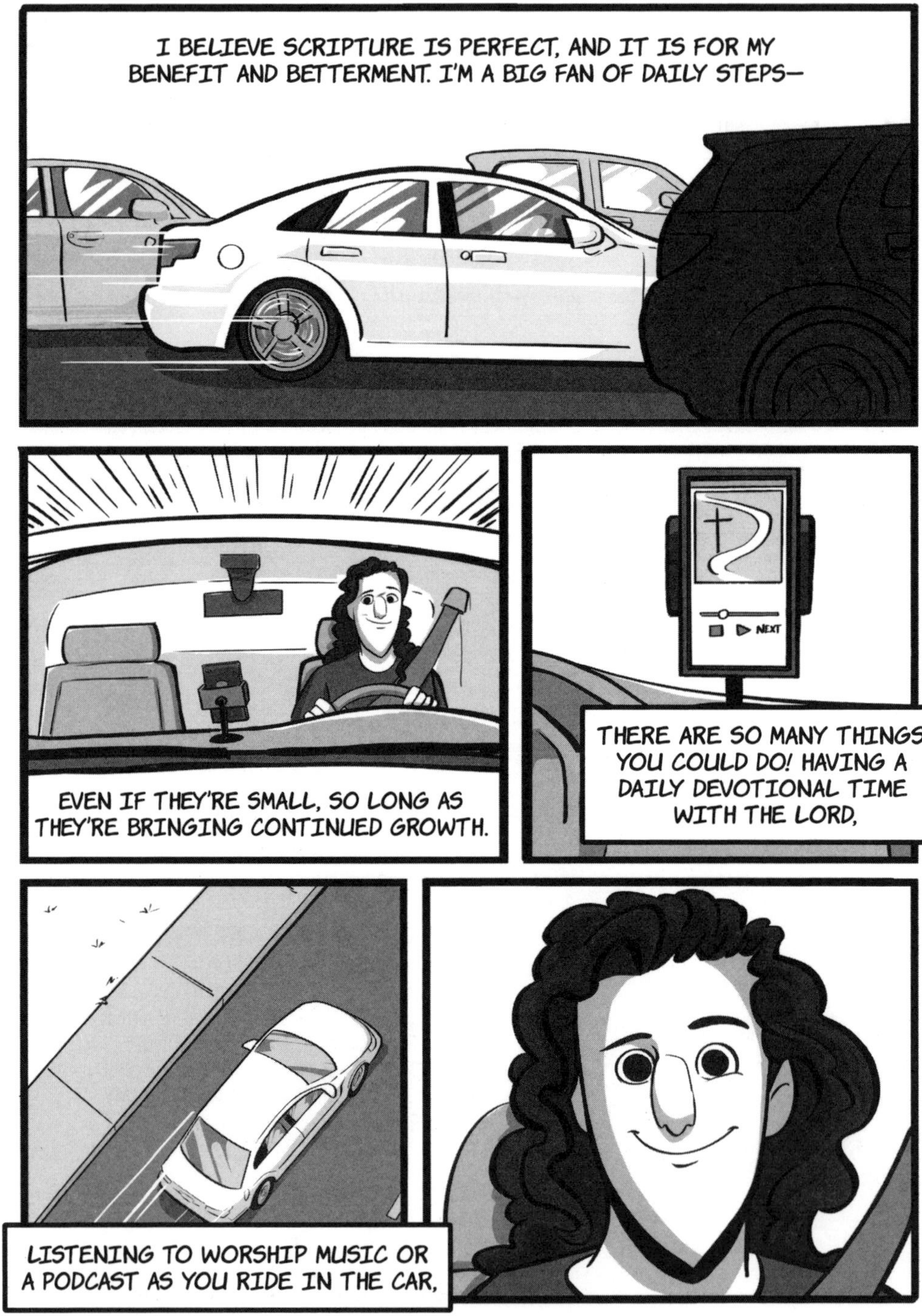
I BELIEVE SCRIPTURE IS PERFECT, AND IT IS FOR MY BENEFIT AND BETTERMENT. I'M A BIG FAN OF DAILY STEPS—
EVEN IF THEY'RE SMALL, SO LONG AS THEY'RE BRINGING CONTINUED GROWTH.
NEXT
THERE ARE SO MANY THINGS YOU COULD DO! HAVING A DAILY DEVOTIONAL TIME WITH THE LORD,
LISTENING TO WORSHIP MUSIC OR A PODCAST AS YOU RIDE IN THE CAR,

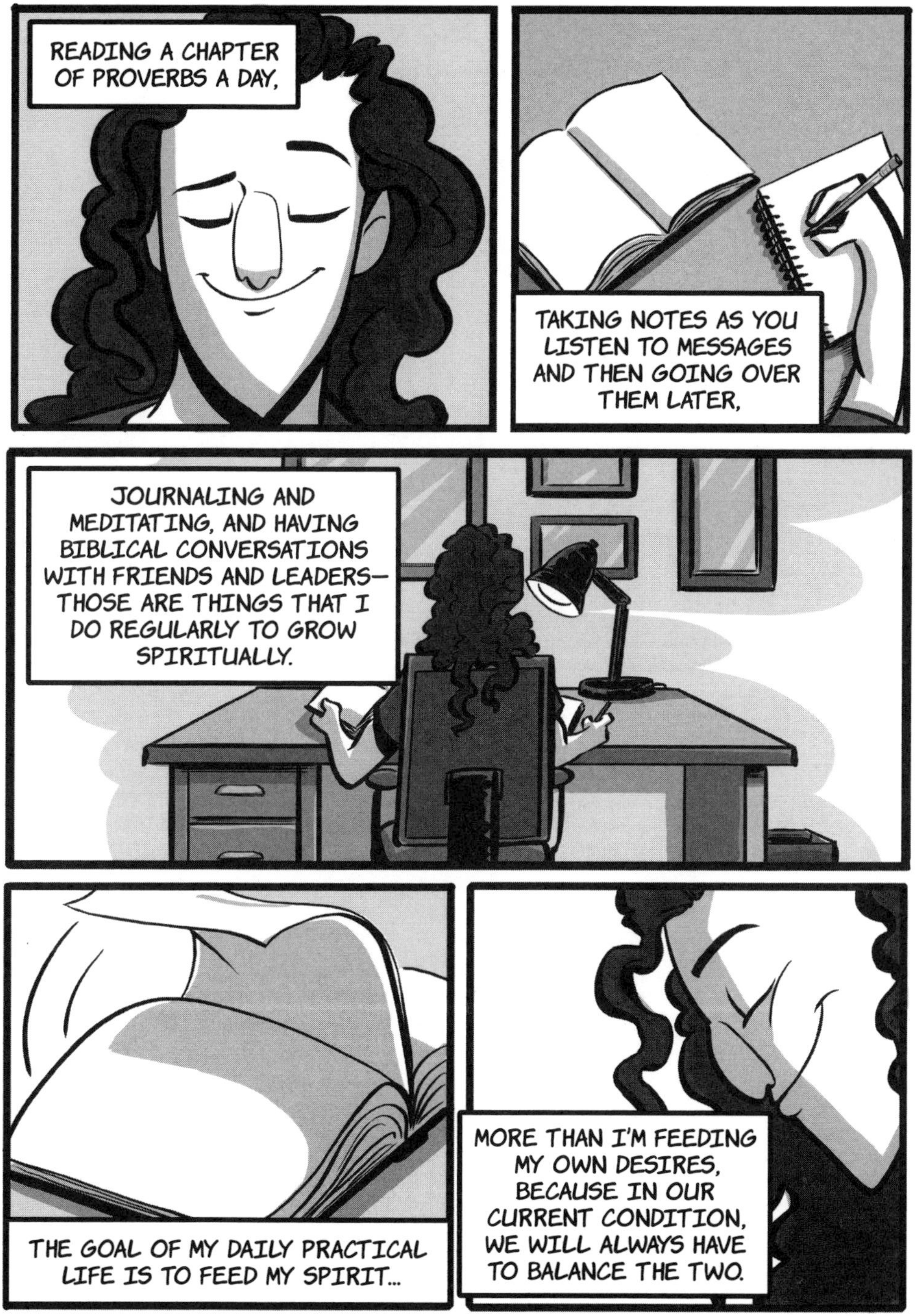
READING A CHAPTER OF PROVERBS A DAY,
TAKING NOTES AS YOU LISTEN TO MESSAGES AND THEN GOING OVER THEM LATER,
JOURNALING AND MEDITATING, AND HAVING BIBLICAL CONVERSATIONS WITH FRIENDS AND LEADERS— THOSE ARE THINGS THAT I DO REGULARLY TO GROW SPIRITUALLY.
THE GOAL OF MY DAILY PRACTICAL LIFE IS TO FEED MY SPIRIT...
MORE THAN I'M FEEDING MY OWN DESIRES, BECAUSE IN OUR CURRENT CONDITION, WE WILL ALWAYS HAVE TO BALANCE THE TWO.

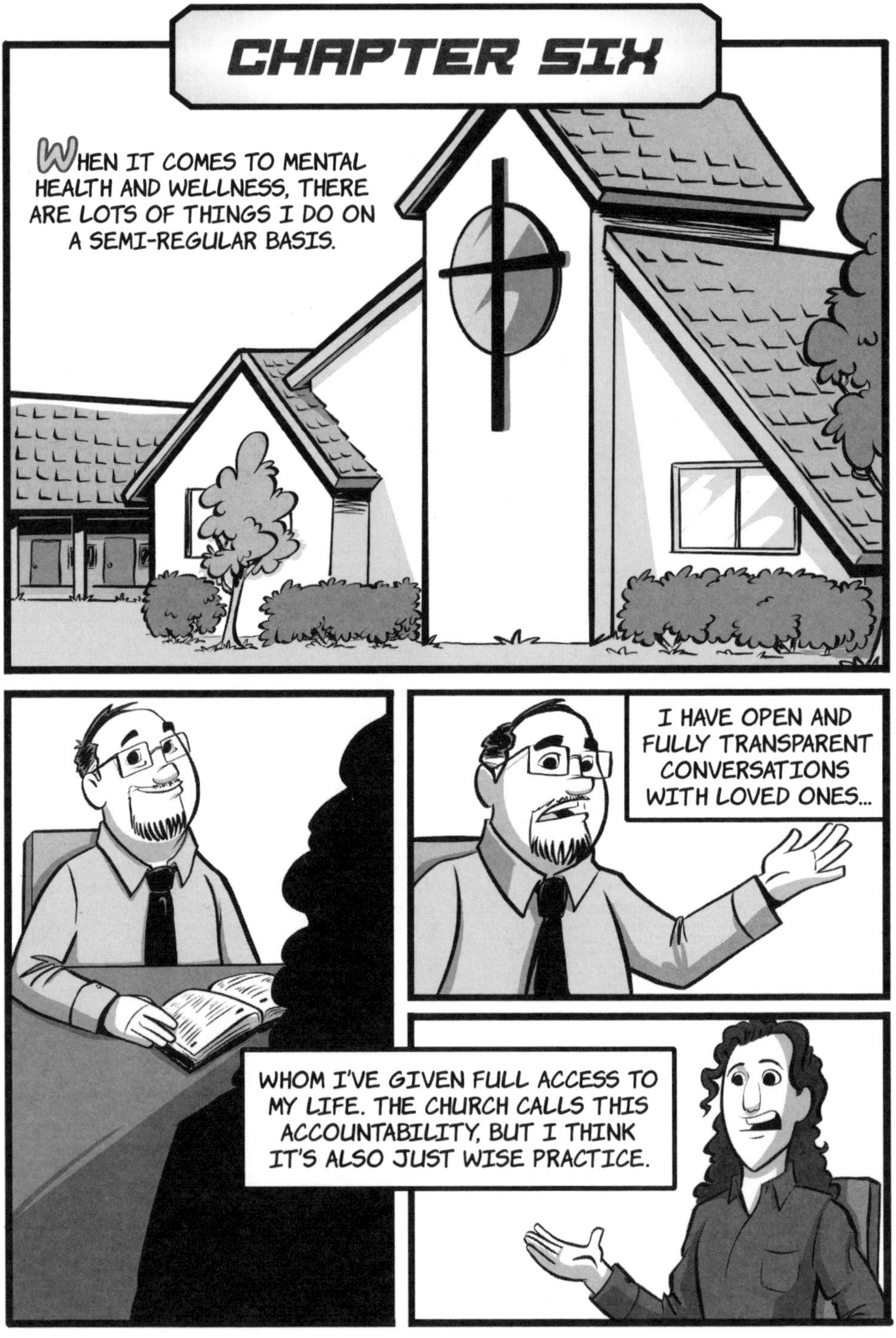
CHAPTER SIX
WHEN IT COMES TO MENTAL HEALTH AND WELLNESS, THERE ARE LOTS OF THINGS I DO ON A SEMI-REGULAR BASIS.
I HAVE OPEN AND FULLY TRANSPARENT CONVERSATIONS WITH LOVED ONES...
WHOM I'VE GIVEN FULL ACCESS TO MY LIFE. THE CHURCH CALLS THIS ACCOUNTABILITY, BUT I THINK IT'S ALSO JUST WISE PRACTICE.

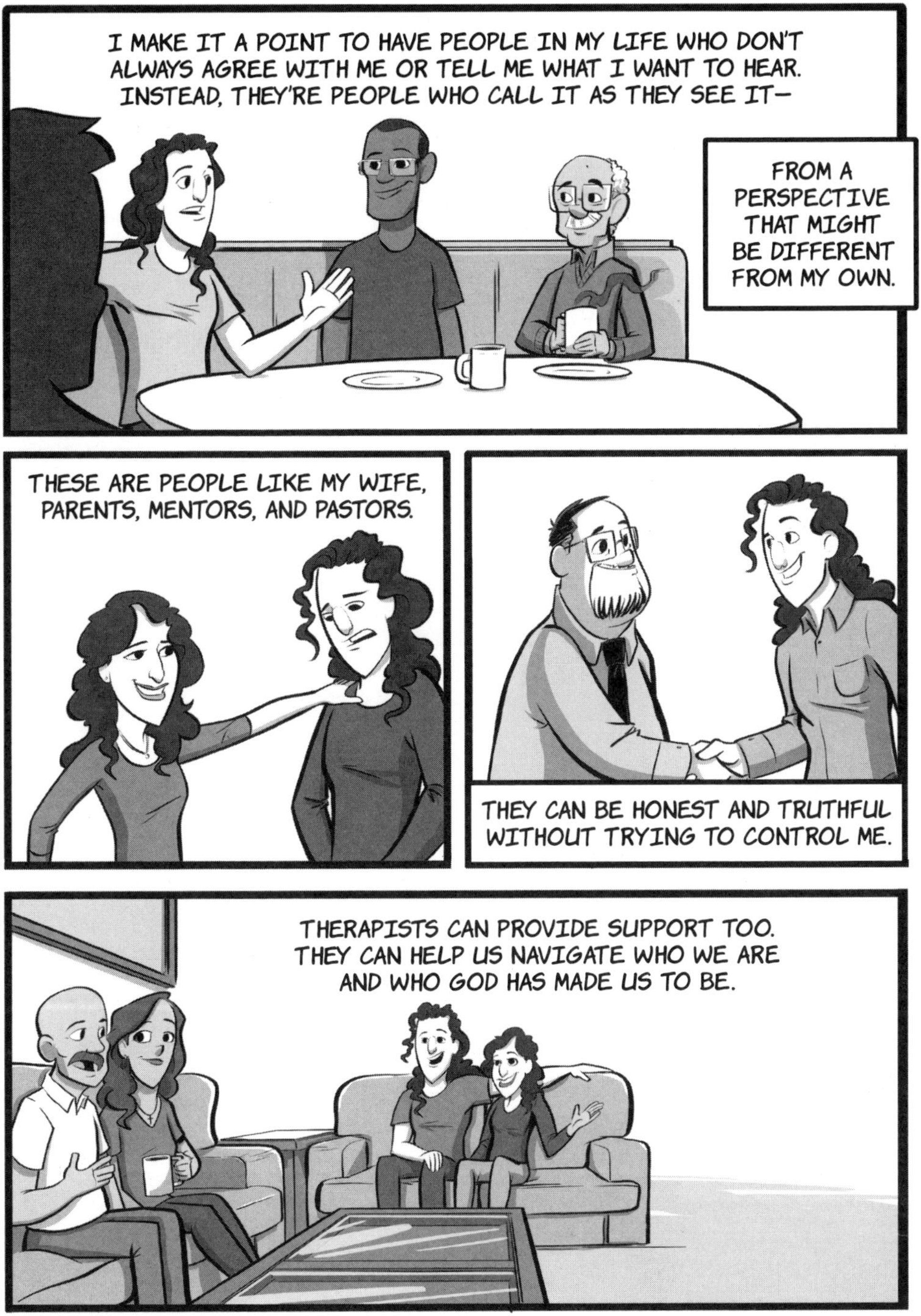
I MAKE IT A POINT TO HAVE PEOPLE IN MY LIFE WHO DON'T ALWAYS AGREE WITH ME OR TELL ME WHAT I WANT TO HEAR. INSTEAD, THEY'RE PEOPLE WHO CALL IT AS THEY SEE IT—
FROM A PERSPECTIVE THAT MIGHT BE DIFFERENT FROM MY OWN.
THESE ARE PEOPLE LIKE MY WIFE, PARENTS, MENTORS, AND PASTORS.
THEY CAN BE HONEST AND TRUTHFUL WITHOUT TRYING TO CONTROL ME.
THERAPISTS CAN PROVIDE SUPPORT TOO. THEY CAN HELP US NAVIGATE WHO WE ARE AND WHO GOD HAS MADE US TO BE.

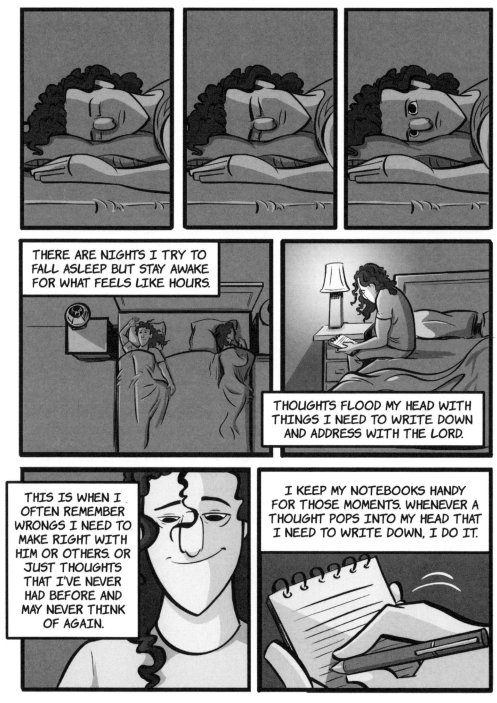

THERE ARE NIGHTS I TRY TO FALL ASLEEP BUT STAY AWAKE FOR WHAT FEELS LIKE HOURS.

THOUGHTS FLOOD MY HEAD WITH THINGS I NEED TO WRITE DOWN AND ADDRESS WITH THE LORD.

THIS IS WHEN I OFTEN REMEMBER WRONGS I NEED TO MAKE RIGHT WITH HIM OR OTHERS. OR JUST THOUGHTS THAT I'VE NEVER HAD BEFORE AND MAY NEVER THINK OF AGAIN.

I KEEP MY NOTEBOOKS HANDY FOR THOSE MOMENTS. WHENEVER A THOUGHT POPS INTO MY HEAD THAT I NEED TO WRITE DOWN, I DO IT.

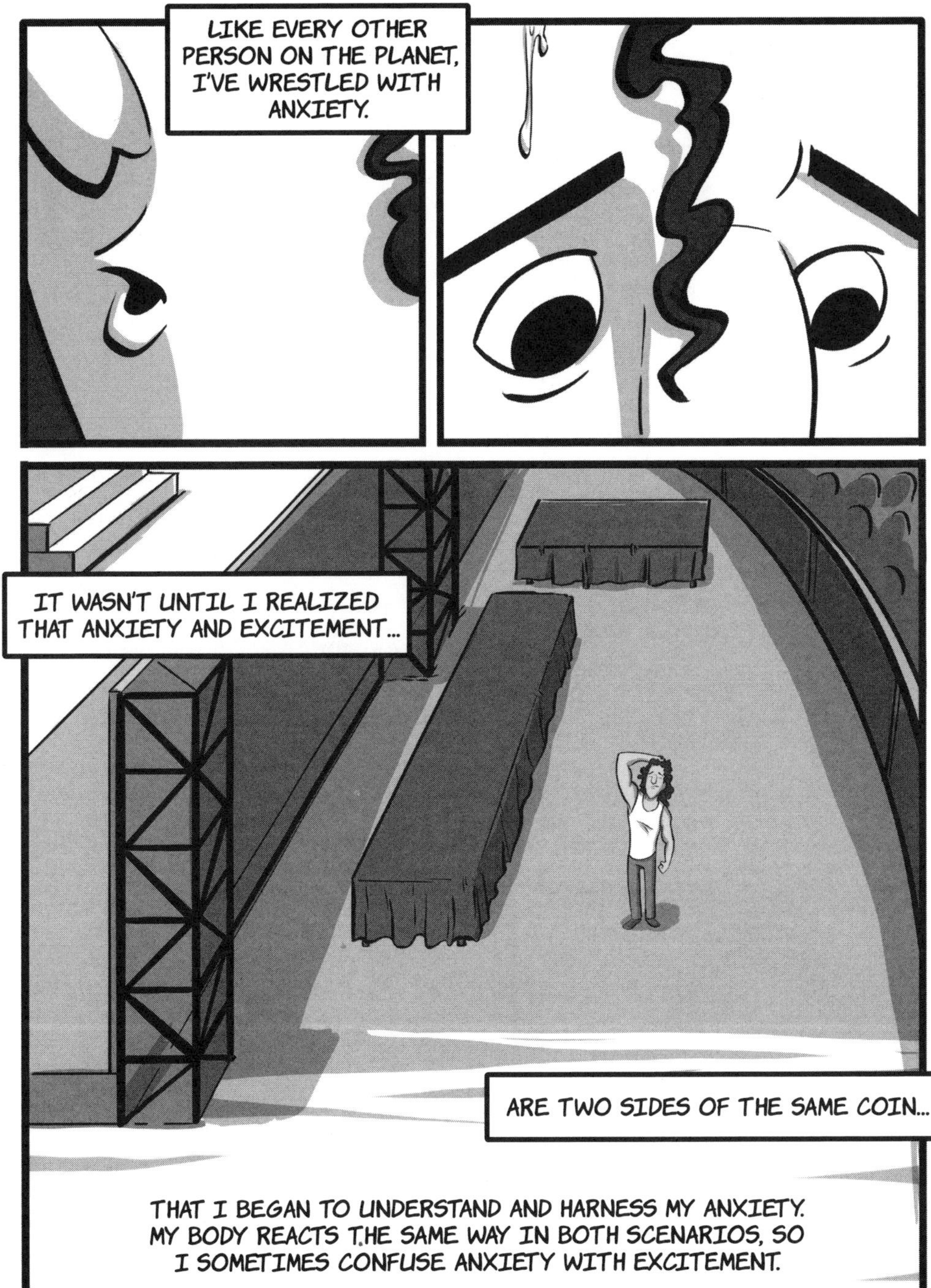
LIKE EVERY OTHER PERSON ON THE PLANET, I'VE WRESTLED WITH ANXIETY.
IT WASN'T UNTIL I REALIZED THAT ANXIETY AND EXCITEMENT...
ARE TWO SIDES OF THE SAME COIN...
THAT I BEGAN TO UNDERSTAND AND HARNESS MY ANXIETY. MY BODY REACTS THE SAME WAY IN BOTH SCENARIOS, SO I SOMETIMES CONFUSE ANXIETY WITH EXCITEMENT.

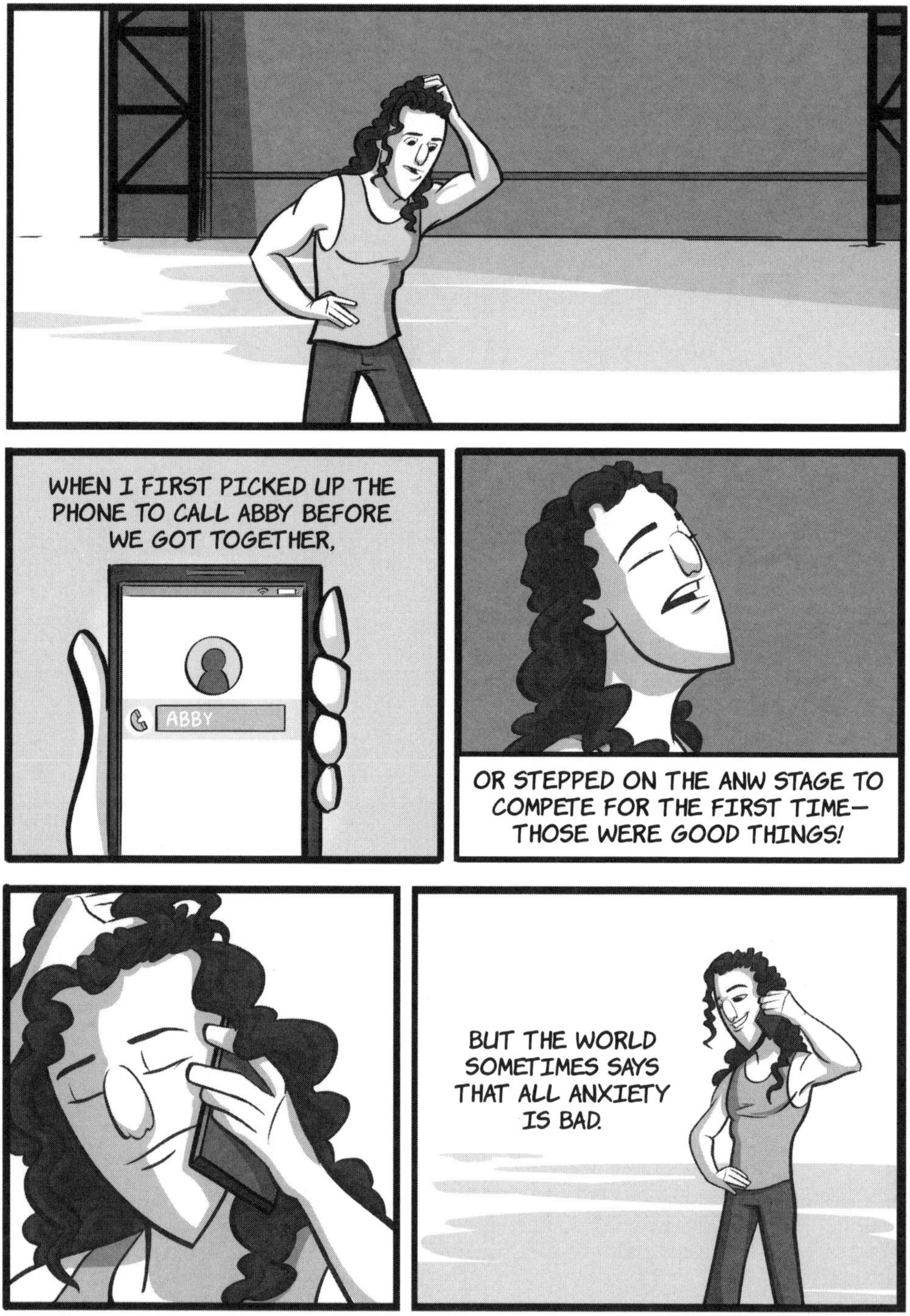
WHEN I FIRST PICKED UP THE PHONE TO CALL ABBY BEFORE WE GOT TOGETHER,
ABBY
OR STEPPED ON THE ANW STAGE TO COMPETE FOR THE FIRST TIME—THOSE WERE GOOD THINGS!
BUT THE WORLD SOMETIMES SAYS THAT ALL ANXIETY IS BAD.

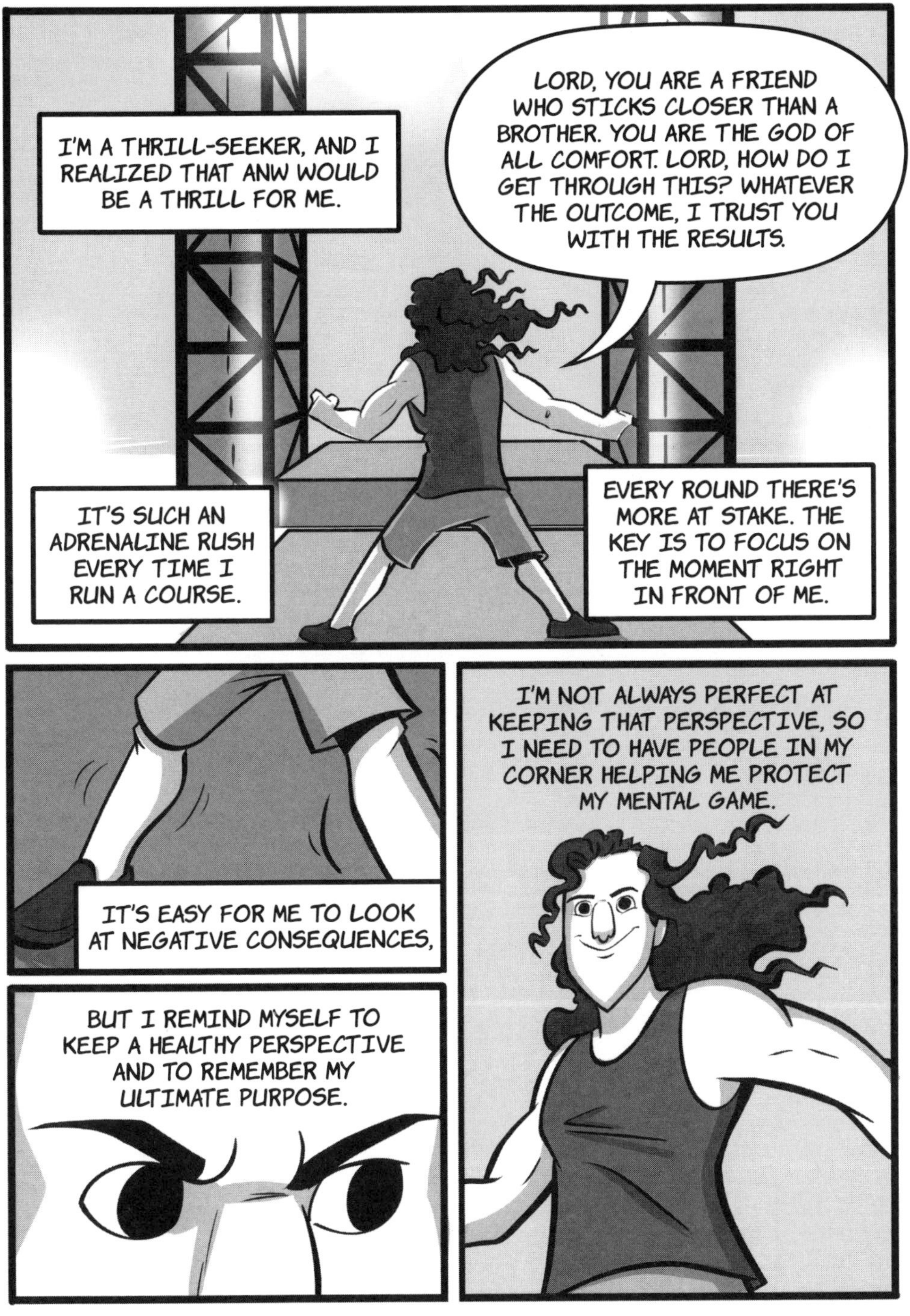
I'M A THRILL-SEEKER, AND I REALIZED THAT ANW WOULD BE A THRILL FOR ME.
LORD, YOU ARE A FRIEND WHO STICKS CLOSER THAN A BROTHER. YOU ARE THE GOD OF ALL COMFORT. LORD, HOW DO I GET THROUGH THIS? WHATEVER THE OUTCOME, I TRUST YOU WITH THE RESULTS.
IT'S SUCH AN ADRENALINE RUSH EVERY TIME I RUN A COURSE.
EVERY ROUND THERE'S MORE AT STAKE. THE KEY IS TO FOCUS ON THE MOMENT RIGHT IN FRONT OF ME.
IT'S EASY FOR ME TO LOOK AT NEGATIVE CONSEQUENCES,
BUT I REMIND MYSELF TO KEEP A HEALTHY PERSPECTIVE AND TO REMEMBER MY ULTIMATE PURPOSE.
I'M NOT ALWAYS PERFECT AT KEEPING THAT PERSPECTIVE, SO I NEED TO HAVE PEOPLE IN MY CORNER HELPING ME PROTECT MY MENTAL GAME.

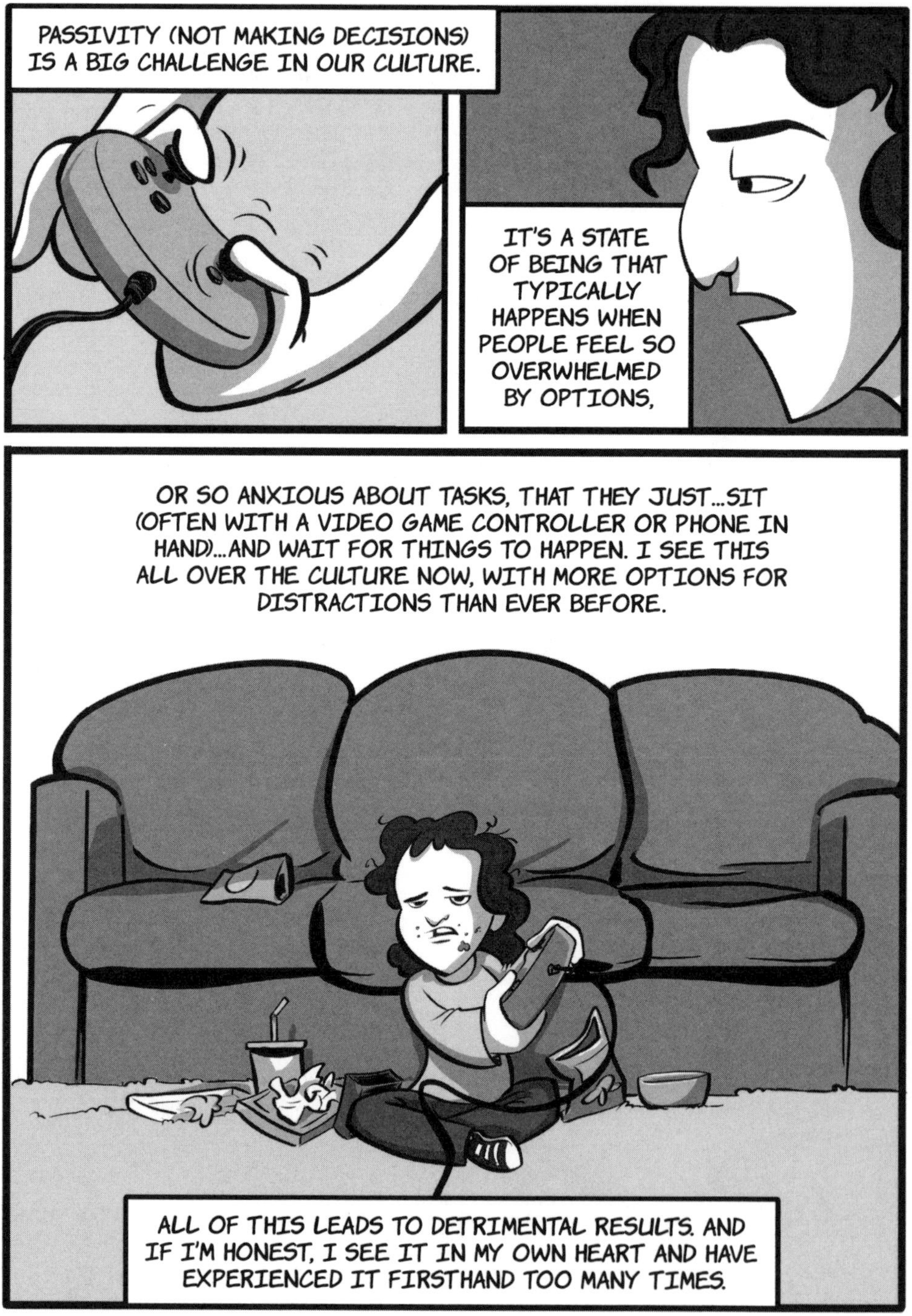
PASSIVITY (NOT MAKING DECISIONS) IS A BIG CHALLENGE IN OUR CULTURE.
IT'S A STATE OF BEING THAT TYPICALLY HAPPENS WHEN PEOPLE FEEL SO OVERWHELMED BY OPTIONS,
OR SO ANXIOUS ABOUT TASKS, THAT THEY JUST...SIT (OFTEN WITH A VIDEO GAME CONTROLLER OR PHONE IN HAND)...AND WAIT FOR THINGS TO HAPPEN. I SEE THIS ALL OVER THE CULTURE NOW, WITH MORE OPTIONS FOR DISTRACTIONS THAN EVER BEFORE.
ALL OF THIS LEADS TO DETRIMENTAL RESULTS. AND IF I'M HONEST, I SEE IT IN MY OWN HEART AND HAVE EXPERIENCED IT FIRSTHAND TOO MANY TIMES.

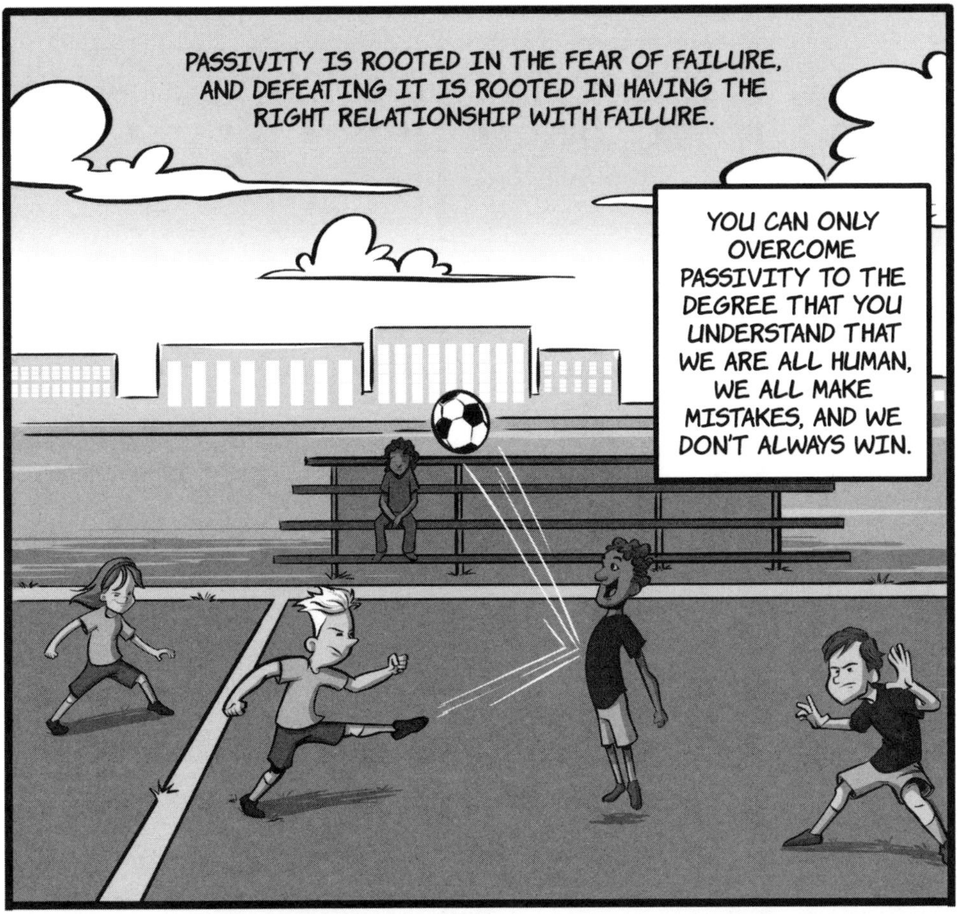
PASSIVITY IS ROOTED IN THE FEAR OF FAILURE, AND DEFEATING IT IS ROOTED IN HAVING THE RIGHT RELATIONSHIP WITH FAILURE.
YOU CAN ONLY OVERCOME PASSIVITY TO THE DEGREE THAT YOU UNDERSTAND THAT WE ARE ALL HUMAN, WE ALL MAKE MISTAKES, AND WE DON'T ALWAYS WIN.

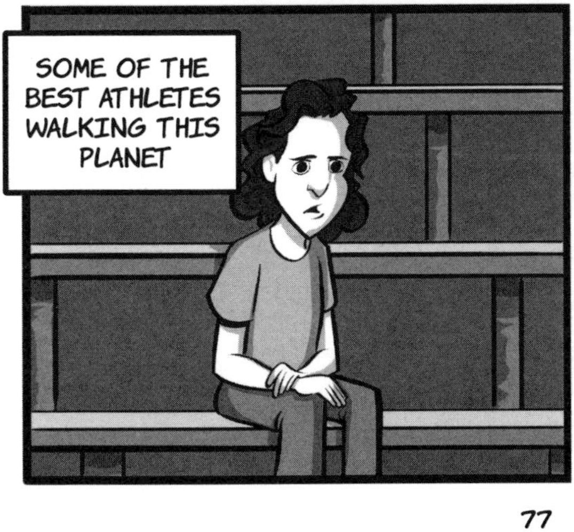
SOME OF THE BEST ATHLETES WALKING THIS PLANET

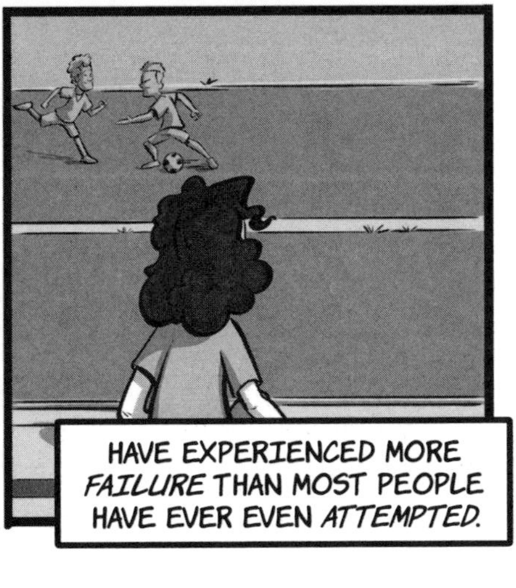
HAVE EXPERIENCED MORE *FAILURE* THAN MOST PEOPLE HAVE EVER EVEN *ATTEMPTED*.

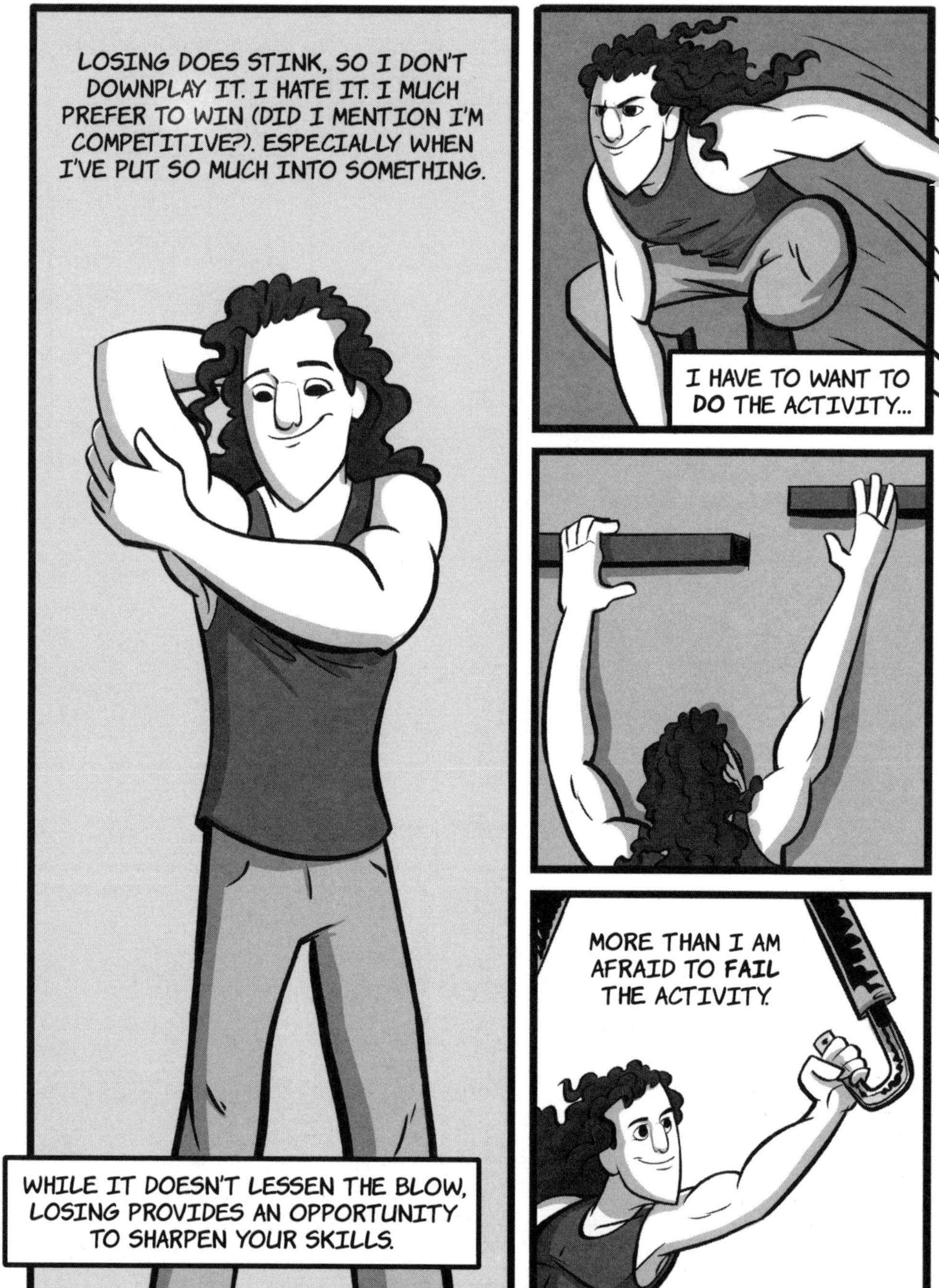
LOSING DOES STINK, SO I DON'T DOWNPLAY IT. I HATE IT. I MUCH PREFER TO WIN (DID I MENTION I'M COMPETITIVE?). ESPECIALLY WHEN I'VE PUT SO MUCH INTO SOMETHING.
WHILE IT DOESN'T LESSEN THE BLOW, LOSING PROVIDES AN OPPORTUNITY TO SHARPEN YOUR SKILLS.
I HAVE TO WANT TO DO THE ACTIVITY...
MORE THAN I AM AFRAID TO FAIL THE ACTIVITY.

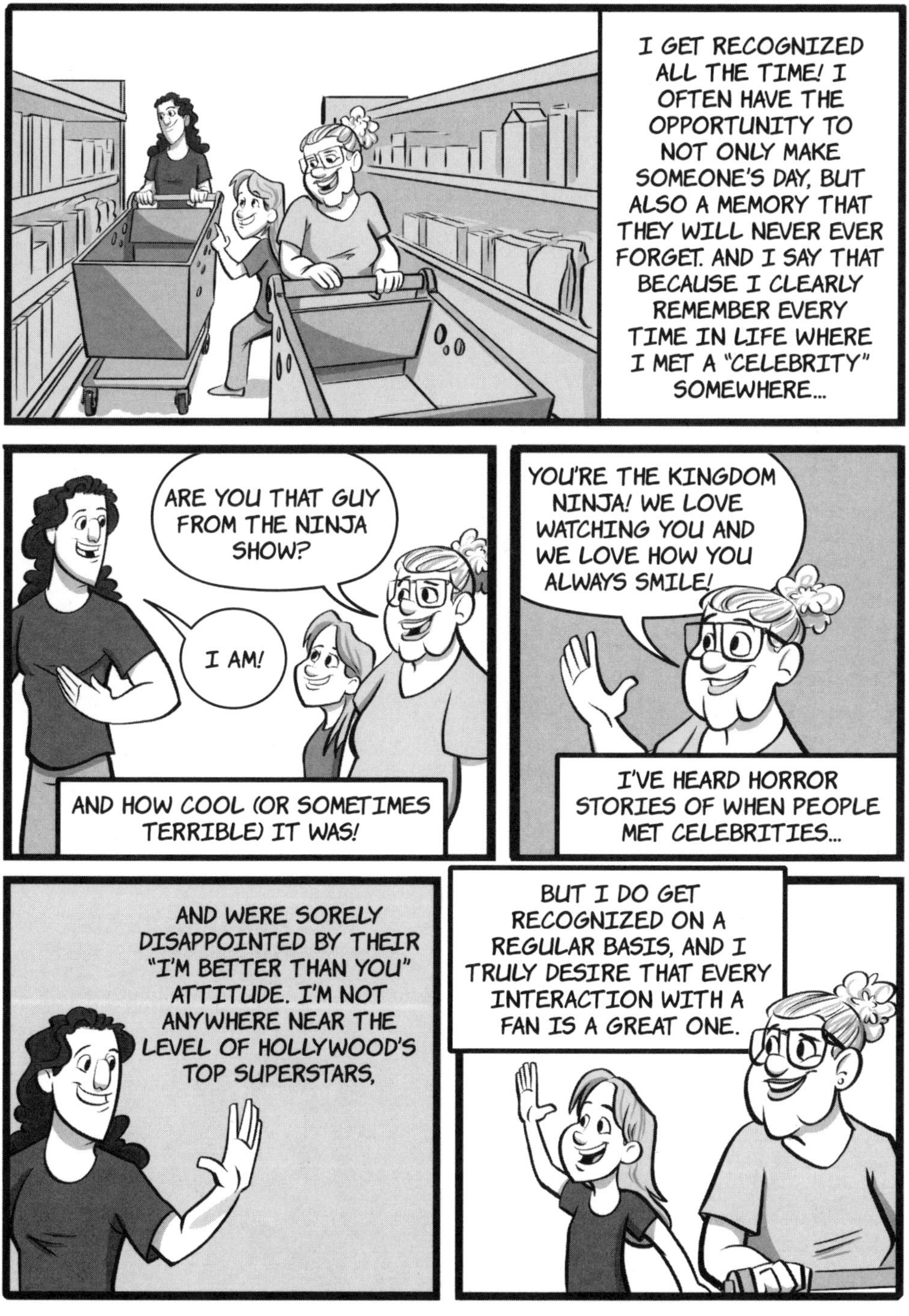
I GET RECOGNIZED ALL THE TIME! I OFTEN HAVE THE OPPORTUNITY TO NOT ONLY MAKE SOMEONE'S DAY, BUT ALSO A MEMORY THAT THEY WILL NEVER EVER FORGET. AND I SAY THAT BECAUSE I CLEARLY REMEMBER EVERY TIME IN LIFE WHERE I MET A "CELEBRITY" SOMEWHERE...
ARE YOU THAT GUY FROM THE NINJA SHOW?
I AM!
AND HOW COOL (OR SOMETIMES TERRIBLE) IT WAS!
YOU'RE THE KINGDOM NINJA! WE LOVE WATCHING YOU AND WE LOVE HOW YOU ALWAYS SMILE!
I'VE HEARD HORROR STORIES OF WHEN PEOPLE MET CELEBRITIES...
AND WERE SORELY DISAPPOINTED BY THEIR "I'M BETTER THAN YOU" ATTITUDE. I'M NOT ANYWHERE NEAR THE LEVEL OF HOLLYWOOD'S TOP SUPERSTARS,
BUT I DO GET RECOGNIZED ON A REGULAR BASIS, AND I TRULY DESIRE THAT EVERY INTERACTION WITH A FAN IS A GREAT ONE.

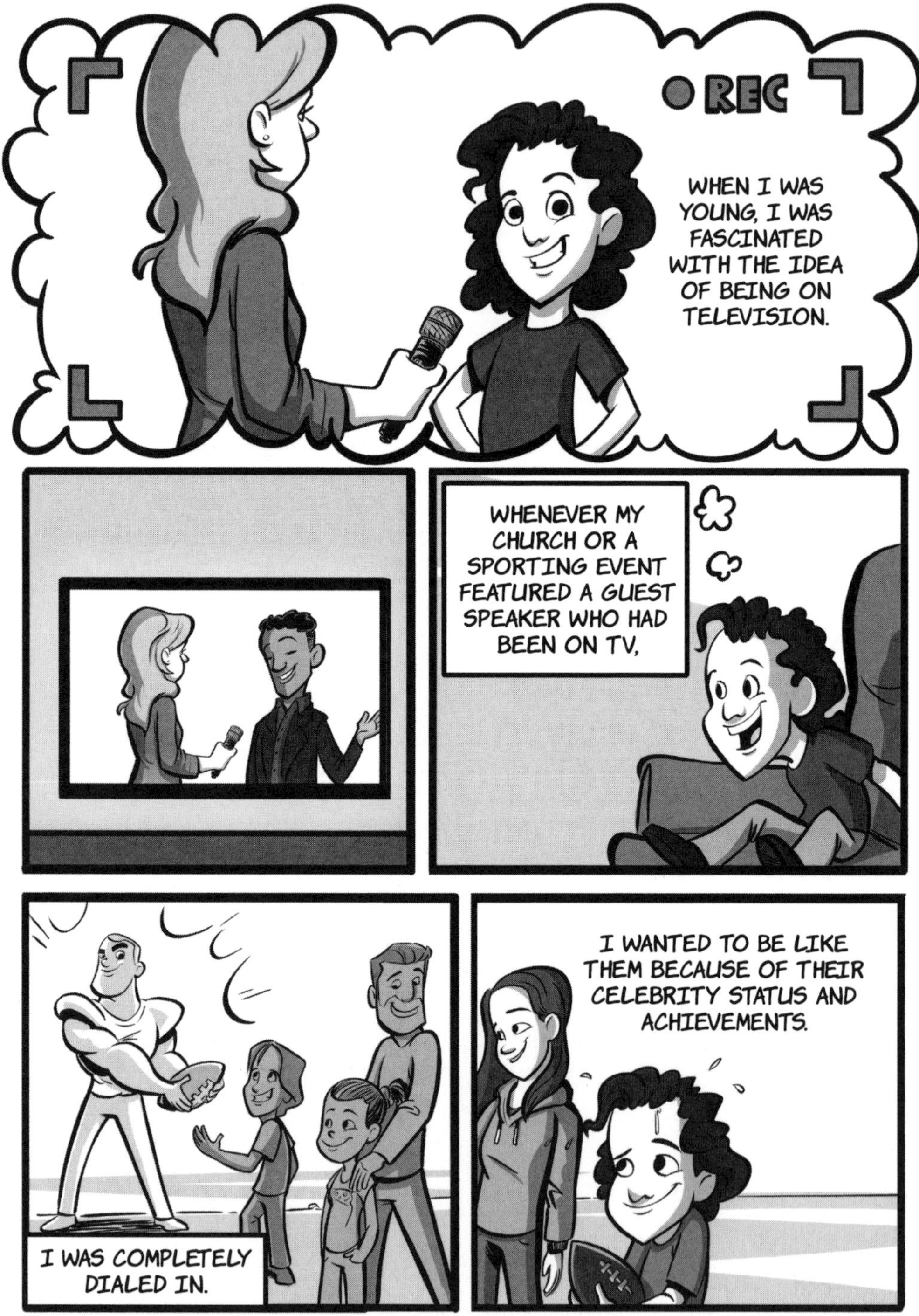
REC
WHEN I WAS YOUNG, I WAS FASCINATED WITH THE IDEA OF BEING ON TELEVISION.
WHENEVER MY CHURCH OR A SPORTING EVENT FEATURED A GUEST SPEAKER WHO HAD BEEN ON TV,
I WAS COMPLETELY DIALED IN.
I WANTED TO BE LIKE THEM BECAUSE OF THEIR CELEBRITY STATUS AND ACHIEVEMENTS.

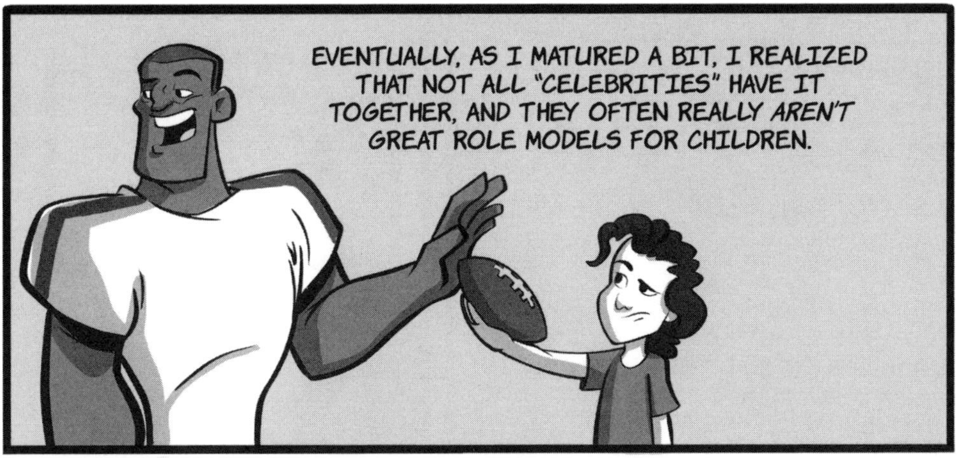
EVENTUALLY, AS I MATURED A BIT, I REALIZED THAT NOT ALL "CELEBRITIES" HAVE IT TOGETHER, AND THEY OFTEN REALLY *AREN'T* GREAT ROLE MODELS FOR CHILDREN.

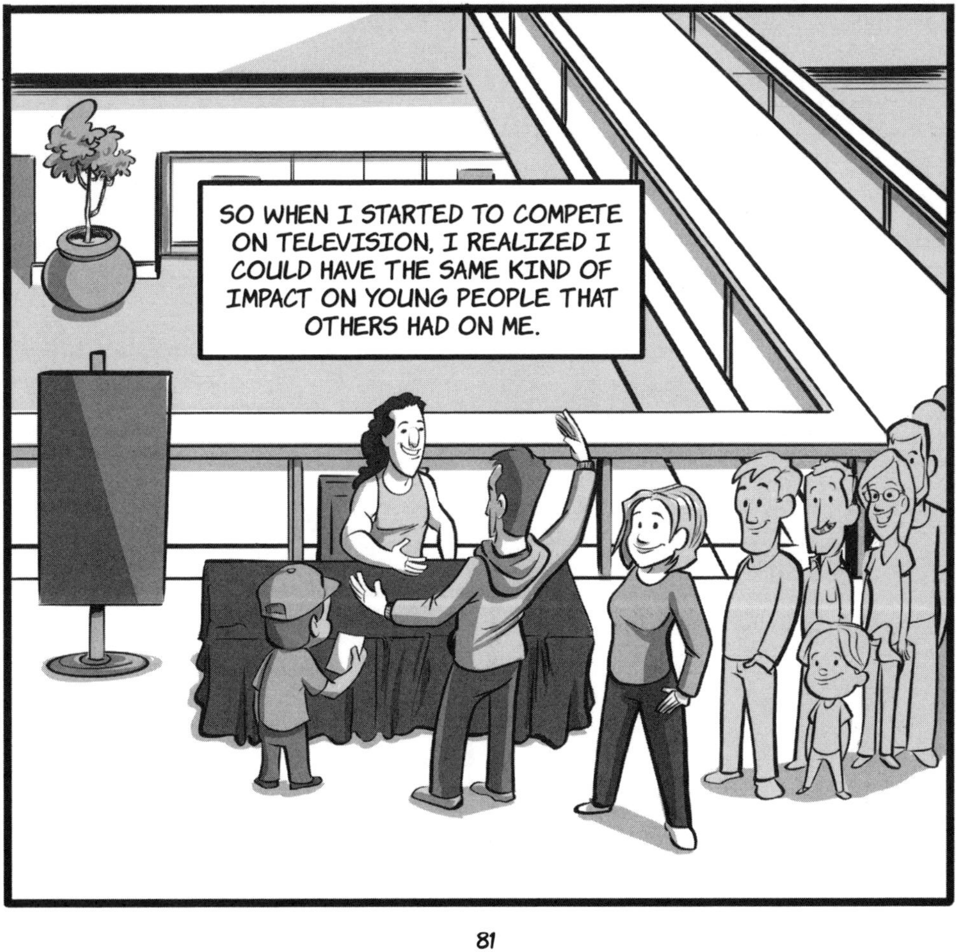
SO WHEN I STARTED TO COMPETE ON TELEVISION, I REALIZED I COULD HAVE THE SAME KIND OF IMPACT ON YOUNG PEOPLE THAT OTHERS HAD ON ME.

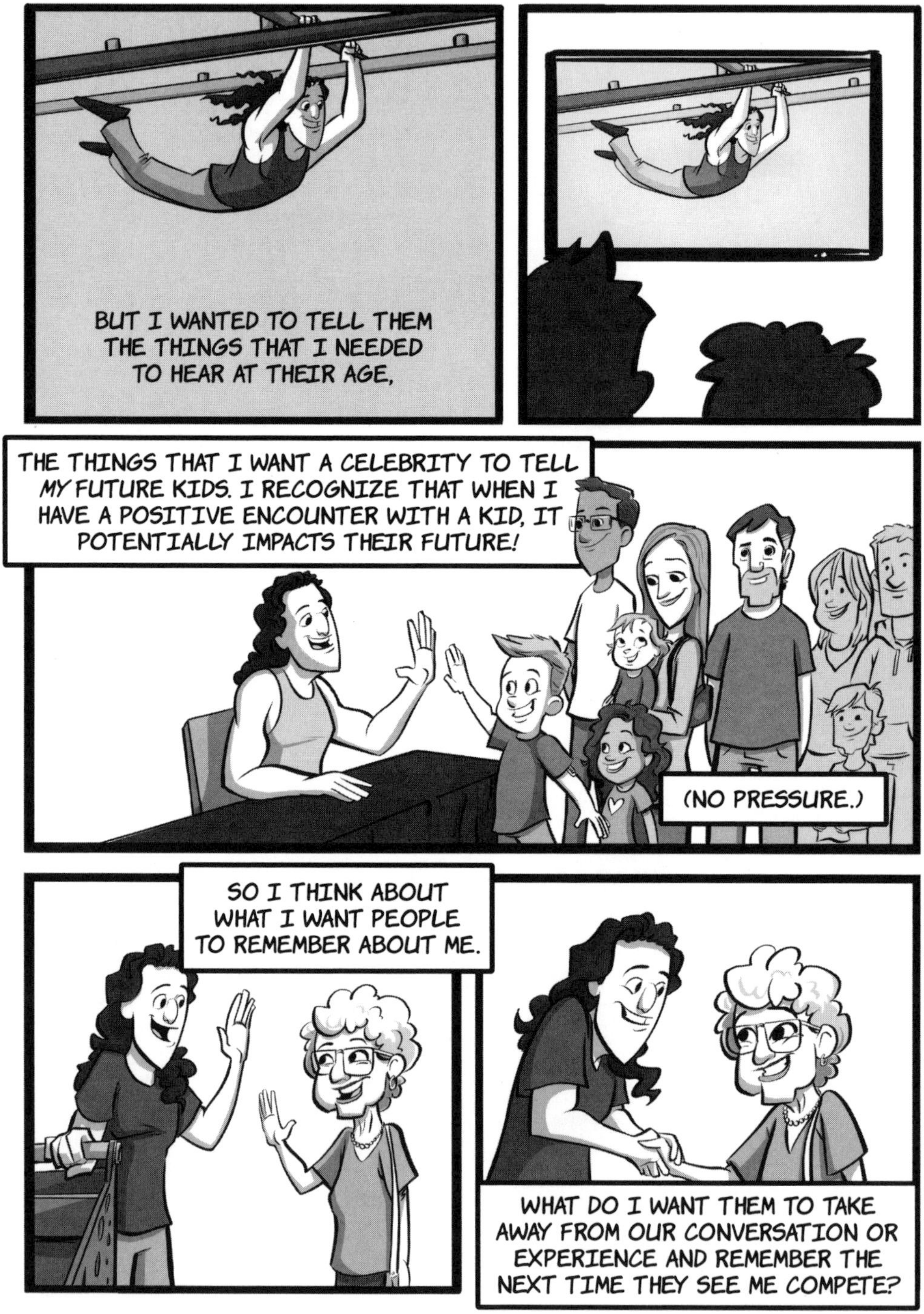
BUT I WANTED TO TELL THEM THE THINGS THAT I NEEDED TO HEAR AT THEIR AGE,
THE THINGS THAT I WANT A CELEBRITY TO TELL *MY* FUTURE KIDS. I RECOGNIZE THAT WHEN I HAVE A POSITIVE ENCOUNTER WITH A KID, IT POTENTIALLY IMPACTS THEIR FUTURE!
(NO PRESSURE.)
SO I THINK ABOUT WHAT I WANT PEOPLE TO REMEMBER ABOUT ME.
WHAT DO I WANT THEM TO TAKE AWAY FROM OUR CONVERSATION OR EXPERIENCE AND REMEMBER THE NEXT TIME THEY SEE ME COMPETE?

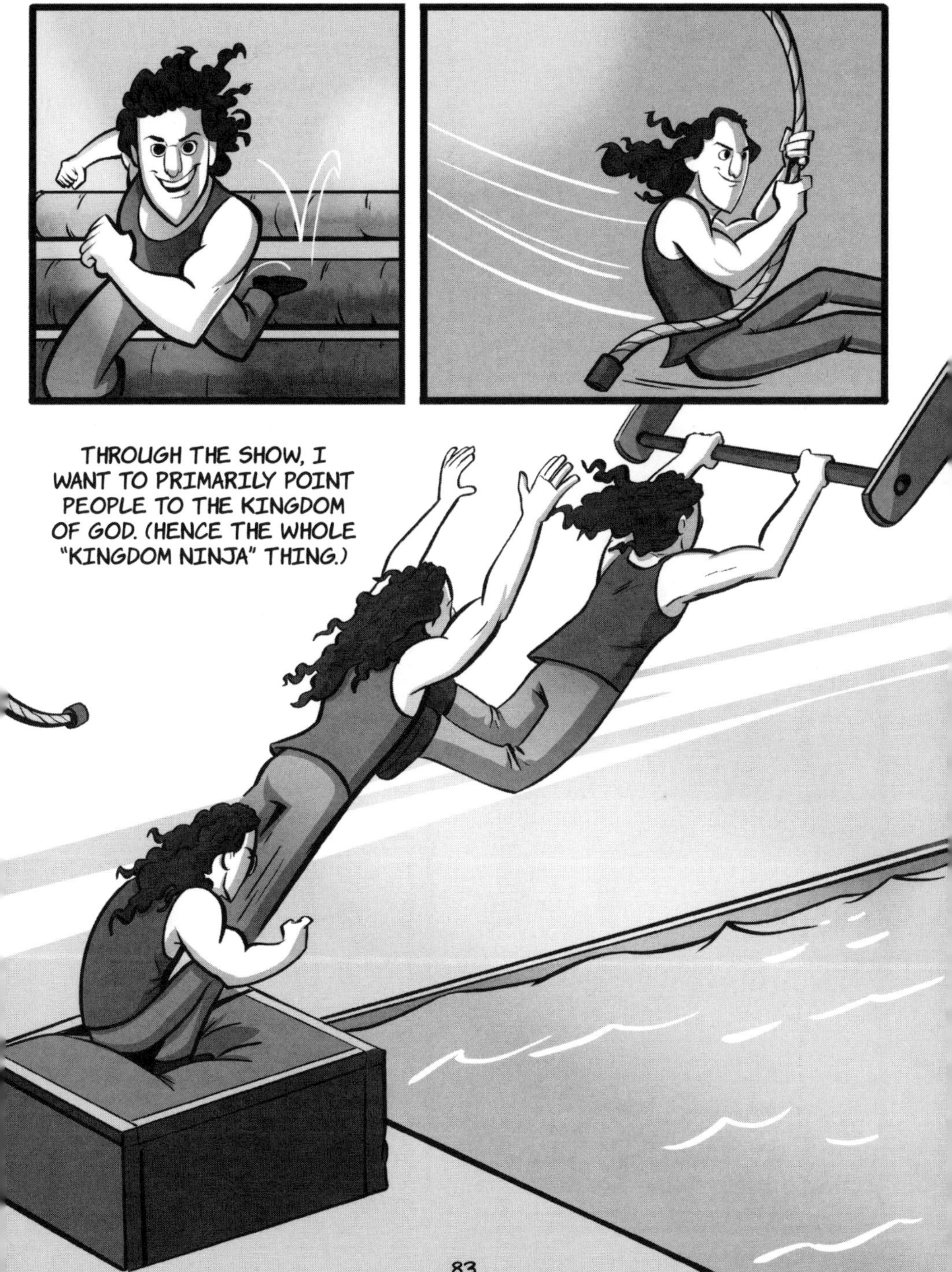
THROUGH THE SHOW, I WANT TO PRIMARILY POINT PEOPLE TO THE KINGDOM OF GOD. (HENCE THE WHOLE "KINGDOM NINJA" THING.)

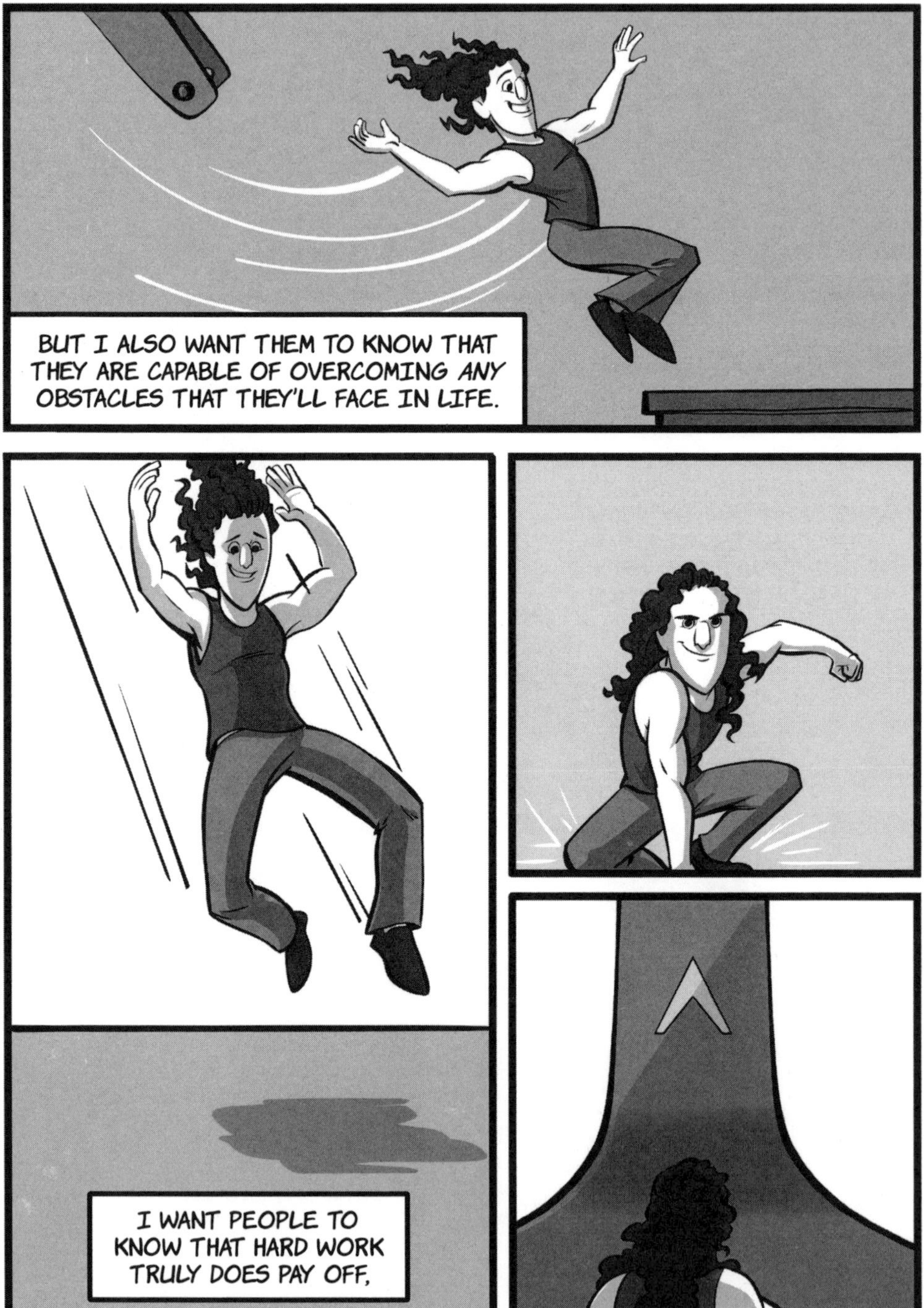
BUT I ALSO WANT THEM TO KNOW THAT THEY ARE CAPABLE OF OVERCOMING *ANY* OBSTACLES THAT THEY'LL FACE IN LIFE.
I WANT PEOPLE TO KNOW THAT HARD WORK TRULY DOES PAY OFF,

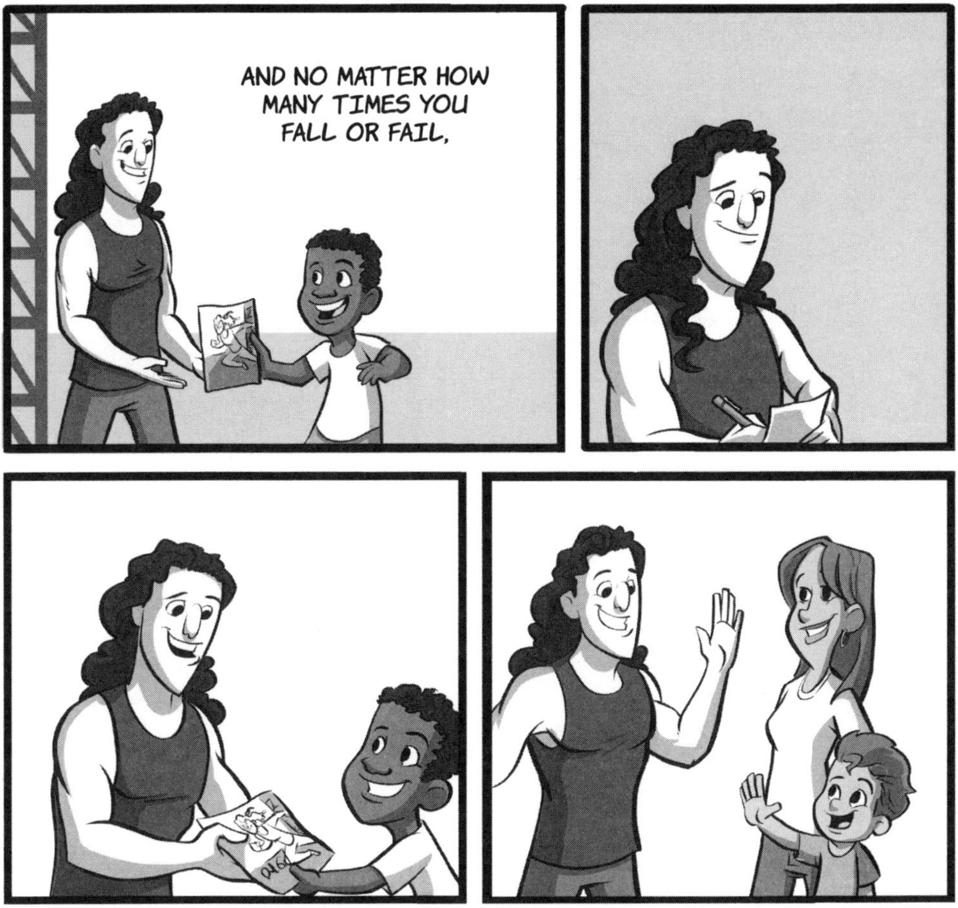
AND NO MATTER HOW MANY TIMES YOU FALL OR FAIL,

YOU CAN LEARN TO GET BACK UP AS QUICKLY AS POSSIBLE SO YOU CAN FINISH WHAT YOU STARTED.

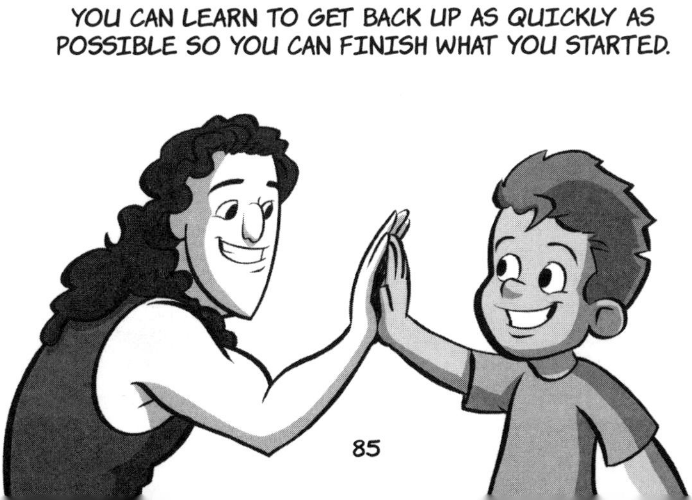

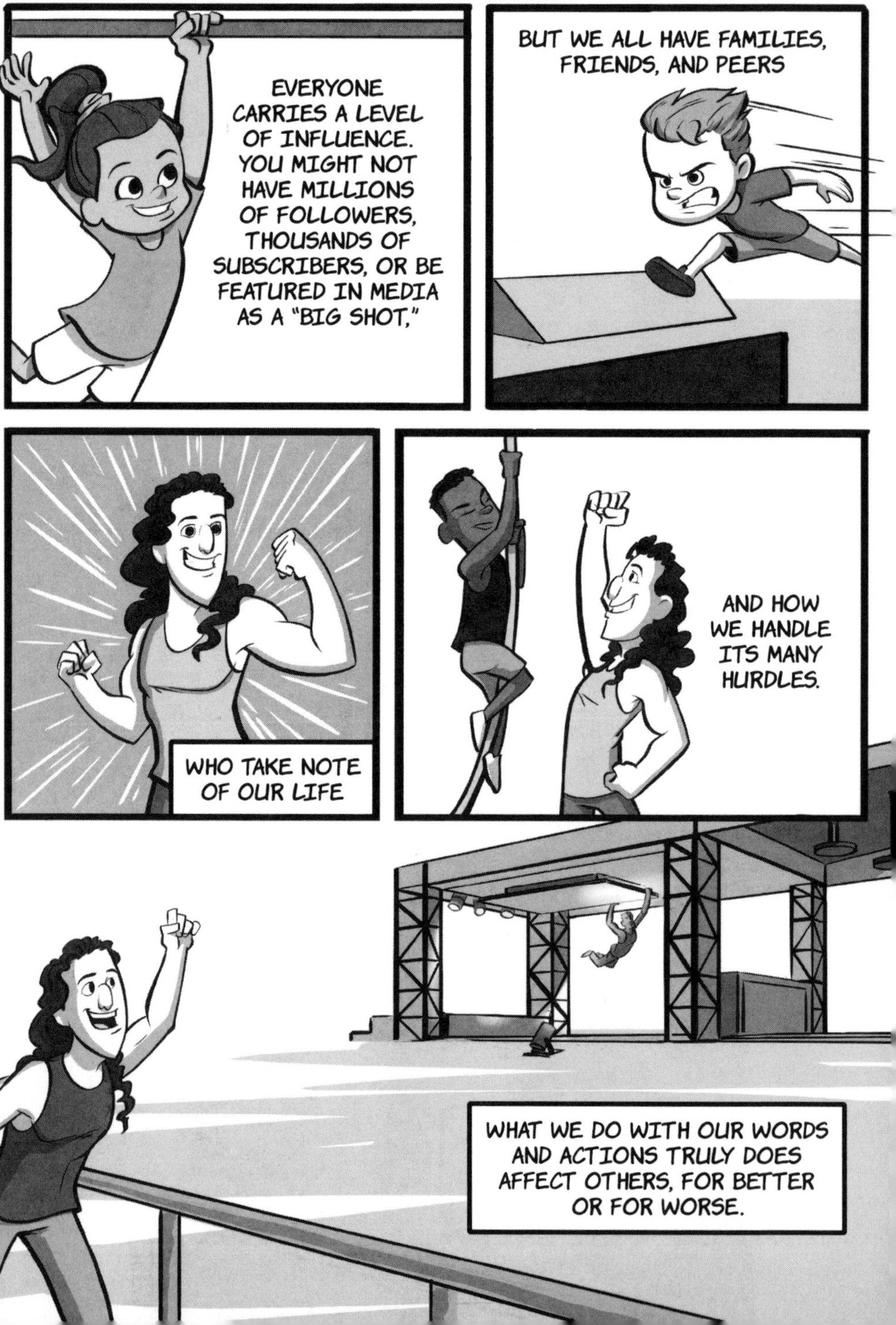
EVERYONE CARRIES A LEVEL OF INFLUENCE. YOU MIGHT NOT HAVE MILLIONS OF FOLLOWERS, THOUSANDS OF SUBSCRIBERS, OR BE FEATURED IN MEDIA AS A "BIG SHOT,"
BUT WE ALL HAVE FAMILIES, FRIENDS, AND PEERS
WHO TAKE NOTE OF OUR LIFE
AND HOW WE HANDLE ITS MANY HURDLES.
WHAT WE DO WITH OUR WORDS AND ACTIONS TRULY DOES AFFECT OTHERS, FOR BETTER OR FOR WORSE.

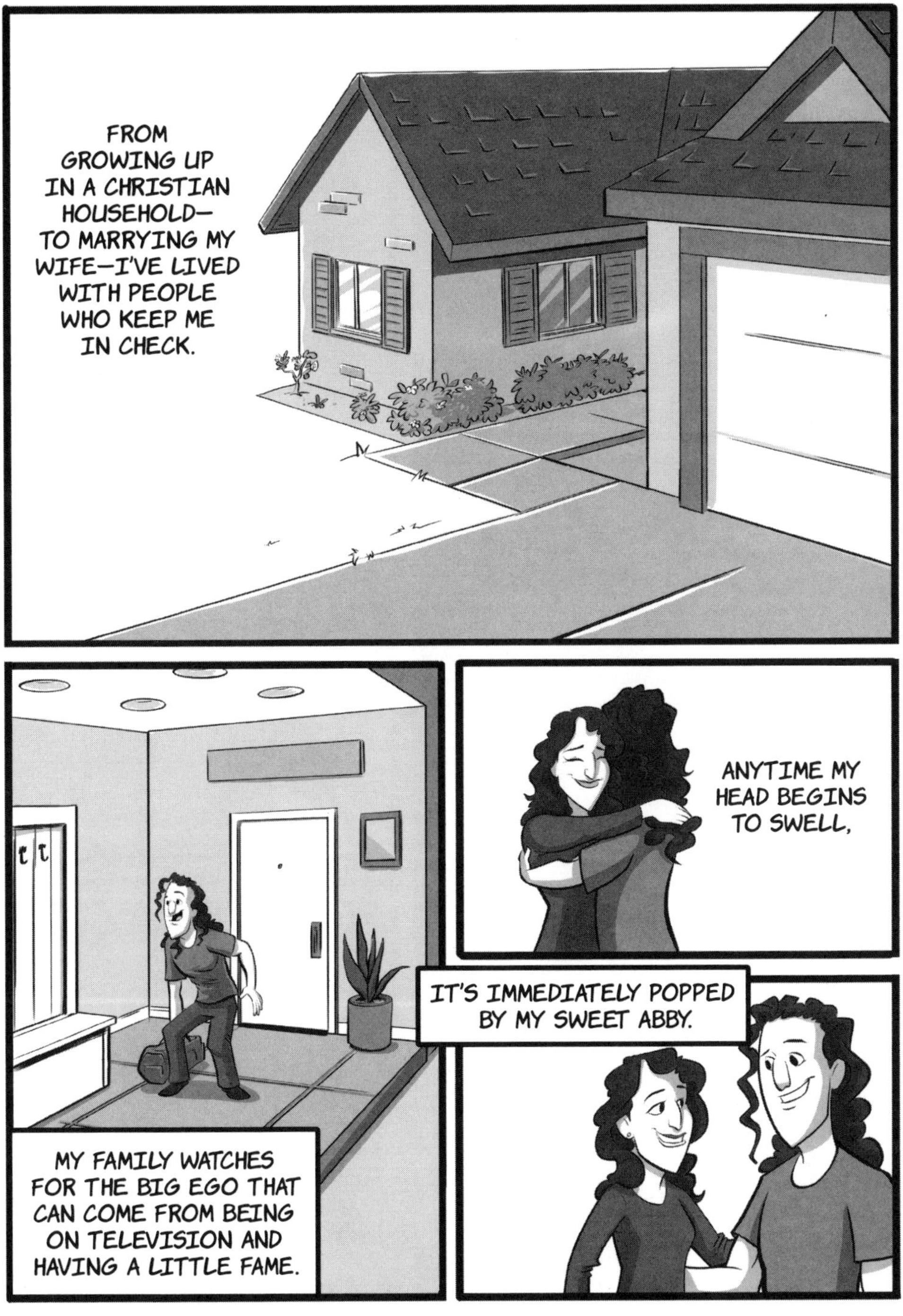
FROM GROWING UP IN A CHRISTIAN HOUSEHOLD—TO MARRYING MY WIFE—I'VE LIVED WITH PEOPLE WHO KEEP ME IN CHECK.
MY FAMILY WATCHES FOR THE BIG EGO THAT CAN COME FROM BEING ON TELEVISION AND HAVING A LITTLE FAME.
ANYTIME MY HEAD BEGINS TO SWELL,
IT'S IMMEDIATELY POPPED BY MY SWEET ABBY.

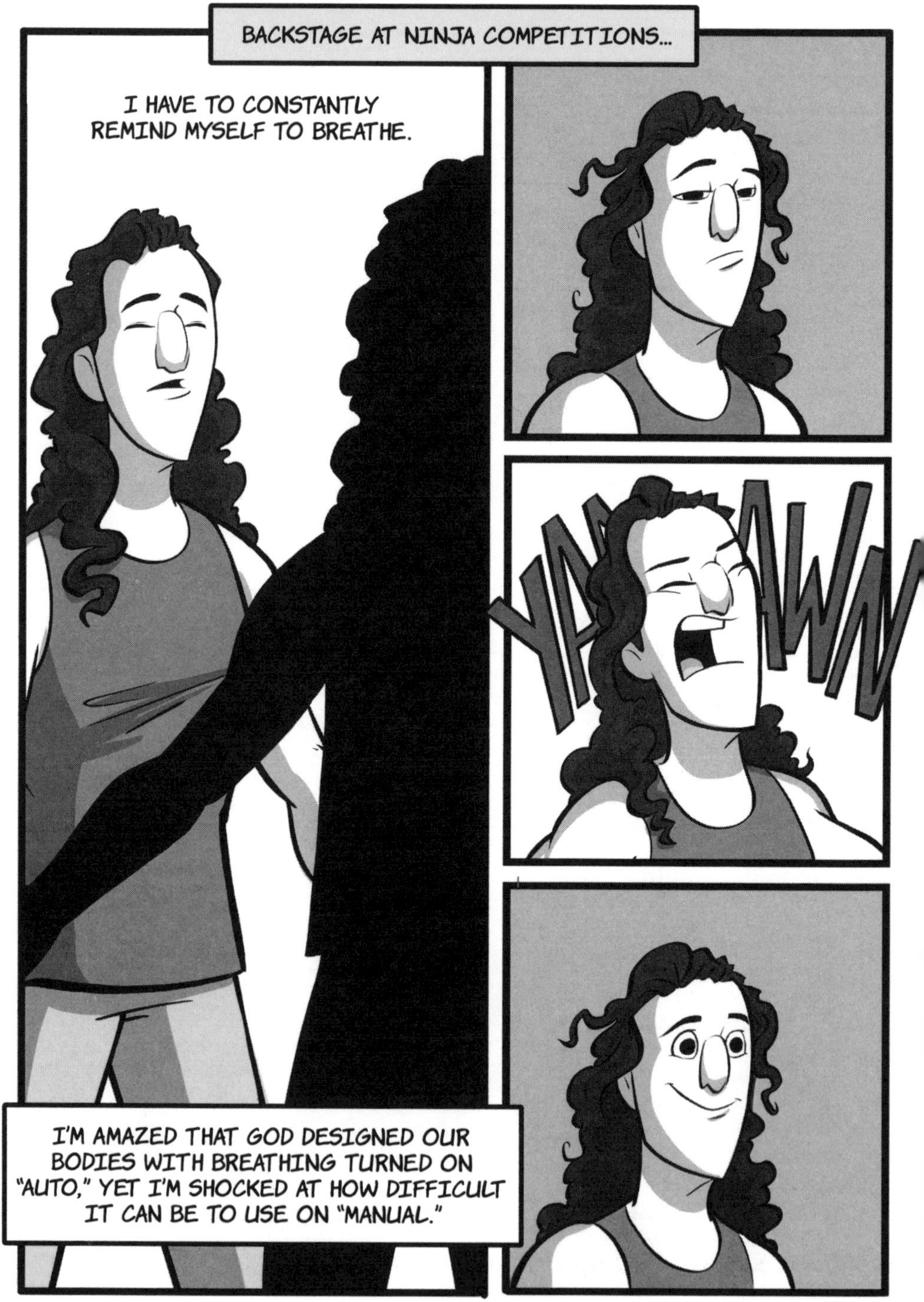
BACKSTAGE AT NINJA COMPETITIONS...
I HAVE TO CONSTANTLY REMIND MYSELF TO BREATHE.
YAAAWN
I'M AMAZED THAT GOD DESIGNED OUR BODIES WITH BREATHING TURNED ON "AUTO," YET I'M SHOCKED AT HOW DIFFICULT IT CAN BE TO USE ON "MANUAL."

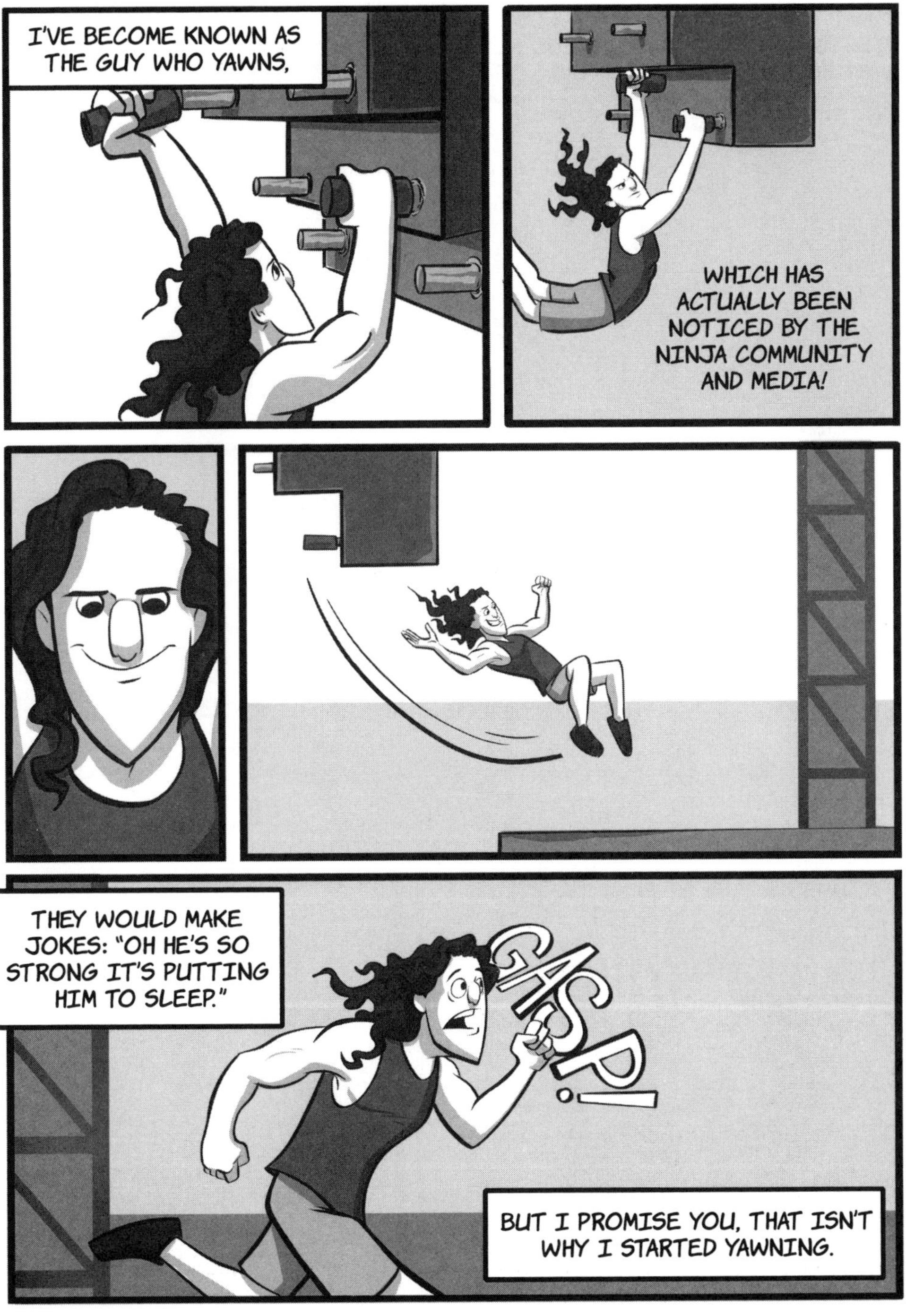
I'VE BECOME KNOWN AS THE GUY WHO YAWNS,
WHICH HAS ACTUALLY BEEN NOTICED BY THE NINJA COMMUNITY AND MEDIA!
THEY WOULD MAKE JOKES: "OH HE'S SO STRONG IT'S PUTTING HIM TO SLEEP."
GASP!
BUT I PROMISE YOU, THAT ISN'T WHY I STARTED YAWNING.

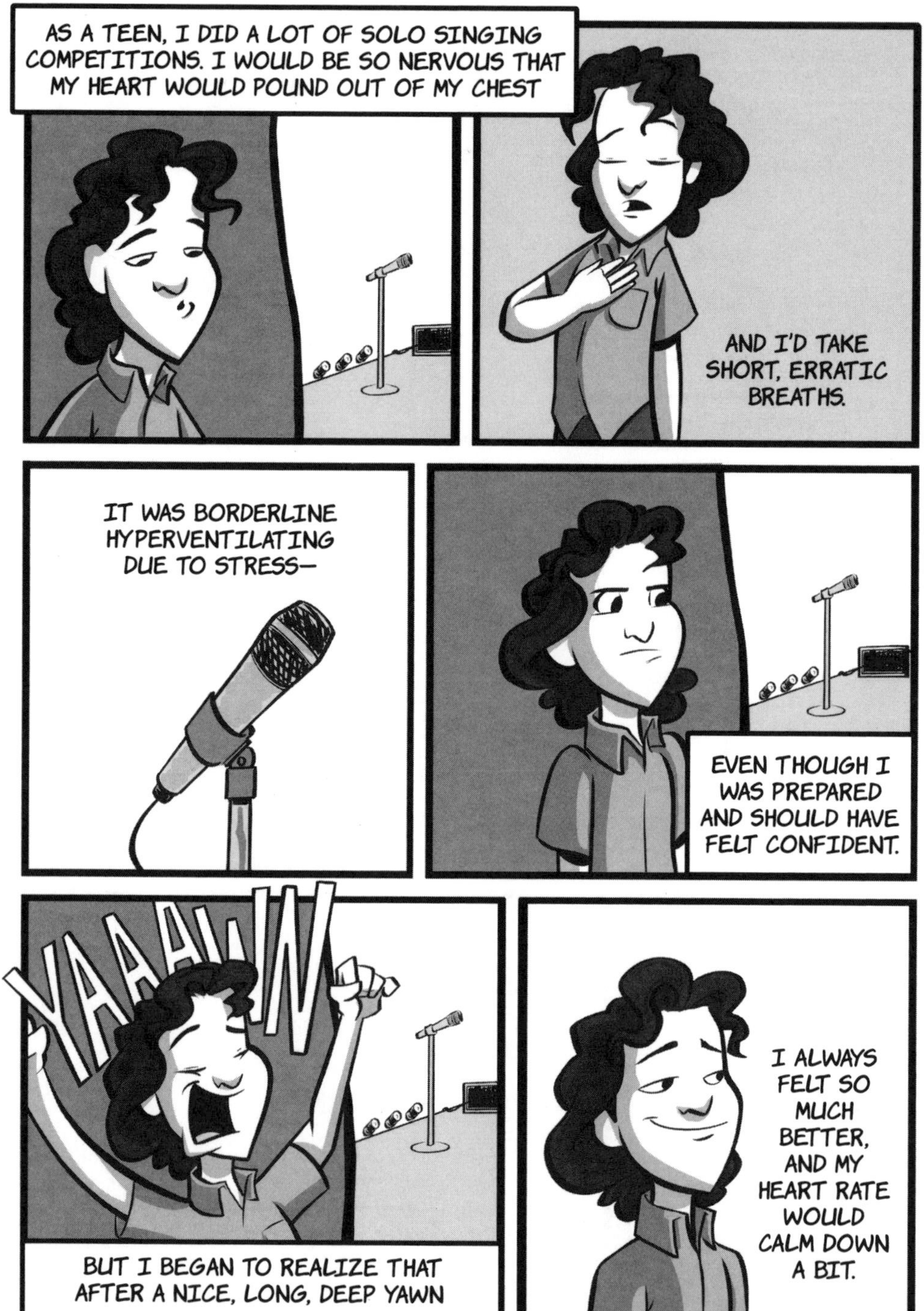
AS A TEEN, I DID A LOT OF SOLO SINGING COMPETITIONS. I WOULD BE SO NERVOUS THAT MY HEART WOULD POUND OUT OF MY CHEST
AND I'D TAKE SHORT, ERRATIC BREATHS.
IT WAS BORDERLINE HYPERVENTILATING DUE TO STRESS—
EVEN THOUGH I WAS PREPARED AND SHOULD HAVE FELT CONFIDENT.
YAAAWN
BUT I BEGAN TO REALIZE THAT AFTER A NICE, LONG, DEEP YAWN
I ALWAYS FELT SO MUCH BETTER, AND MY HEART RATE WOULD CALM DOWN A BIT.

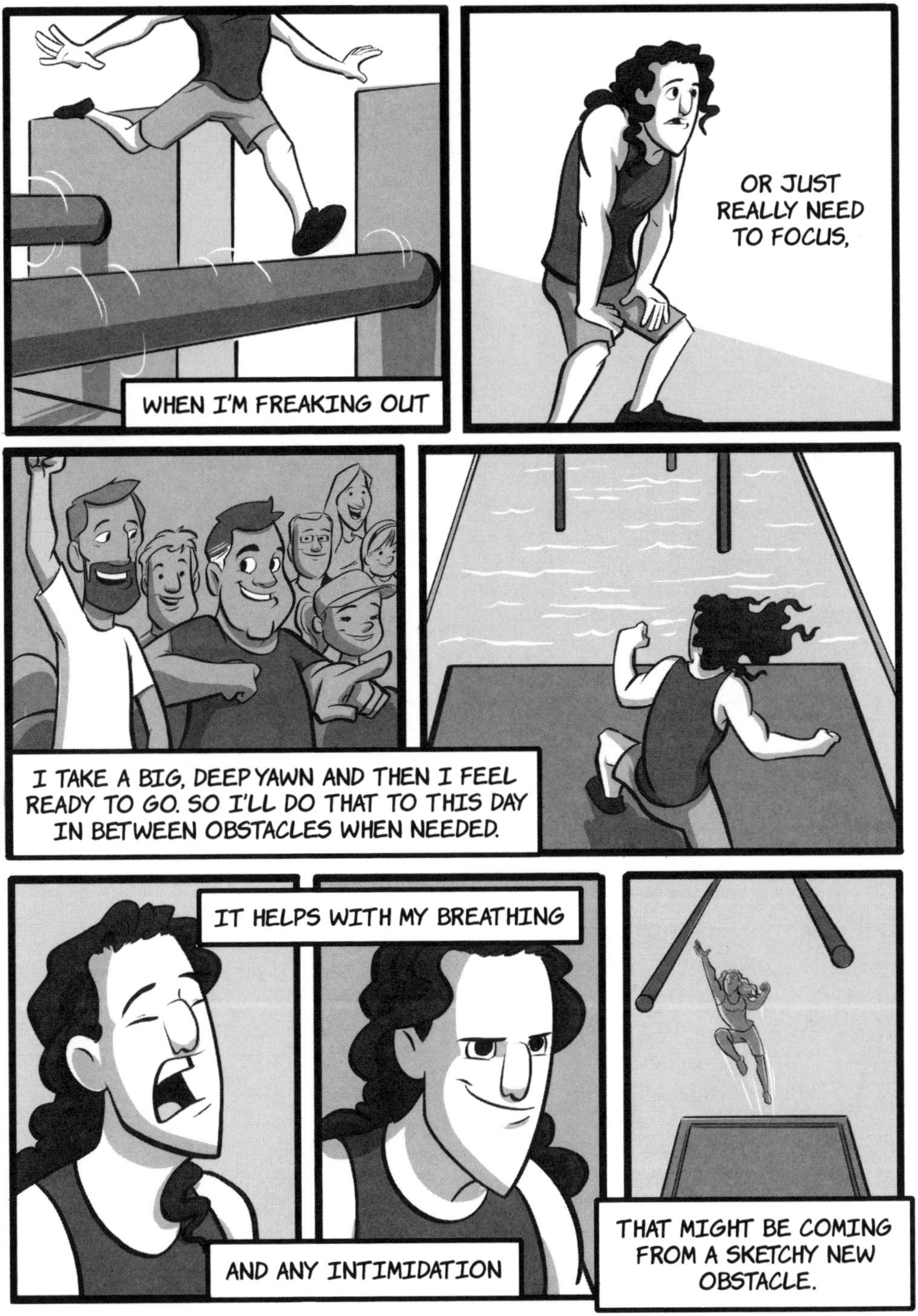
WHEN I'M FREAKING OUT
OR JUST REALLY NEED TO FOCUS,
I TAKE A BIG, DEEP YAWN AND THEN I FEEL READY TO GO. SO I'LL DO THAT TO THIS DAY IN BETWEEN OBSTACLES WHEN NEEDED.
IT HELPS WITH MY BREATHING
AND ANY INTIMIDATION
THAT MIGHT BE COMING FROM A SKETCHY NEW OBSTACLE.

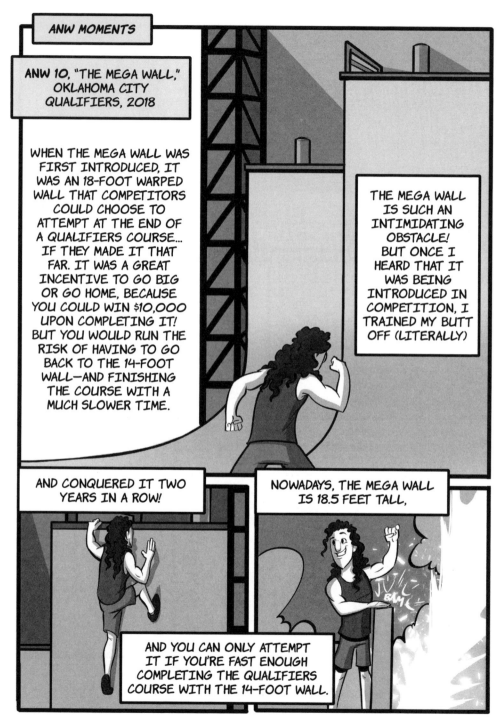

ANW 10, "THE MEGA WALL," OKLAHOMA CITY QUALIFIERS, 2018

WHEN THE MEGA WALL WAS FIRST INTRODUCED, IT WAS AN 18-FOOT WARPED WALL THAT COMPETITORS COULD CHOOSE TO ATTEMPT AT THE END OF A QUALIFIERS COURSE... IF THEY MADE IT THAT FAR. IT WAS A GREAT INCENTIVE TO GO BIG OR GO HOME, BECAUSE YOU COULD WIN $10,000 UPON COMPLETING IT! BUT YOU WOULD RUN THE RISK OF HAVING TO GO BACK TO THE 14-FOOT WALL—AND FINISHING THE COURSE WITH A MUCH SLOWER TIME.

THE MEGA WALL IS SUCH AN INTIMIDATING OBSTACLE! BUT ONCE I HEARD THAT IT WAS BEING INTRODUCED IN COMPETITION, I TRAINED MY BUTT OFF (LITERALLY)

AND CONQUERED IT TWO YEARS IN A ROW!

NOWADAYS, THE MEGA WALL IS 18.5 FEET TALL,

AND YOU CAN ONLY ATTEMPT IT IF YOU'RE FAST ENOUGH COMPLETING THE QUALIFIERS COURSE WITH THE 14-FOOT WALL.

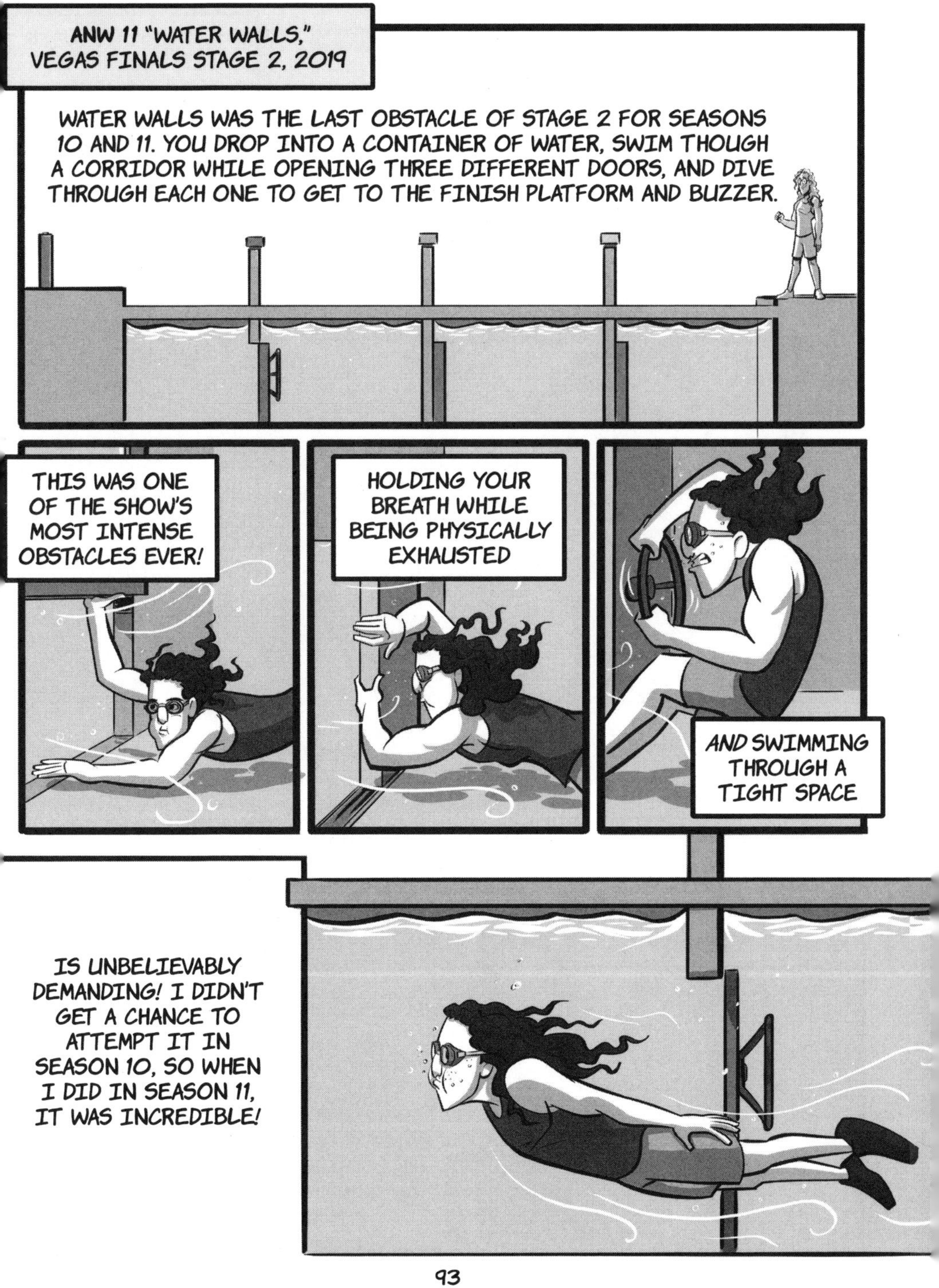
ANW 11 "WATER WALLS," VEGAS FINALS STAGE 2, 2019
WATER WALLS WAS THE LAST OBSTACLE OF STAGE 2 FOR SEASONS 10 AND 11. YOU DROP INTO A CONTAINER OF WATER, SWIM THOUGH A CORRIDOR WHILE OPENING THREE DIFFERENT DOORS, AND DIVE THROUGH EACH ONE TO GET TO THE FINISH PLATFORM AND BUZZER.
THIS WAS ONE OF THE SHOW'S MOST INTENSE OBSTACLES EVER!
HOLDING YOUR BREATH WHILE BEING PHYSICALLY EXHAUSTED
AND SWIMMING THROUGH A TIGHT SPACE
IS UNBELIEVABLY DEMANDING! I DIDN'T GET A CHANCE TO ATTEMPT IT IN SEASON 10, SO WHEN I DID IN SEASON 11, IT WAS INCREDIBLE!

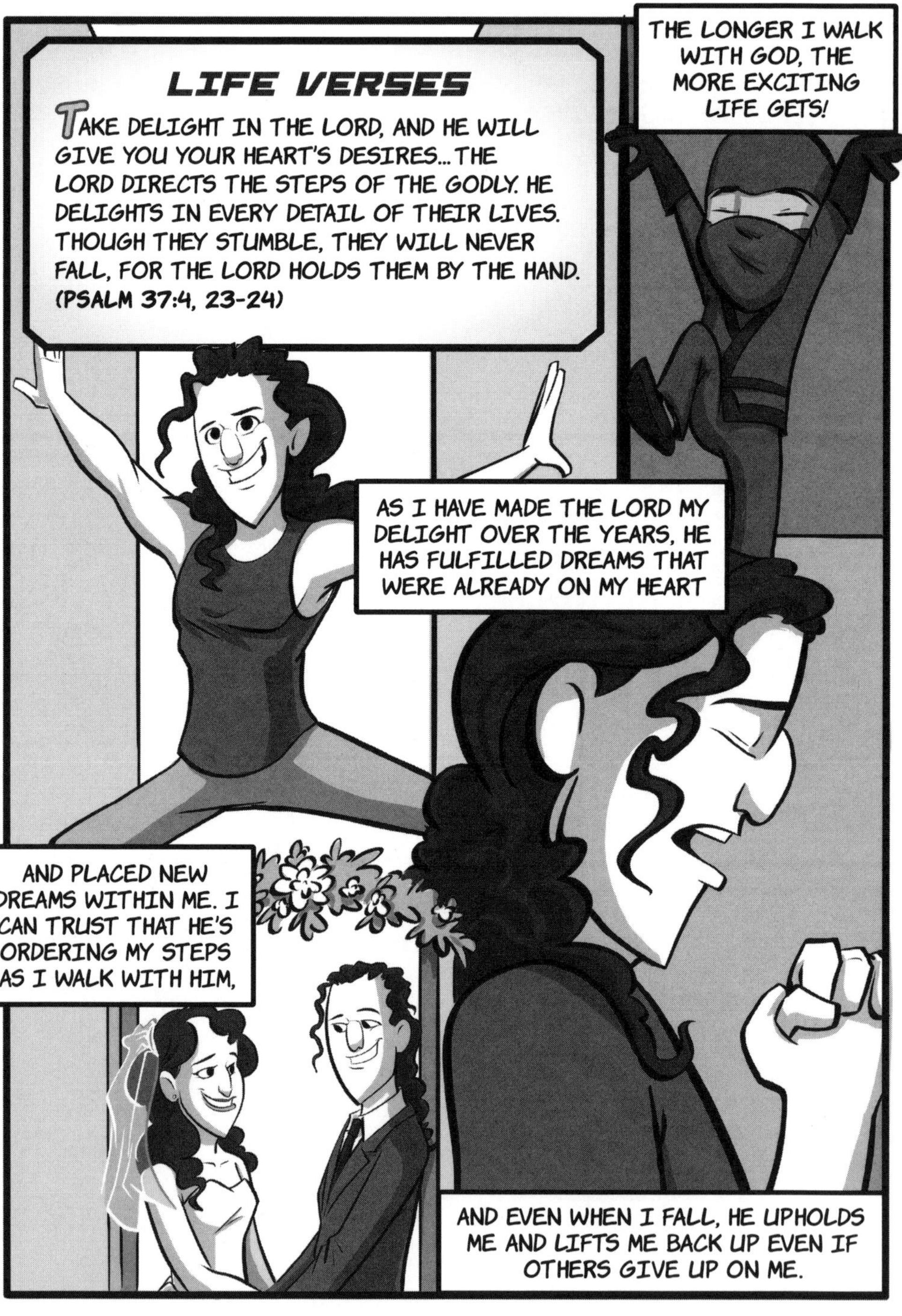
LIFE VERSES
TAKE DELIGHT IN THE LORD, AND HE WILL GIVE YOU YOUR HEART'S DESIRES... THE LORD DIRECTS THE STEPS OF THE GODLY. HE DELIGHTS IN EVERY DETAIL OF THEIR LIVES. THOUGH THEY STUMBLE, THEY WILL NEVER FALL, FOR THE LORD HOLDS THEM BY THE HAND. (PSALM 37:4, 23-24)
THE LONGER I WALK WITH GOD, THE MORE EXCITING LIFE GETS!
AS I HAVE MADE THE LORD MY DELIGHT OVER THE YEARS, HE HAS FULFILLED DREAMS THAT WERE ALREADY ON MY HEART
AND PLACED NEW DREAMS WITHIN ME. I CAN TRUST THAT HE'S ORDERING MY STEPS AS I WALK WITH HIM,
AND EVEN WHEN I FALL, HE UPHOLDS ME AND LIFTS ME BACK UP EVEN IF OTHERS GIVE UP ON ME.

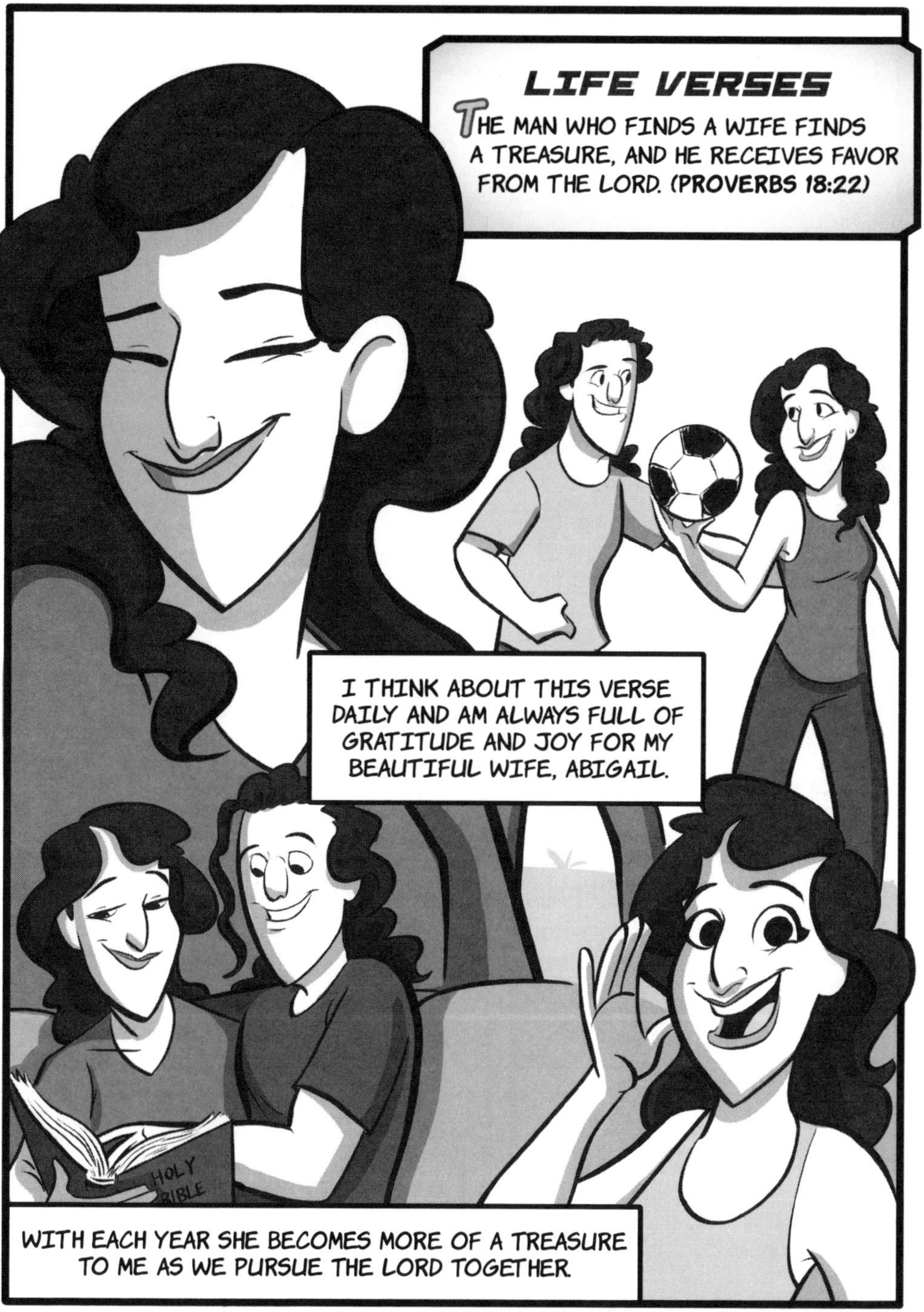
LIFE VERSES
THE MAN WHO FINDS A WIFE FINDS A TREASURE, AND HE RECEIVES FAVOR FROM THE LORD. (PROVERBS 18:22)
I THINK ABOUT THIS VERSE DAILY AND AM ALWAYS FULL OF GRATITUDE AND JOY FOR MY BEAUTIFUL WIFE, ABIGAIL.
HOLY BIBLE
WITH EACH YEAR SHE BECOMES MORE OF A TREASURE TO ME AS WE PURSUE THE LORD TOGETHER.

CHAPTER SEVEN

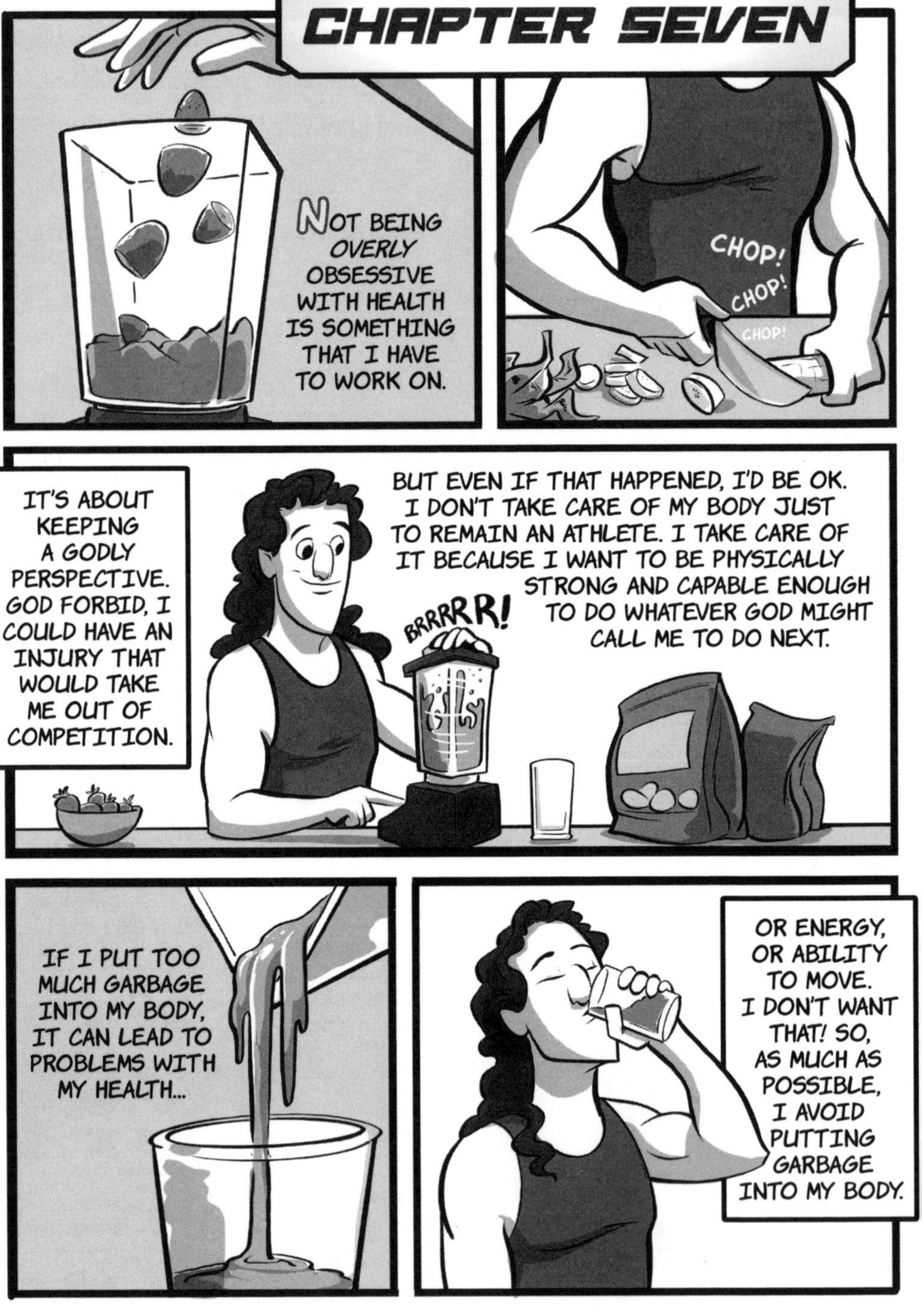

NOT BEING OVERLY OBSESSIVE WITH HEALTH IS SOMETHING THAT I HAVE TO WORK ON.
CHOP!
CHOP!
CHOP!
IT'S ABOUT KEEPING A GODLY PERSPECTIVE. GOD FORBID, I COULD HAVE AN INJURY THAT WOULD TAKE ME OUT OF COMPETITION.
BUT EVEN IF THAT HAPPENED, I'D BE OK. I DON'T TAKE CARE OF MY BODY JUST TO REMAIN AN ATHLETE. I TAKE CARE OF IT BECAUSE I WANT TO BE PHYSICALLY STRONG AND CAPABLE ENOUGH TO DO WHATEVER GOD MIGHT CALL ME TO DO NEXT.
BRRRRR!
IF I PUT TOO MUCH GARBAGE INTO MY BODY, IT CAN LEAD TO PROBLEMS WITH MY HEALTH...
OR ENERGY, OR ABILITY TO MOVE. I DON'T WANT THAT! SO, AS MUCH AS POSSIBLE, I AVOID PUTTING GARBAGE INTO MY BODY.

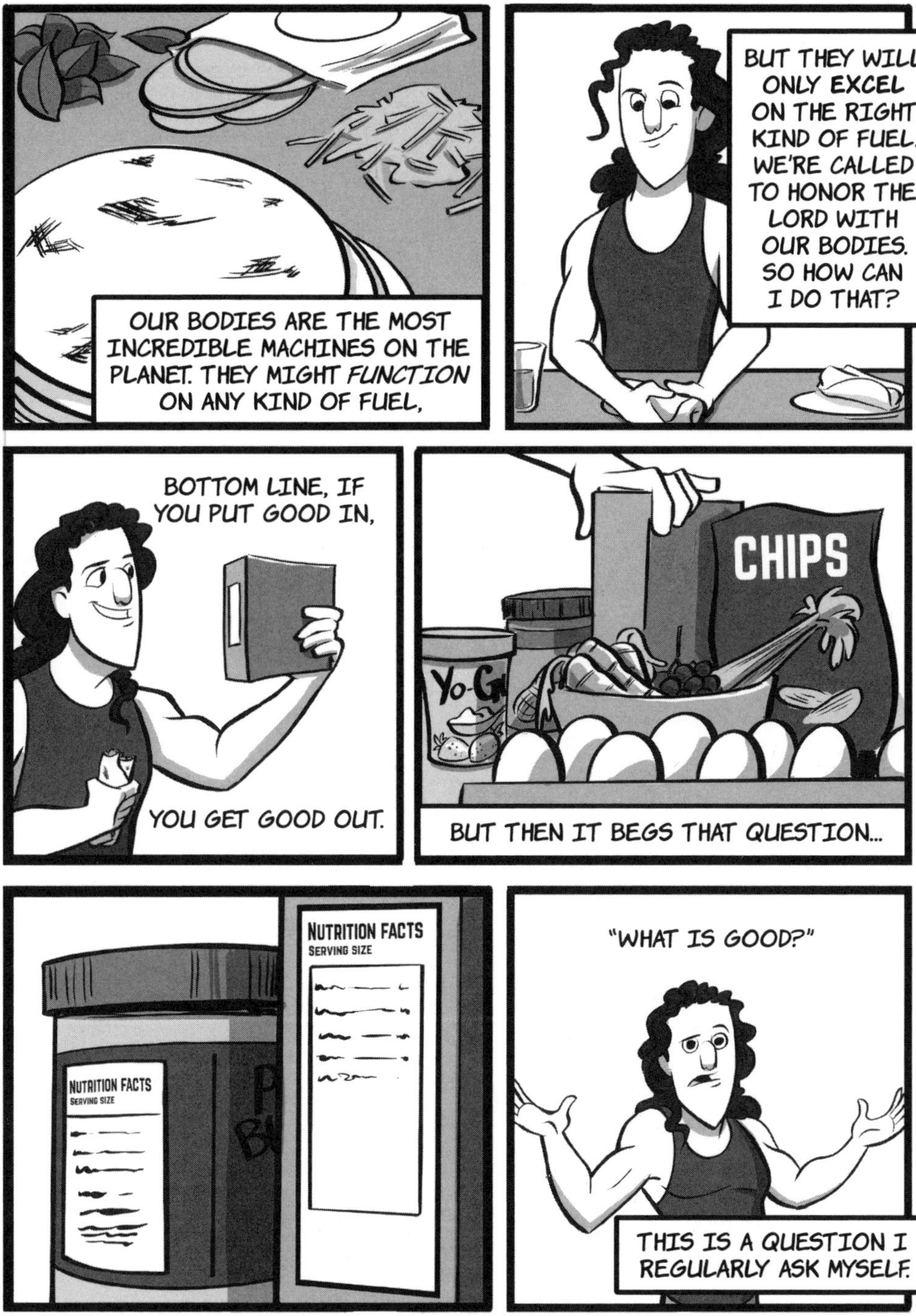
OUR BODIES ARE THE MOST INCREDIBLE MACHINES ON THE PLANET. THEY MIGHT *FUNCTION* ON ANY KIND OF FUEL,
BUT THEY WILL ONLY **EXCEL** ON THE RIGHT KIND OF FUEL. WE'RE CALLED TO HONOR THE LORD WITH OUR BODIES. SO HOW CAN I DO THAT?
BOTTOM LINE, IF YOU PUT GOOD IN,
YOU GET GOOD OUT.
CHIPS
BUT THEN IT BEGS THAT QUESTION...
NUTRITION FACTS
SERVING SIZE
NUTRITION FACTS
SERVING SIZE
"WHAT IS GOOD?"
THIS IS A QUESTION I REGULARLY ASK MYSELF.

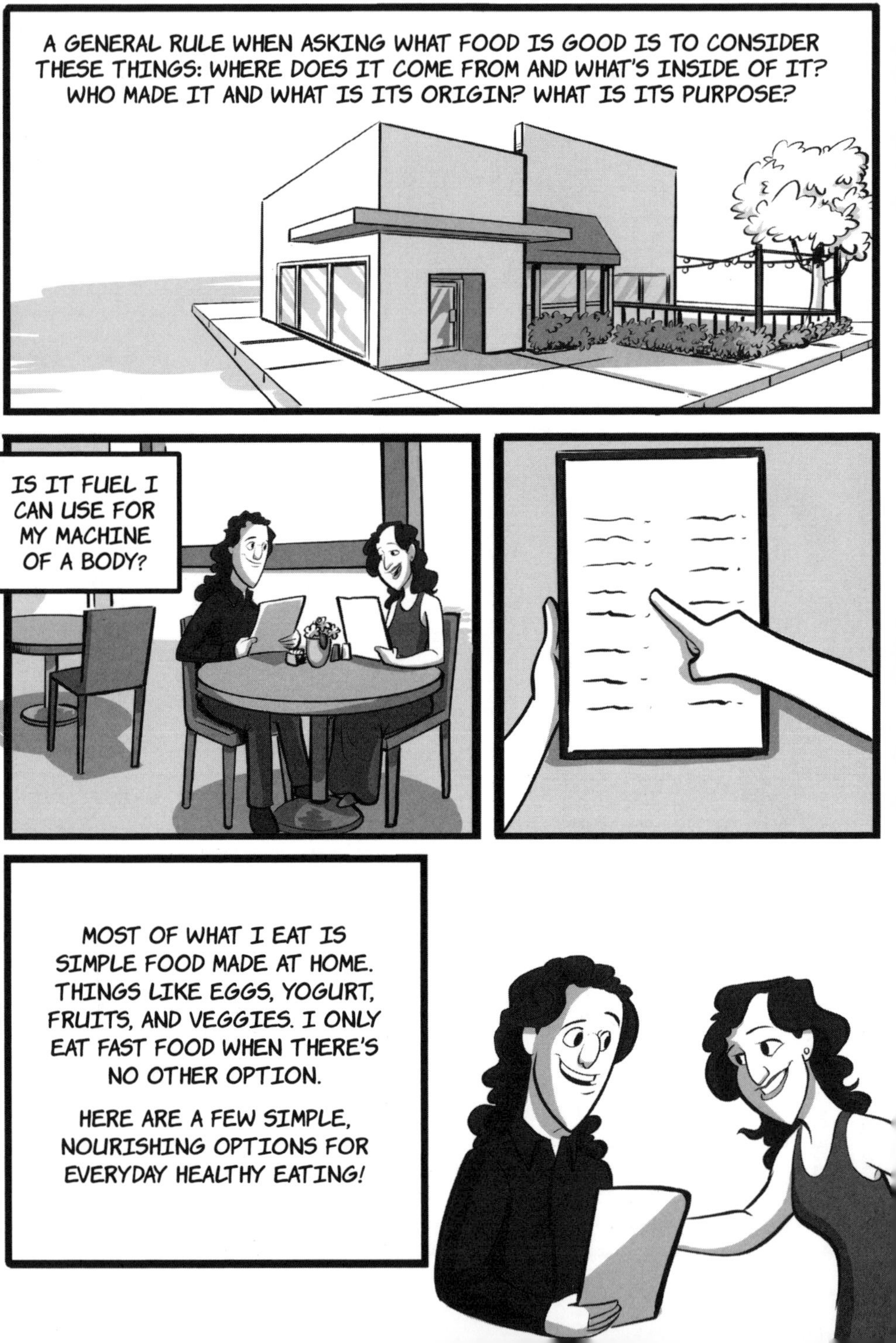
A GENERAL RULE WHEN ASKING WHAT FOOD IS GOOD IS TO CONSIDER THESE THINGS: WHERE DOES IT COME FROM AND WHAT'S INSIDE OF IT? WHO MADE IT AND WHAT IS ITS ORIGIN? WHAT IS ITS PURPOSE?
IS IT FUEL I CAN USE FOR MY MACHINE OF A BODY?
MOST OF WHAT I EAT IS SIMPLE FOOD MADE AT HOME. THINGS LIKE EGGS, YOGURT, FRUITS, AND VEGGIES. I ONLY EAT FAST FOOD WHEN THERE'S NO OTHER OPTION.
HERE ARE A FEW SIMPLE, NOURISHING OPTIONS FOR EVERYDAY HEALTHY EATING!

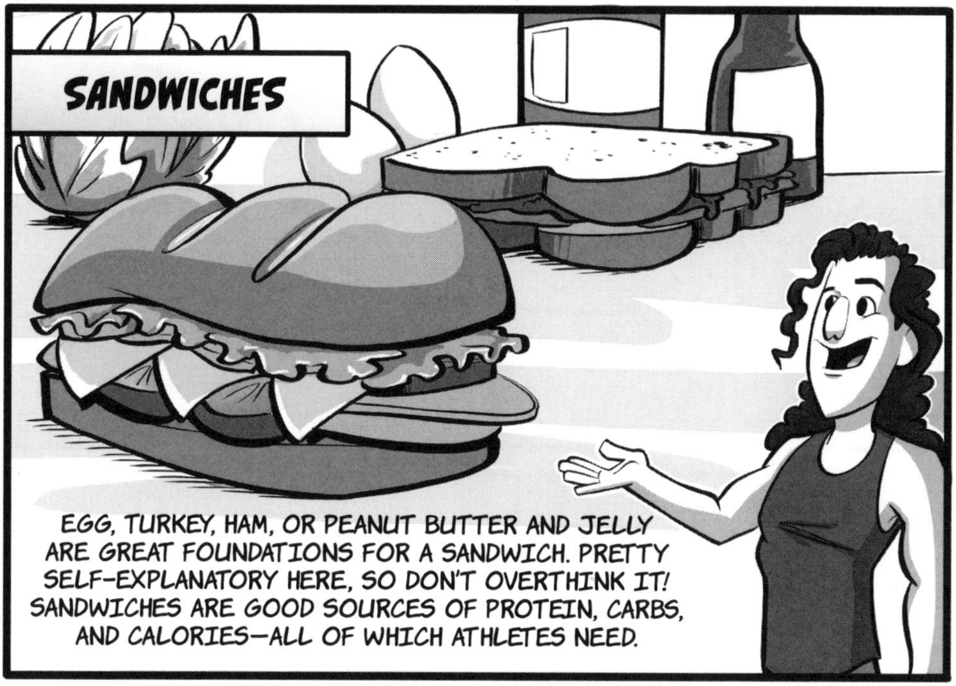
SANDWICHES
EGG, TURKEY, HAM, OR PEANUT BUTTER AND JELLY ARE GREAT FOUNDATIONS FOR A SANDWICH. PRETTY SELF-EXPLANATORY HERE, SO DON'T OVERTHINK IT! SANDWICHES ARE GOOD SOURCES OF PROTEIN, CARBS, AND CALORIES—ALL OF WHICH ATHLETES NEED.

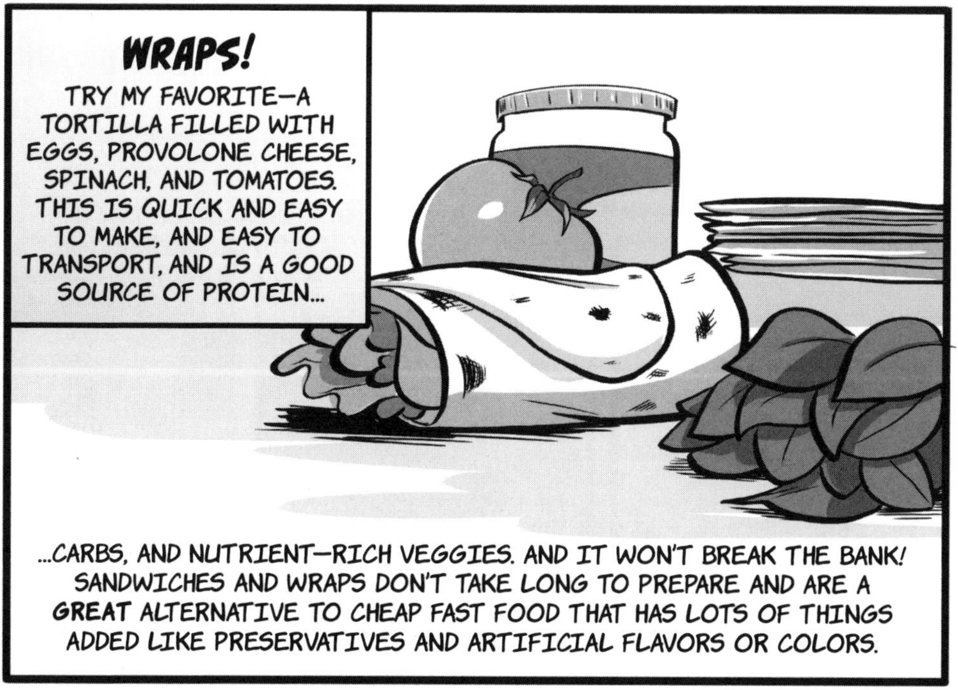
WRAPS!
TRY MY FAVORITE—A TORTILLA FILLED WITH EGGS, PROVOLONE CHEESE, SPINACH, AND TOMATOES. THIS IS QUICK AND EASY TO MAKE, AND EASY TO TRANSPORT, AND IS A GOOD SOURCE OF PROTEIN...
...CARBS, AND NUTRIENT-RICH VEGGIES. AND IT WON'T BREAK THE BANK! SANDWICHES AND WRAPS DON'T TAKE LONG TO PREPARE AND ARE A GREAT ALTERNATIVE TO CHEAP FAST FOOD THAT HAS LOTS OF THINGS ADDED LIKE PRESERVATIVES AND ARTIFICIAL FLAVORS OR COLORS.

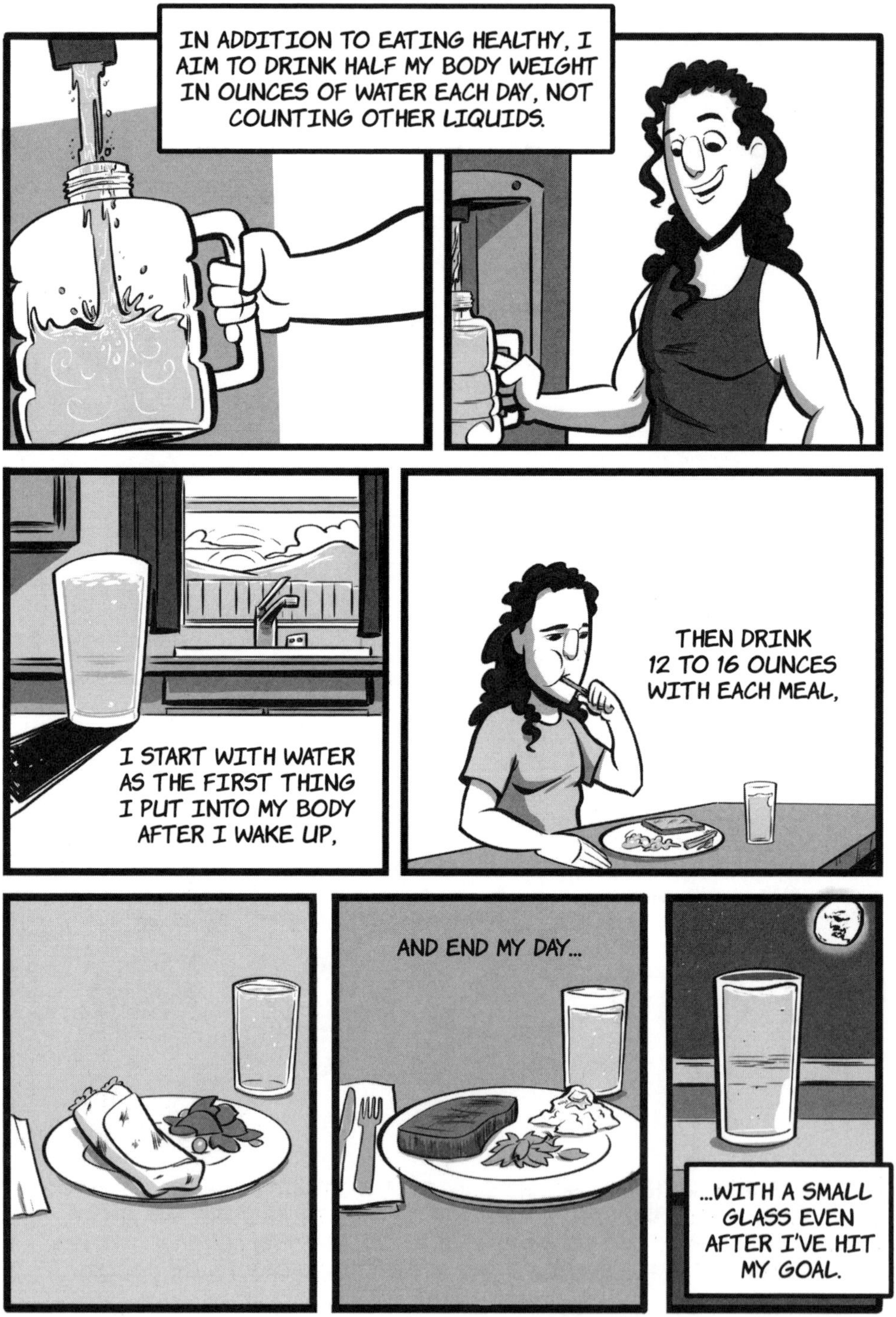
IN ADDITION TO EATING HEALTHY, I AIM TO DRINK HALF MY BODY WEIGHT IN OUNCES OF WATER EACH DAY, NOT COUNTING OTHER LIQUIDS.
I START WITH WATER AS THE FIRST THING I PUT INTO MY BODY AFTER I WAKE UP,
THEN DRINK 12 TO 16 OUNCES WITH EACH MEAL,
AND END MY DAY...
...WITH A SMALL GLASS EVEN AFTER I'VE HIT MY GOAL.

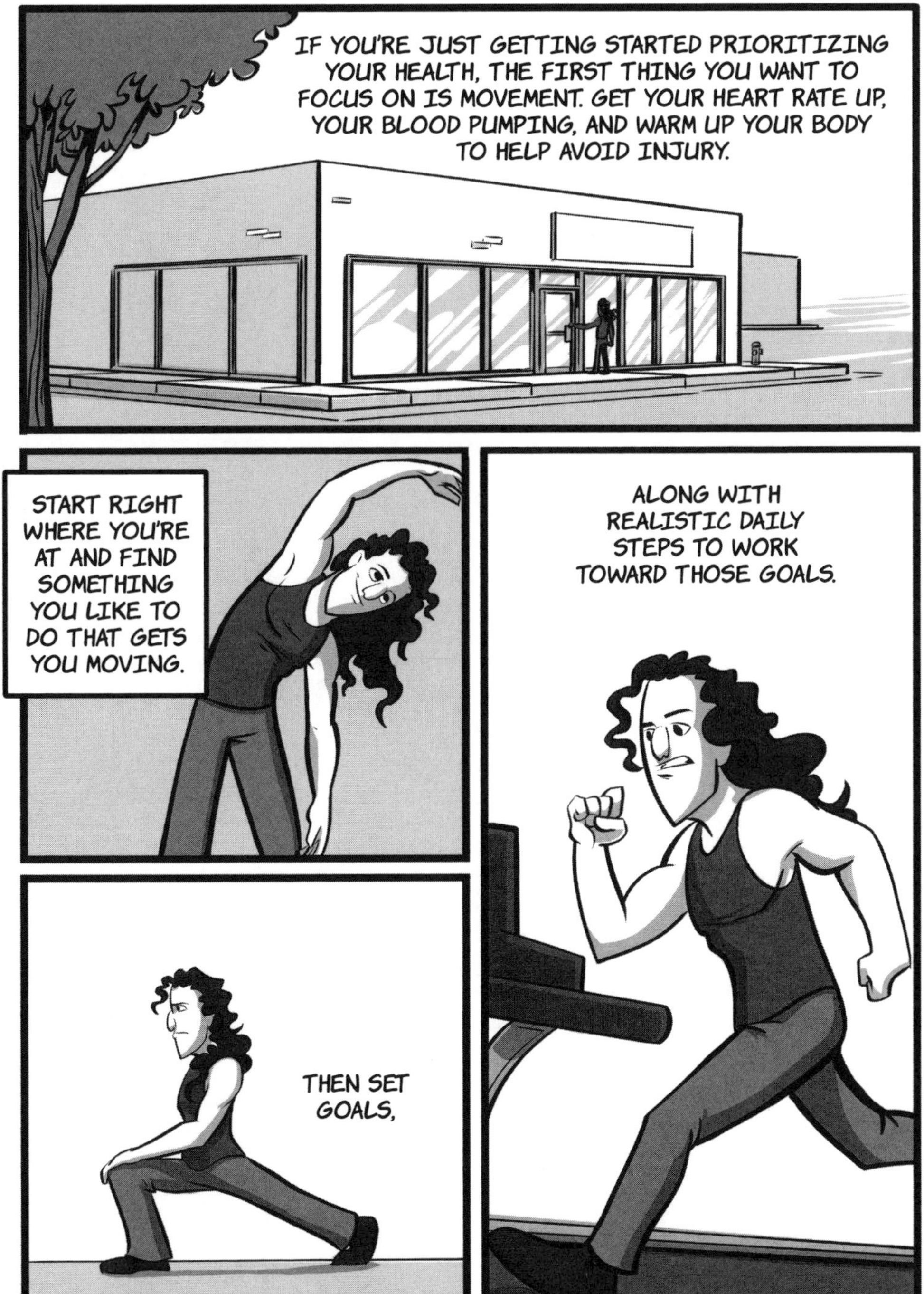
IF YOU'RE JUST GETTING STARTED PRIORITIZING YOUR HEALTH, THE FIRST THING YOU WANT TO FOCUS ON IS MOVEMENT. GET YOUR HEART RATE UP, YOUR BLOOD PUMPING, AND WARM UP YOUR BODY TO HELP AVOID INJURY.
START RIGHT WHERE YOU'RE AT AND FIND SOMETHING YOU LIKE TO DO THAT GETS YOU MOVING.
THEN SET GOALS,
ALONG WITH REALISTIC DAILY STEPS TO WORK TOWARD THOSE GOALS.

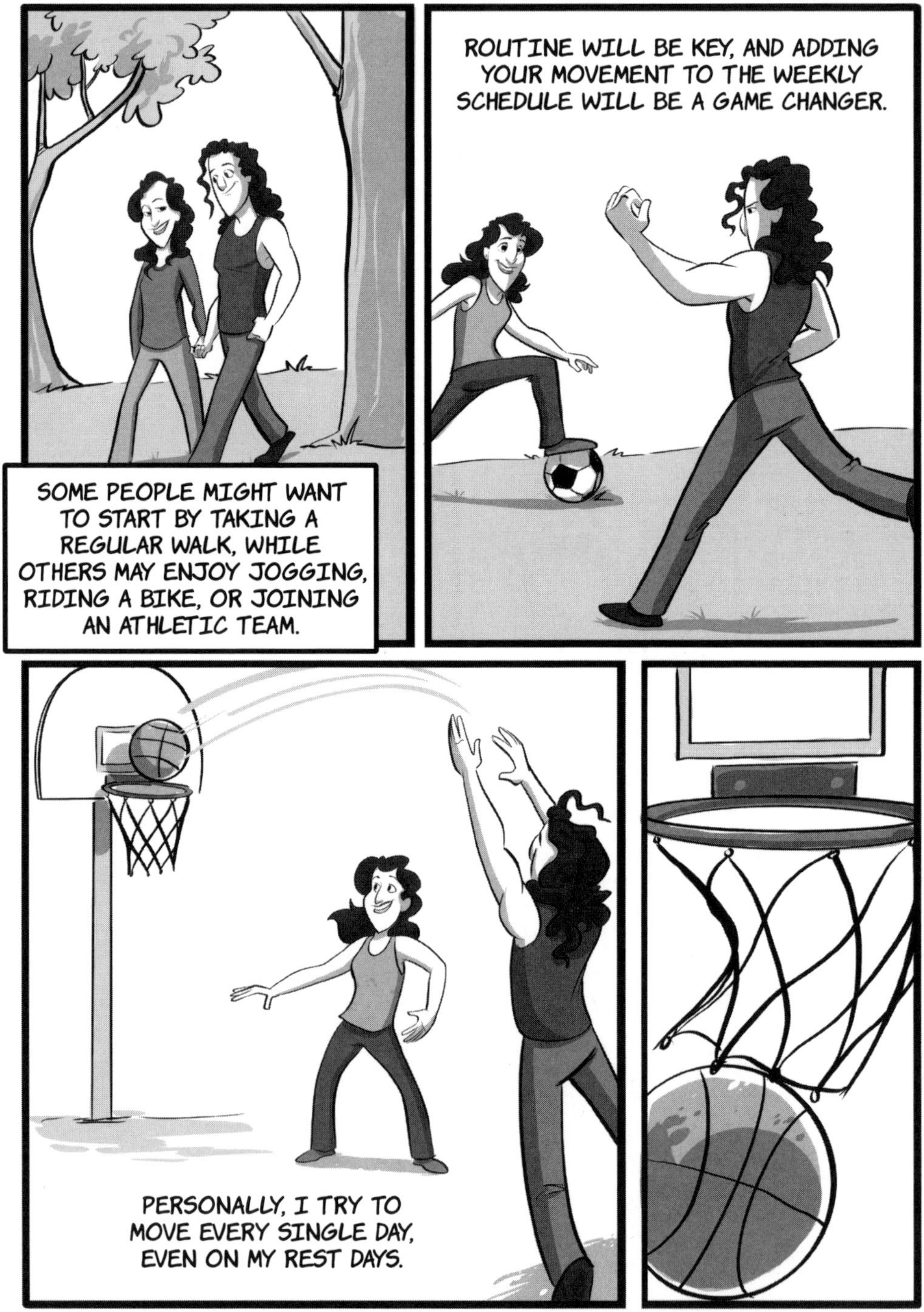
SOME PEOPLE MIGHT WANT TO START BY TAKING A REGULAR WALK, WHILE OTHERS MAY ENJOY JOGGING, RIDING A BIKE, OR JOINING AN ATHLETIC TEAM.
ROUTINE WILL BE KEY, AND ADDING YOUR MOVEMENT TO THE WEEKLY SCHEDULE WILL BE A GAME CHANGER.
PERSONALLY, I TRY TO MOVE EVERY SINGLE DAY, EVEN ON MY REST DAYS.

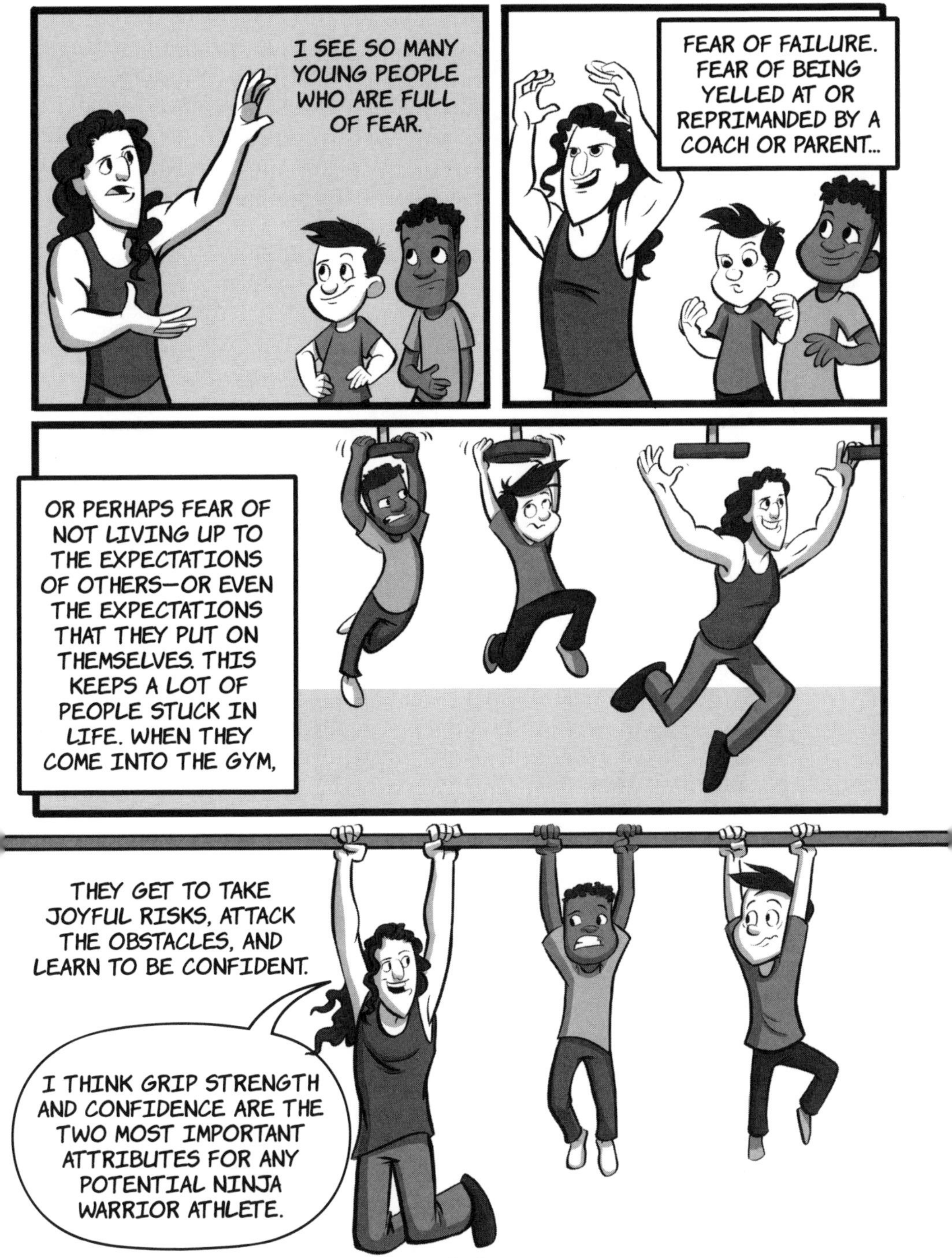

I SEE SO MANY YOUNG PEOPLE WHO ARE FULL OF FEAR.
FEAR OF FAILURE. FEAR OF BEING YELLED AT OR REPRIMANDED BY A COACH OR PARENT...
OR PERHAPS FEAR OF NOT LIVING UP TO THE EXPECTATIONS OF OTHERS—OR EVEN THE EXPECTATIONS THAT THEY PUT ON THEMSELVES. THIS KEEPS A LOT OF PEOPLE STUCK IN LIFE. WHEN THEY COME INTO THE GYM,
THEY GET TO TAKE JOYFUL RISKS, ATTACK THE OBSTACLES, AND LEARN TO BE CONFIDENT.
I THINK GRIP STRENGTH AND CONFIDENCE ARE THE TWO MOST IMPORTANT ATTRIBUTES FOR ANY POTENTIAL NINJA WARRIOR ATHLETE.

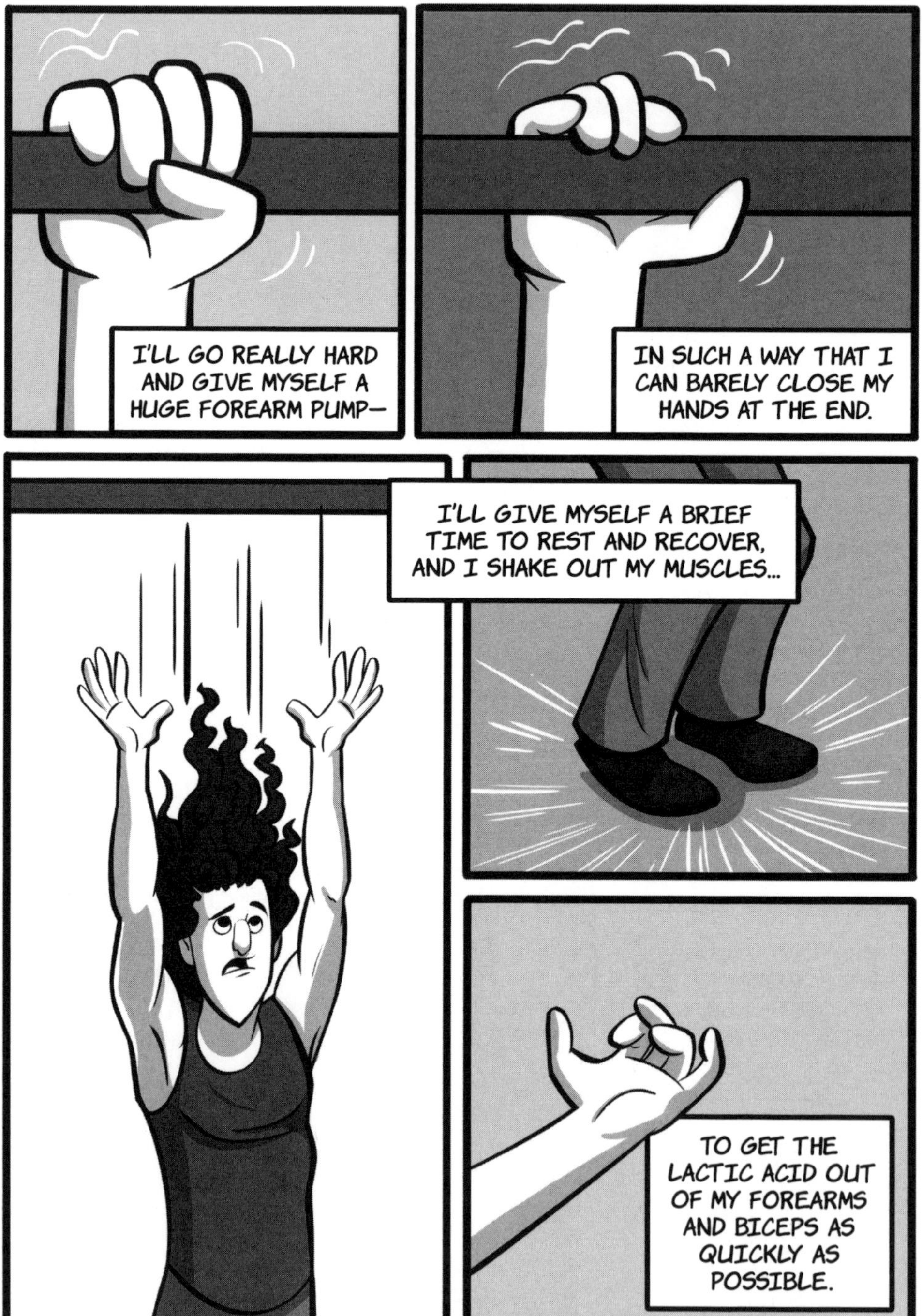
I'LL GO REALLY HARD AND GIVE MYSELF A HUGE FOREARM PUMP—
IN SUCH A WAY THAT I CAN BARELY CLOSE MY HANDS AT THE END.
I'LL GIVE MYSELF A BRIEF TIME TO REST AND RECOVER, AND I SHAKE OUT MY MUSCLES...
TO GET THE LACTIC ACID OUT OF MY FOREARMS AND BICEPS AS QUICKLY AS POSSIBLE.

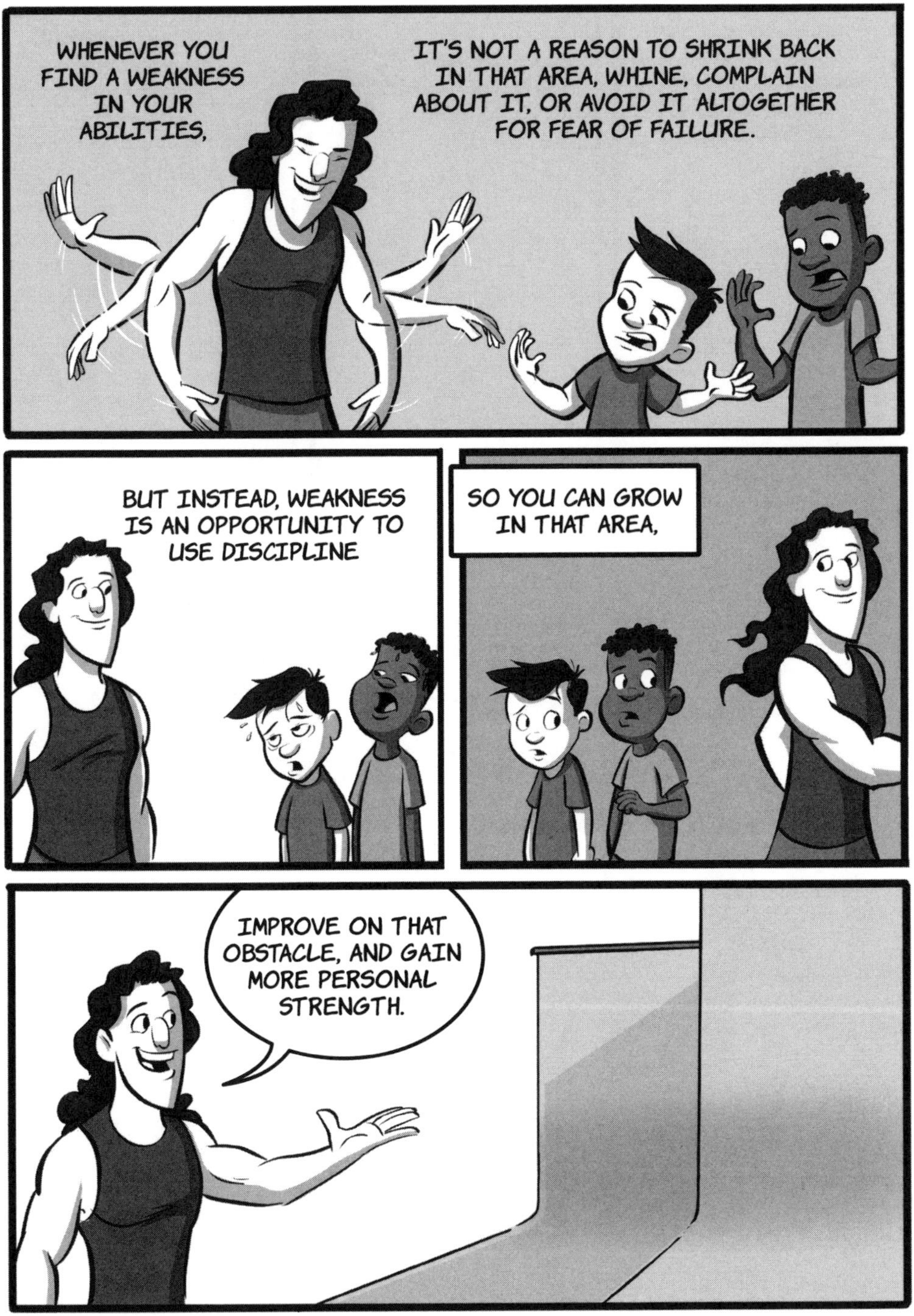
WHENEVER YOU FIND A WEAKNESS IN YOUR ABILITIES,
IT'S NOT A REASON TO SHRINK BACK IN THAT AREA, WHINE, COMPLAIN ABOUT IT, OR AVOID IT ALTOGETHER FOR FEAR OF FAILURE.
BUT INSTEAD, WEAKNESS IS AN OPPORTUNITY TO USE DISCIPLINE
SO YOU CAN GROW IN THAT AREA,
IMPROVE ON THAT OBSTACLE, AND GAIN MORE PERSONAL STRENGTH.

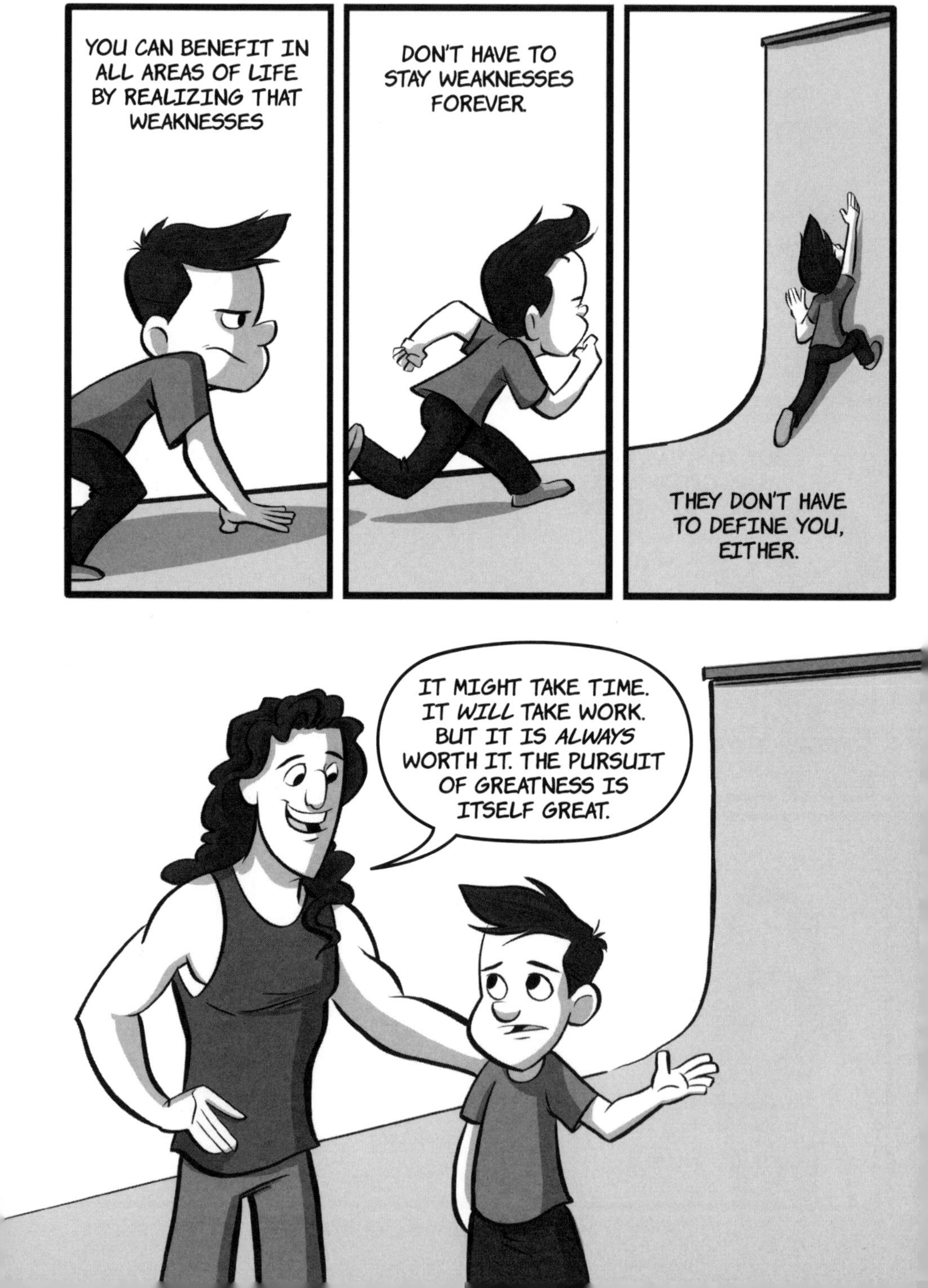
YOU CAN BENEFIT IN ALL AREAS OF LIFE BY REALIZING THAT WEAKNESSES
DON'T HAVE TO STAY WEAKNESSES FOREVER.
THEY DON'T HAVE TO DEFINE YOU, EITHER.
IT MIGHT TAKE TIME. IT *WILL* TAKE WORK. BUT IT IS *ALWAYS* WORTH IT. THE PURSUIT OF GREATNESS IS ITSELF GREAT.

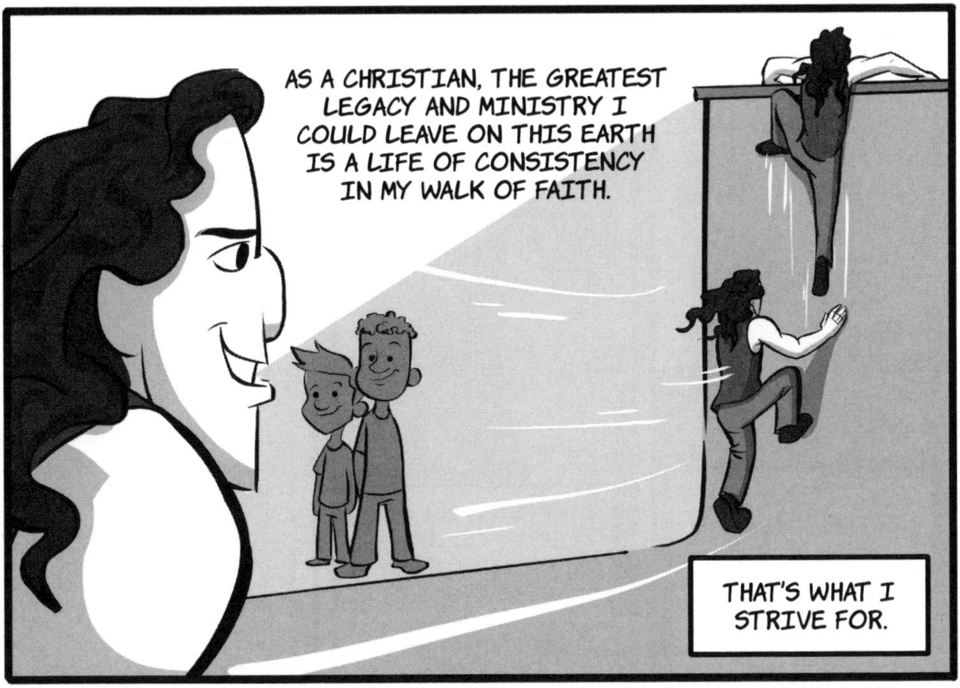
AS A CHRISTIAN, THE GREATEST LEGACY AND MINISTRY I COULD LEAVE ON THIS EARTH IS A LIFE OF CONSISTENCY IN MY WALK OF FAITH.
THAT'S WHAT I STRIVE FOR.

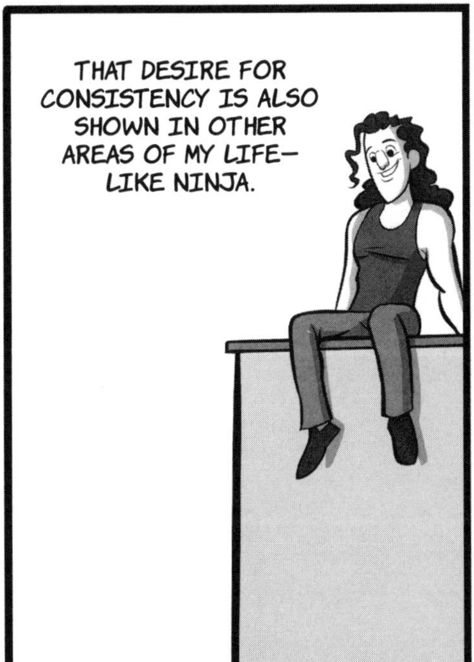
THAT DESIRE FOR CONSISTENCY IS ALSO SHOWN IN OTHER AREAS OF MY LIFE—LIKE NINJA.

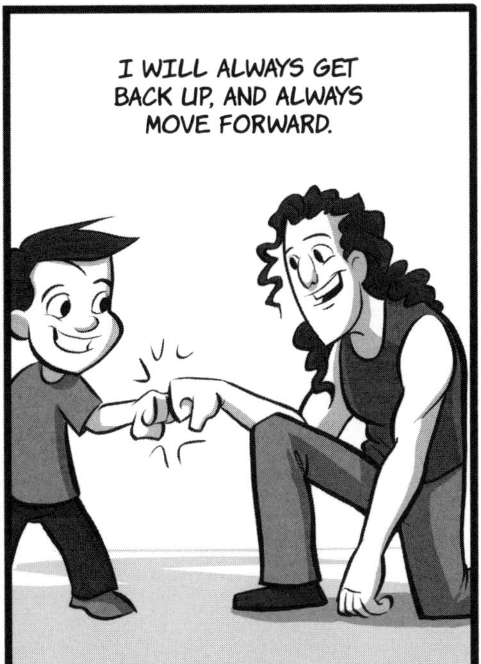
I WILL ALWAYS GET BACK UP, AND ALWAYS MOVE FORWARD.

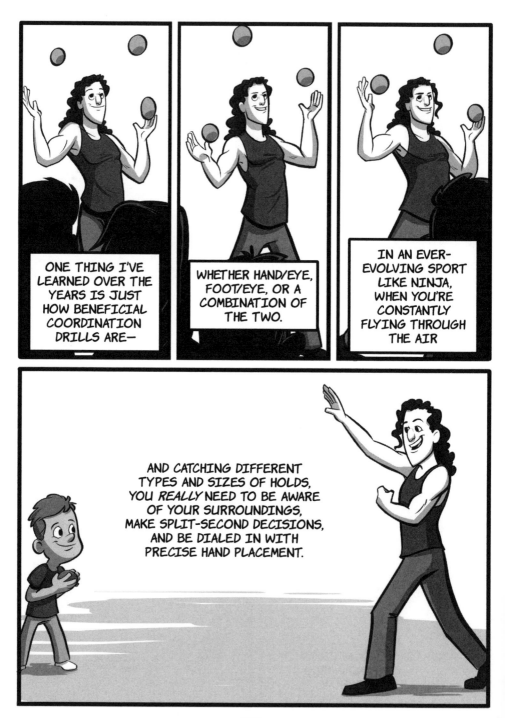

ONE THING I'VE LEARNED OVER THE YEARS IS JUST HOW BENEFICIAL COORDINATION DRILLS ARE—

WHETHER HAND/EYE, FOOT/EYE, OR A COMBINATION OF THE TWO.

IN AN EVER-EVOLVING SPORT LIKE NINJA, WHEN YOU'RE CONSTANTLY FLYING THROUGH THE AIR

AND CATCHING DIFFERENT TYPES AND SIZES OF HOLDS, YOU *REALLY* NEED TO BE AWARE OF YOUR SURROUNDINGS, MAKE SPLIT-SECOND DECISIONS, AND BE DIALED IN WITH PRECISE HAND PLACEMENT.

ONE OF MY PERSONAL FAVORITE DRILLS INVOLVES MAKING A SMALL "+" OUT OF PVC PIPING.

I ADD A DIFFERENT COLOR TO EACH OF THE FOUR ENDS (DUCT TAPE WORKS GREAT!).

THEN MY TRAINING PARTNER AND I WILL MAKE A GAME OF TOSSING IT TO EACH OTHER AND CALLING OUT

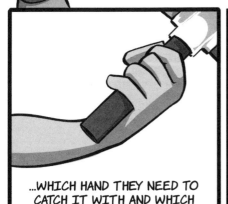

...WHICH HAND THEY NEED TO CATCH IT WITH AND WHICH COLOR PIPE TO GRAB.

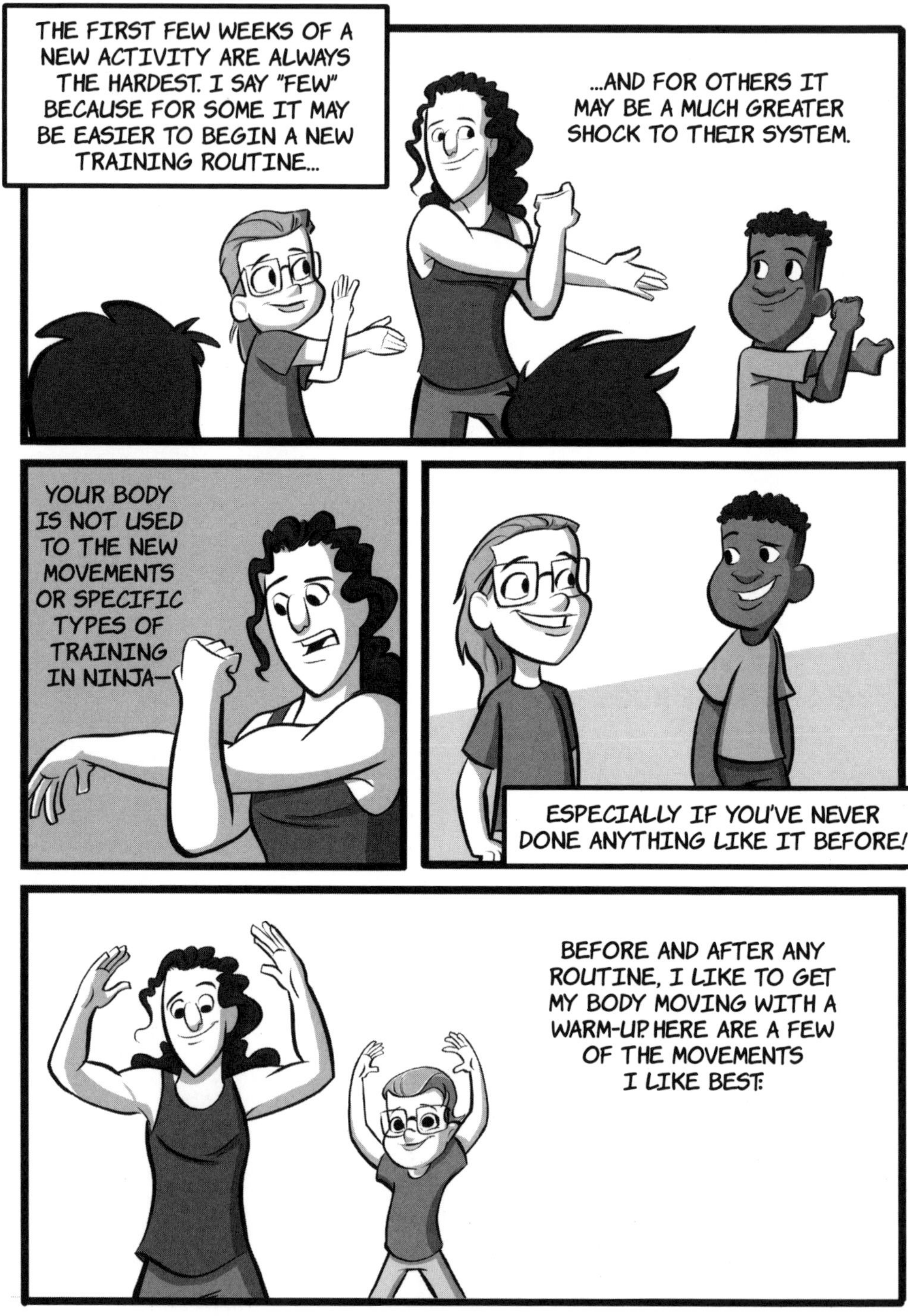
THE FIRST FEW WEEKS OF A NEW ACTIVITY ARE ALWAYS THE HARDEST. I SAY "FEW" BECAUSE FOR SOME IT MAY BE EASIER TO BEGIN A NEW TRAINING ROUTINE...
...AND FOR OTHERS IT MAY BE A MUCH GREATER SHOCK TO THEIR SYSTEM.
YOUR BODY IS NOT USED TO THE NEW MOVEMENTS OR SPECIFIC TYPES OF TRAINING IN NINJA—
ESPECIALLY IF YOU'VE NEVER DONE ANYTHING LIKE IT BEFORE!
BEFORE AND AFTER ANY ROUTINE, I LIKE TO GET MY BODY MOVING WITH A WARM-UP. HERE ARE A FEW OF THE MOVEMENTS I LIKE BEST:

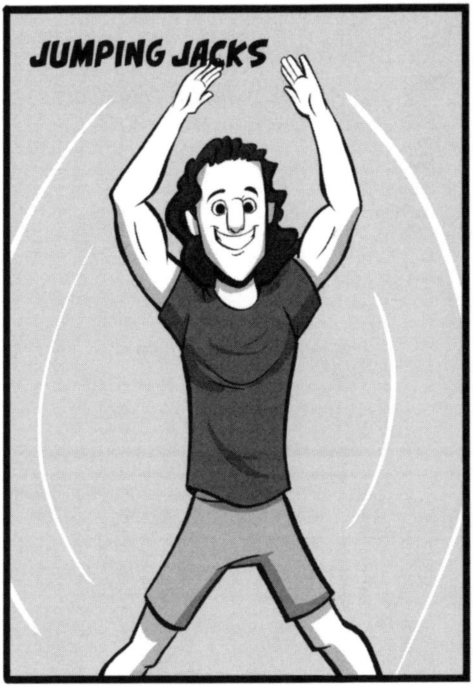
JUMPING JACKS

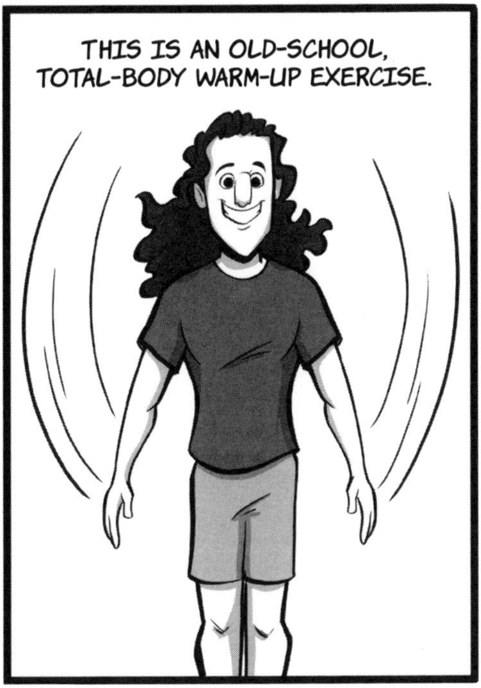
THIS IS AN OLD-SCHOOL, TOTAL-BODY WARM-UP EXERCISE.

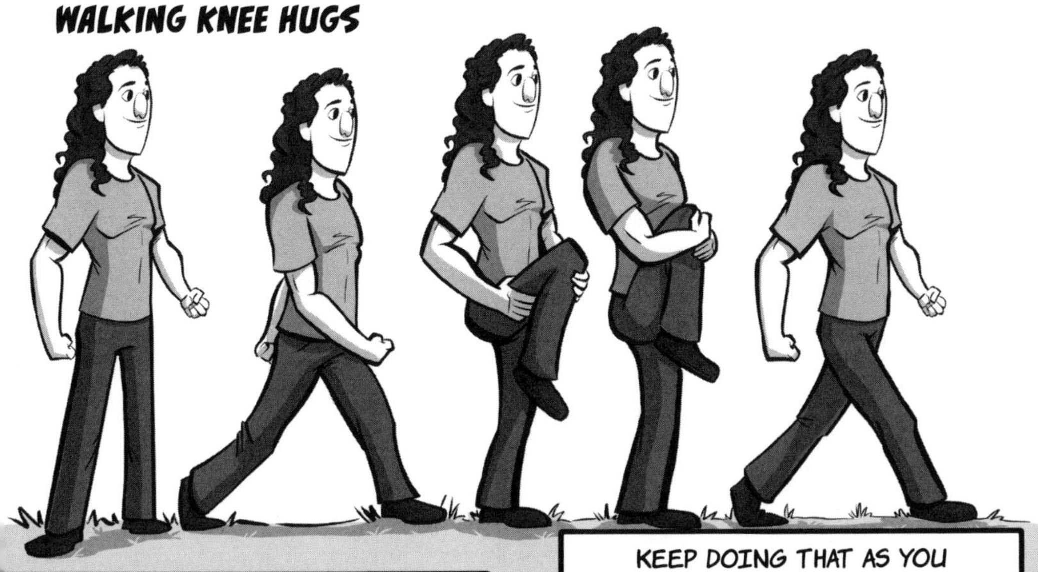
WALKING KNEE HUGS
IT'S JUST LIKE THEY SOUND: TAKE A STEP FORWARD, RAISE YOUR KNEE TO YOUR CHEST, AND GRAB IT.
KEEP DOING THAT AS YOU WALK AROUND THE ROOM. THIS MOVEMENT IS MEANT TO ENGAGE YOUR STABILIZER MUSCLES, BUILD BETTER BALANCE, AND WARM UP THE HAMSTRINGS AND GLUTES.

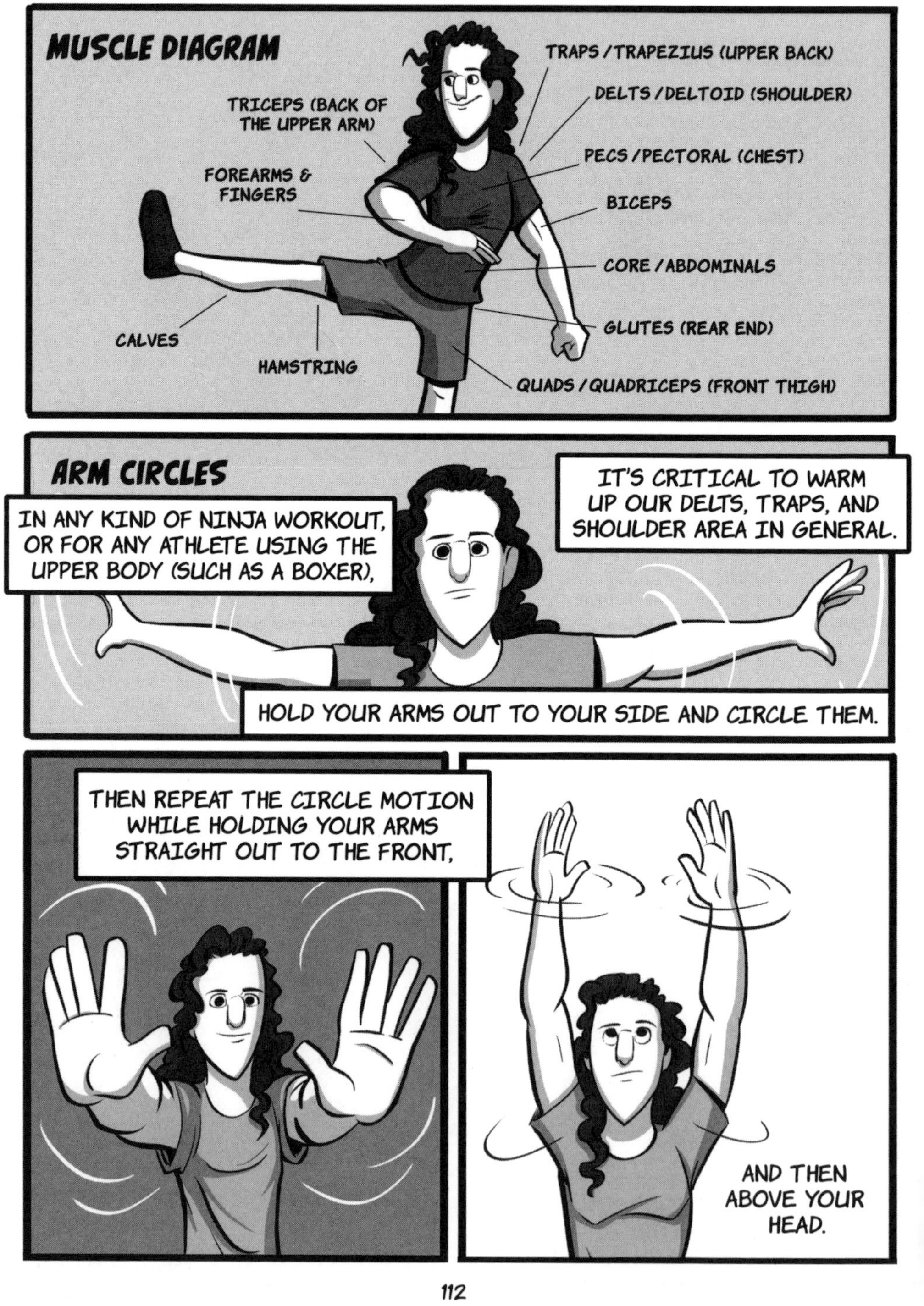
MUSCLE DIAGRAM
TRAPS / TRAPEZIUS (UPPER BACK)
TRICEPS (BACK OF THE UPPER ARM)
DELTS / DELTOID (SHOULDER)
FOREARMS & FINGERS
PECS / PECTORAL (CHEST)
BICEPS
CORE / ABDOMINALS
CALVES
GLUTES (REAR END)
HAMSTRING
QUADS / QUADRICEPS (FRONT THIGH)
ARM CIRCLES
IN ANY KIND OF NINJA WORKOUT, OR FOR ANY ATHLETE USING THE UPPER BODY (SUCH AS A BOXER),
IT'S CRITICAL TO WARM UP OUR DELTS, TRAPS, AND SHOULDER AREA IN GENERAL.
HOLD YOUR ARMS OUT TO YOUR SIDE AND CIRCLE THEM.
THEN REPEAT THE CIRCLE MOTION WHILE HOLDING YOUR ARMS STRAIGHT OUT TO THE FRONT,
AND THEN ABOVE YOUR HEAD.

SIDE SHUFFLES

SIDE SHUFFLES ENGAGE THE QUADS, GLUTES, AND CALVES.

START WITH YOUR FEET ABOUT SHOULDER-WIDTH APART, LOWER YOUR BUTT DOWN,

KEEP YOUR EYES UP, AND SHUFFLE TO THE SIDE—TAKING CARE NOT TO CROSS YOUR FEET.

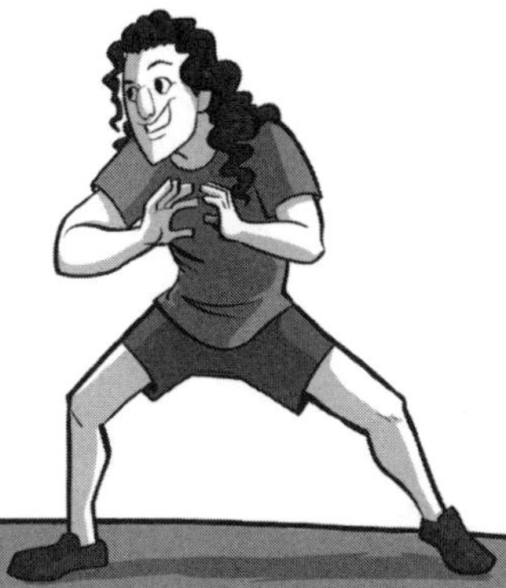

ARM SWINGS

SWING YOUR ARMS IN FRONT OF YOU AT ABOUT CHEST LEVEL, CROSSING THEM IN FRONT, AND THEN SWING TO THE BACK, TRYING TO CLAP BEHIND YOUR BACK.

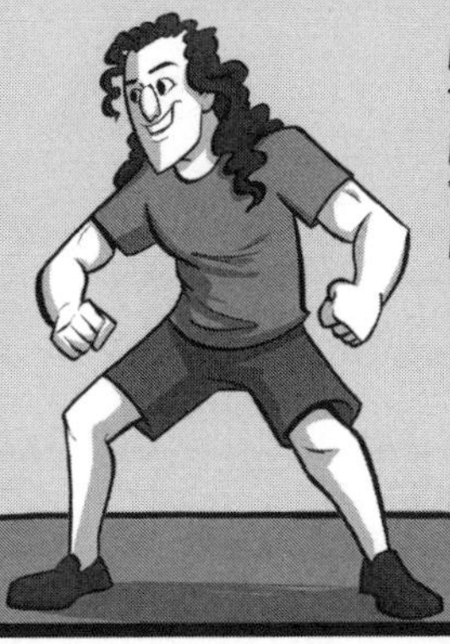

DO THIS 6 TO 10 TIMES, THEN CHANGE DIRECTION TO SWING YOUR ARMS UP AND DOWN 6 TO 10 TIMES.

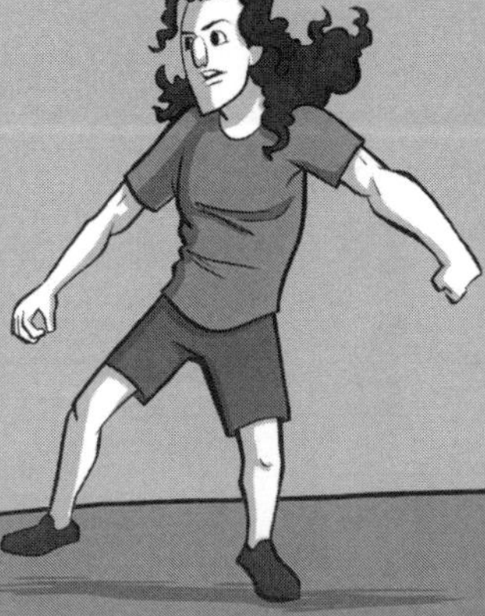

KEEP YOUR ELBOWS STRAIGHT AND TRY TO GET YOUR SHOULDERS TO GO BEHIND YOUR EARS WHEN YOU SWING UPWARD.

THIS WILL HELP YOU TO WARM UP FOR DIFFERENT DIRECTIONS YOU MAY BE SWINGING IN NINJA TRAINING.

BACKPEDALING

WITH YOUR FEET ABOUT SHOULDER-WIDTH APART...
AND TAKING CARE TO NOT GET YOUR CHEST TOO FAR
FORWARD... PUMP YOUR ARMS AND RUN BACKWARD.
START SLOW, SO AS TO KEEP YOUR BALANCE.

WALKING TOE TOUCHES

WALKING FORWARD, SWING A
LEG UP HIGH WITH EACH STEP
AND TRY TO TOUCH YOUR TOE
WITH YOUR OPPOSITE HAND.
LEFT HAND TO RIGHT FOOT, AND
RIGHT HAND TO LEFT FOOT.

BEAR CRAWL

CRAWL AROUND ON ALL FOURS
(NO KNEES TOUCHING THE
GROUND) TO WARM UP YOUR
UPPER AND LOWER BODY.

KONG THROUGH

JUMP FORWARD LIKE A FROG.
LAND ON BOTH HANDS, AND SWING
YOUR LEGS BETWEEN YOUR
HANDS BEFORE JUMPING AGAIN.
CONTINUE ACROSS THE ROOM.

PULL-UPS

PULL-UPS ARE GREAT FOR BUILDING SHOULDER AND GRIP STRENGTH,

BUT THEY ALSO WORK YOUR WHOLE UPPER BODY.

TRY THESE WORKOUTS TWICE EACH WEEK.

KEEP TRACK OF YOUR REPS (REPETITIONS) AND YOUR TIME RECORDS, AND YOU'LL SEE A DIFFERENCE IF YOU KEEP AT IT!

BEGINNING PULL-UP ROUTINE: SIMPLY PERFORM 10 SETS OF PULL-UPS TO FAILURE (WHEN YOU CAN'T DO ANY MORE). TAKE 90 OR 120 SECONDS OF REST BETWEEN SETS, EVEN IF THIS MEANS 10 SETS OF JUST 1 REP!

BAR HANGS: IF YOU CAN'T DO A PULL-UP YET, START HERE. SIMPLY HANG ON THE BAR WITH YOUR ARMS STRAIGHT ABOVE YOU. USE A TIMER TO SEE HOW LONG YOU CAN HOLD. ADD IN SHOULDER SHRUGS TO ALSO STRENGTHEN SHOULDERS AND FOREARMS!

NEGATIVE PULL-UPS: THESE WILL HELP YOU GET REALLY STRONG, REALLY FAST. USE A CHAIR TO GET INTO POSITION IF NEEDED. START AT THE TOP OF THE CHIN-UP OR PULL-UP POSITION WITH YOUR CHIN ABOVE THE BAR. LOWER YOURSELF DOWN AS SLOWLY AS POSSIBLE WHILE SQUEEZING YOUR ARMS, BACK, AND CORE MUSCLES. COUNT 3 TO 5 SECONDS BEFORE GETTING TO THE BOTTOM, MAKING SURE NOT TO DROP TOO QUICKLY AT THE BOTTOM, WHICH COULD HURT YOUR SHOULDERS. STAY TIGHT AND IN CONTROL THE ENTIRE TIME. DO THREE TO FIVE SETS WITH 30 TO 60 SECONDS OF REST BETWEEN EACH SET.

WANT TO GET EVEN STRONGER? MAKE SURE THE BAR IS SECURE (AND ADD A CRASH PAD BENEATH FOR SAFETY), THEN ADD SMALL SWINGS AS YOU HANG ON THE BAR. THAT WILL REALLY BUILD THE STRENGTH IN YOUR FINGERS AND FOREARMS AS YOU TIME HOW LONG YOU CAN HANG PLUS HOW MANY SWINGS YOU CAN DO WHILE HANGING! AS AN ADDED BONUS, YOU WILL BUILD UP STRONG CALLUSES ON YOUR HANDS THIS WAY.

YOGA PLANK

A YOGA PLANK IS LIKE THE "UP" PART OF THE PUSH-UP POSITION. GET IN THIS POSITION AND HOLD IT. TRY TO HOLD FOR 30 SECONDS, AND WORK UP TO A MINUTE. TAKE A BREAK, THEN TRY AGAIN!

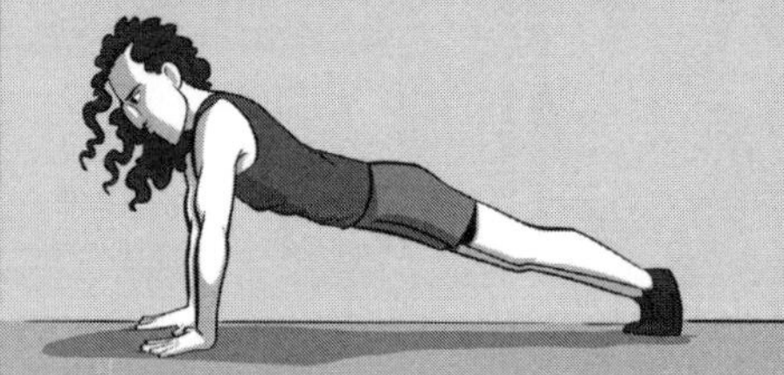

CORE PLANK

A CORE PLANK IS SIMILAR TO A YOGA PLANK, BUT THIS TIME YOU REST ON YOUR ELBOWS AND TOES. THIS CENTERS MOST OF YOUR BODYWEIGHT ON THE CORE AND IS MORE CHALLENGING.

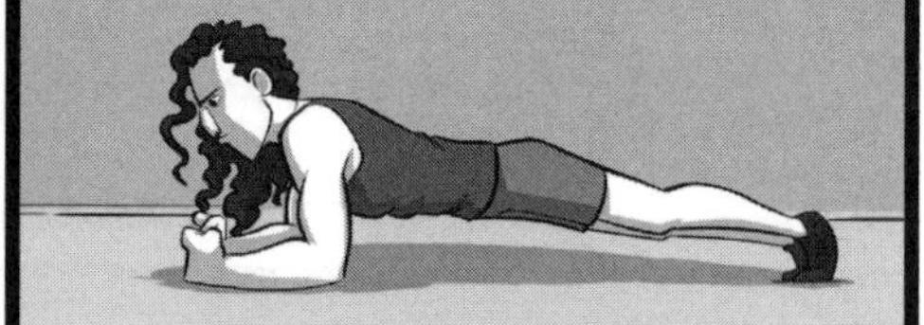

LEG LIFTS

LIE ON YOUR BACK, HANDS FLAT ON YOUR STOMACH, HOLD YOUR HEELS TOGETHER, AND LIFT YOUR HEELS 6 INCHES OFF THE GROUND. HOLD THE POSITION, THEN SPREAD YOUR HEELS APART AND HOLD THAT POSITION.

FINALLY, BRING YOUR FEET BACK TOGETHER AND LIFT YOUR LEGS STRAIGHT UP TO THE CEILING, WITH THE BOTTOM OF YOUR FEET STRAIGHT IN THE AIR. TRY EACH POSITION FOR A COUNT OF 20, AND WORK UP TO DOING LONGER SETS.

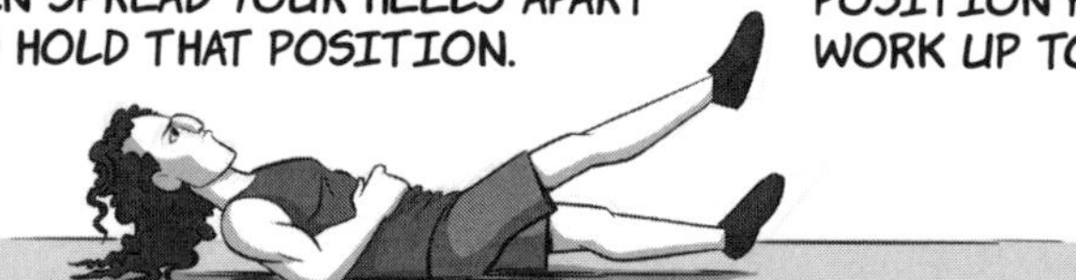

SQUATS, SQUAT JUMPS, AND LUNGE JUMPS

THESE BUILD EXPLOSIVE LEG POWER TO HELP YOU GET BETTER AT THE WARPED WALL AND REACH NEW HEIGHTS! FOR A **SQUAT**, PLACE YOUR FEET JUST PAST HIP WIDTH. JUST REMEMBER TO KEEP YOUR CHEST UP, BACK STRAIGHT, HEELS ON THE GROUND, AND TOES POINTED SLIGHTLY OUT. WHEN YOU CAN DO A STEADY SQUAT, TRY ADDING A JUMP. A **LUNGE** IS SIMILAR, BUT WITH ONE FOOT FORWARD AND ONE BACK. WHEN YOU DO A LUNGE **JUMP**, DON'T LET YOUR KNEES HIT THE GROUND WHEN YOU JUMP. AFTER EACH SET, DON'T FORGET TO SWITCH WHICH LEG IS IN FRONT!

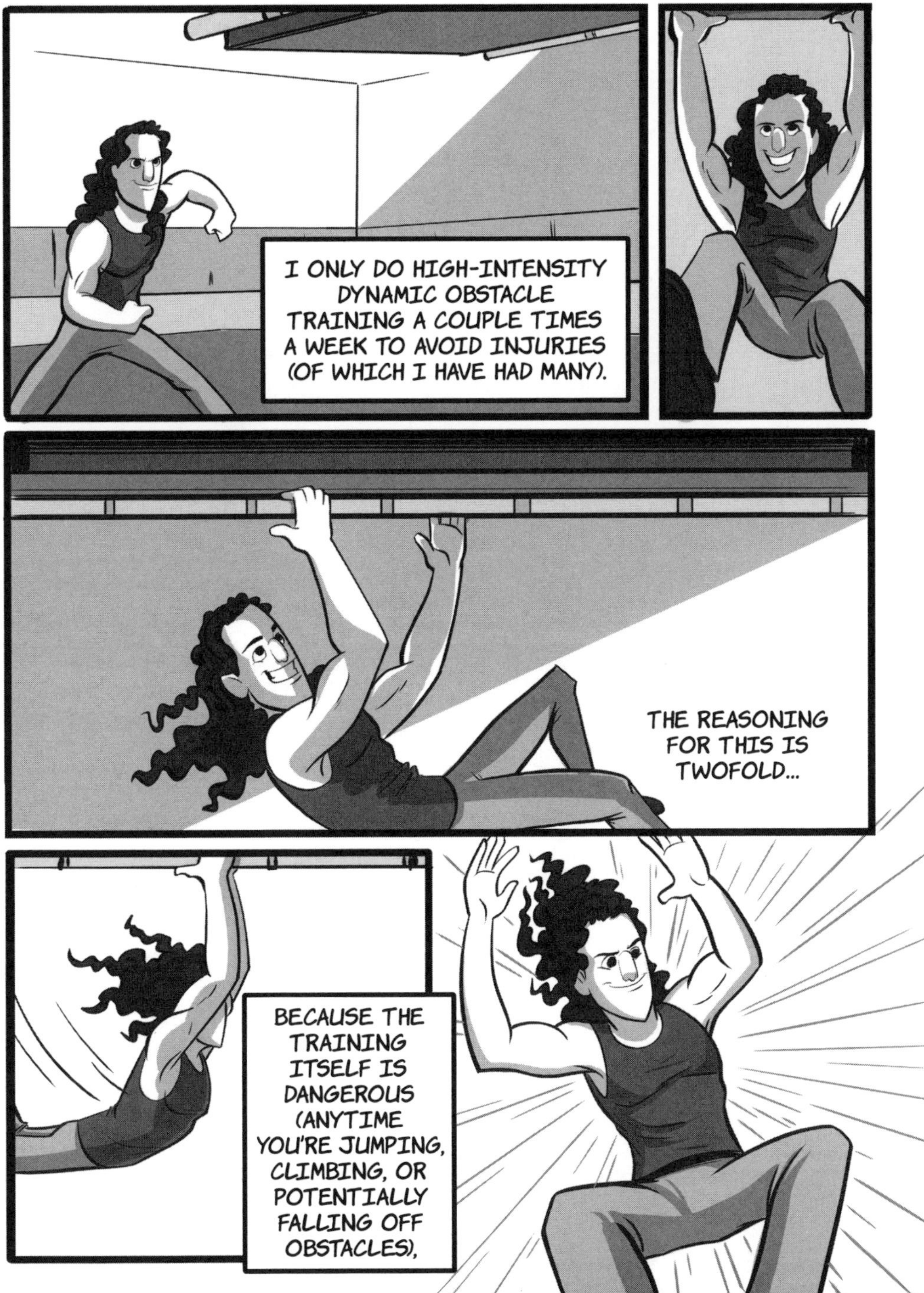
I ONLY DO HIGH-INTENSITY DYNAMIC OBSTACLE TRAINING A COUPLE TIMES A WEEK TO AVOID INJURIES (OF WHICH I HAVE HAD MANY).
THE REASONING FOR THIS IS TWOFOLD...
BECAUSE THE TRAINING ITSELF IS DANGEROUS (ANYTIME YOU'RE JUMPING, CLIMBING, OR POTENTIALLY FALLING OFF OBSTACLES),

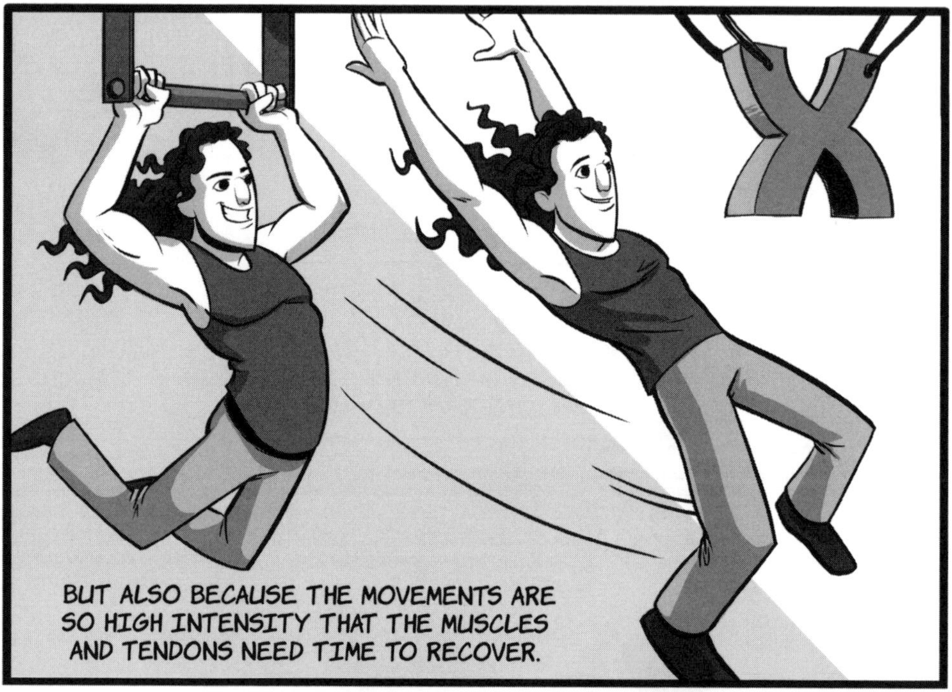
BUT ALSO BECAUSE THE MOVEMENTS ARE SO HIGH INTENSITY THAT THE MUSCLES AND TENDONS NEED TIME TO RECOVER.

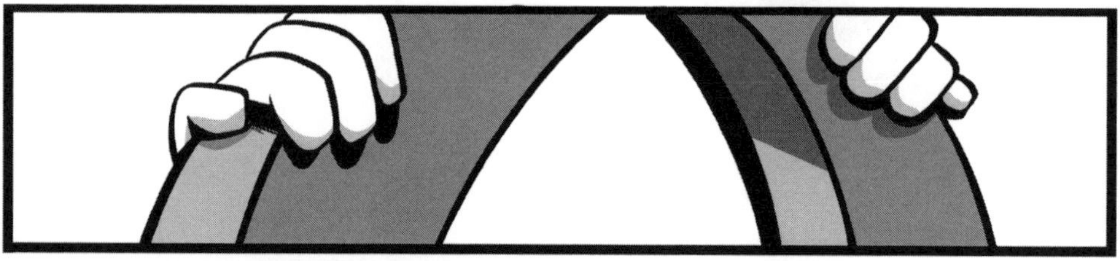

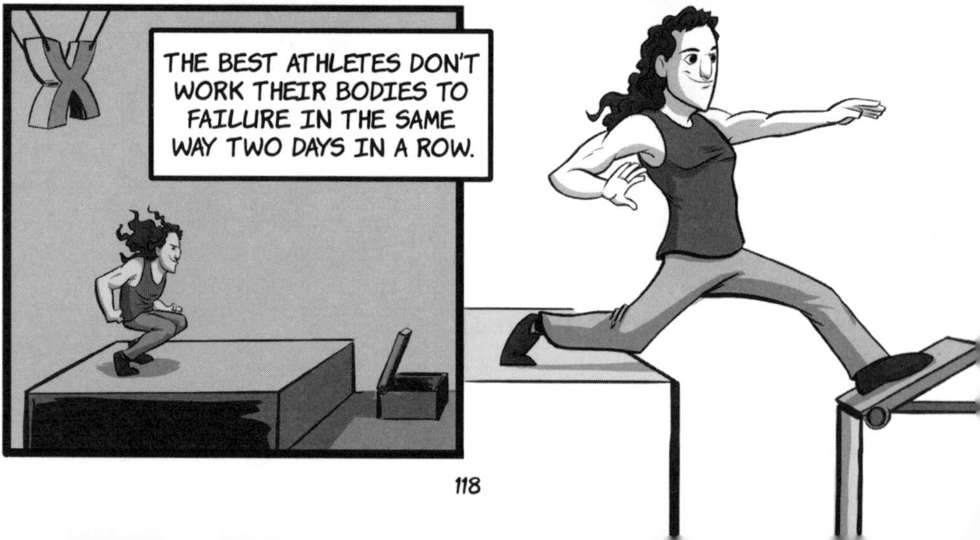
THE BEST ATHLETES DON'T WORK THEIR BODIES TO FAILURE IN THE SAME WAY TWO DAYS IN A ROW.

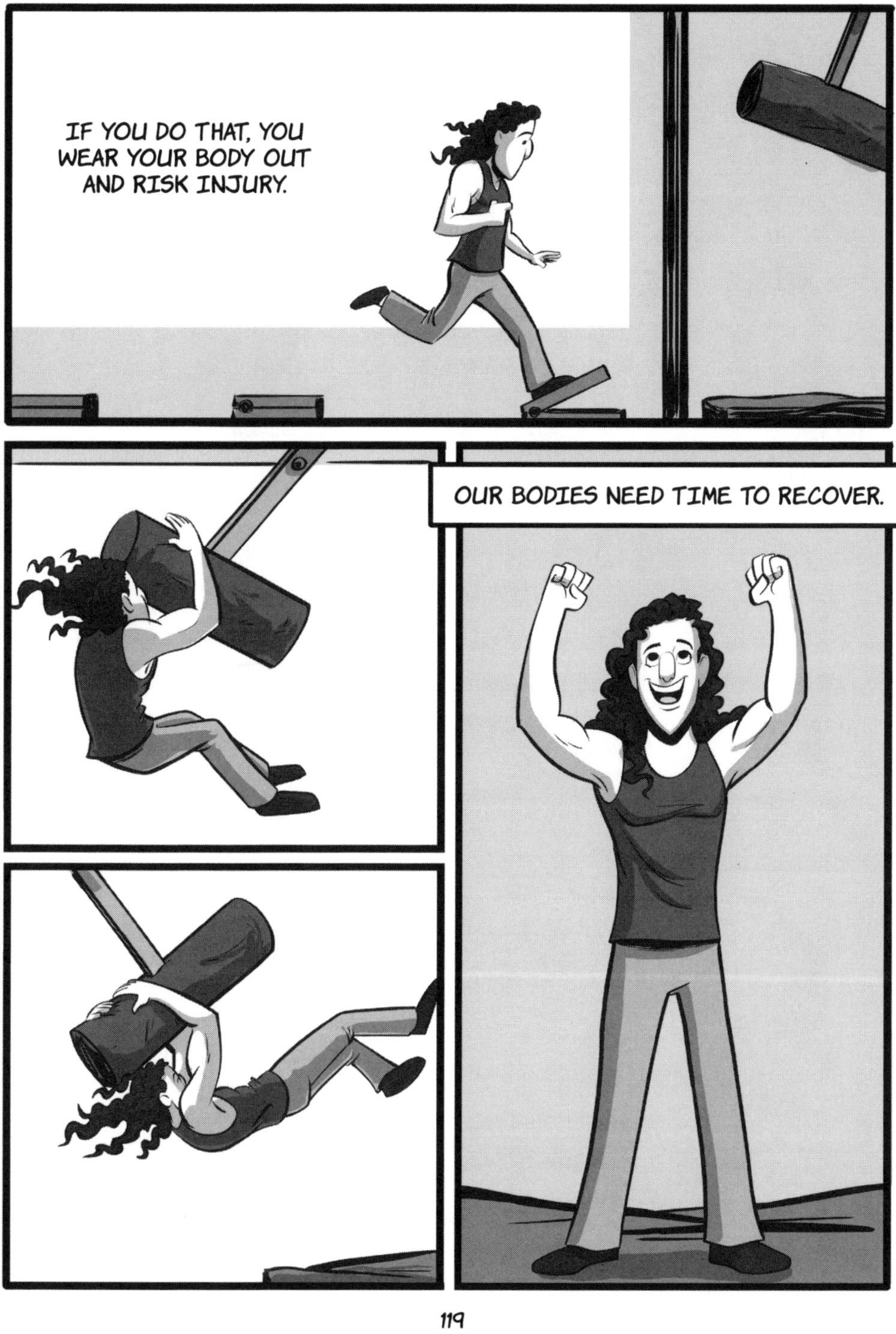
IF YOU DO THAT, YOU WEAR YOUR BODY OUT AND RISK INJURY.
OUR BODIES NEED TIME TO RECOVER.

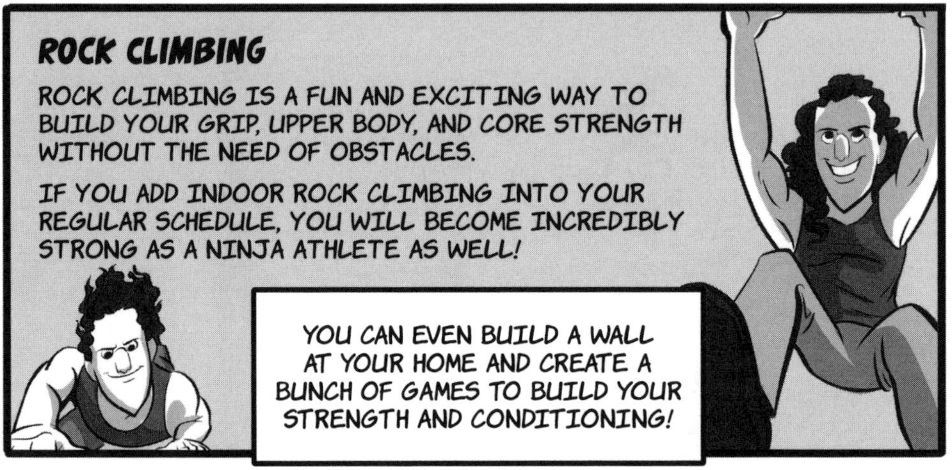
ROCK CLIMBING
ROCK CLIMBING IS A FUN AND EXCITING WAY TO BUILD YOUR GRIP, UPPER BODY, AND CORE STRENGTH WITHOUT THE NEED OF OBSTACLES.
IF YOU ADD INDOOR ROCK CLIMBING INTO YOUR REGULAR SCHEDULE, YOU WILL BECOME INCREDIBLY STRONG AS A NINJA ATHLETE AS WELL!
YOU CAN EVEN BUILD A WALL AT YOUR HOME AND CREATE A BUNCH OF GAMES TO BUILD YOUR STRENGTH AND CONDITIONING!

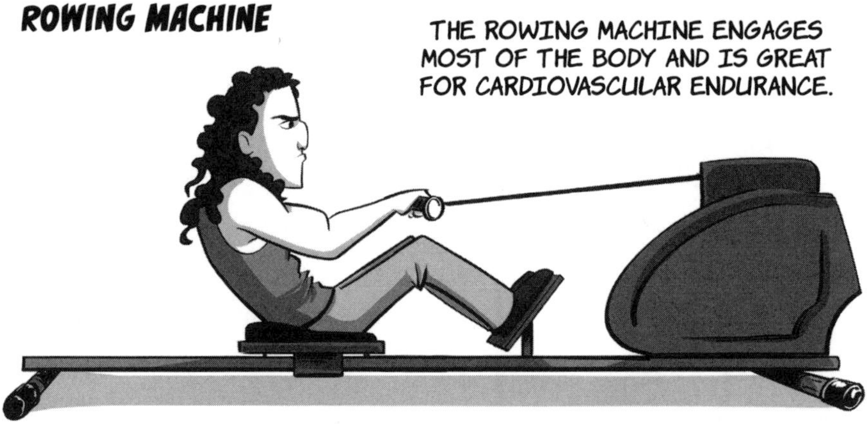
ROWING MACHINE
THE ROWING MACHINE ENGAGES MOST OF THE BODY AND IS GREAT FOR CARDIOVASCULAR ENDURANCE.

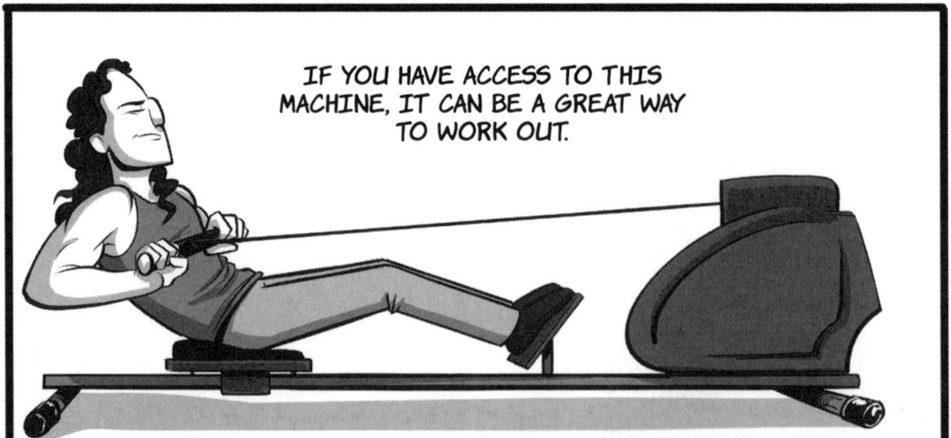
IF YOU HAVE ACCESS TO THIS MACHINE, IT CAN BE A GREAT WAY TO WORK OUT.

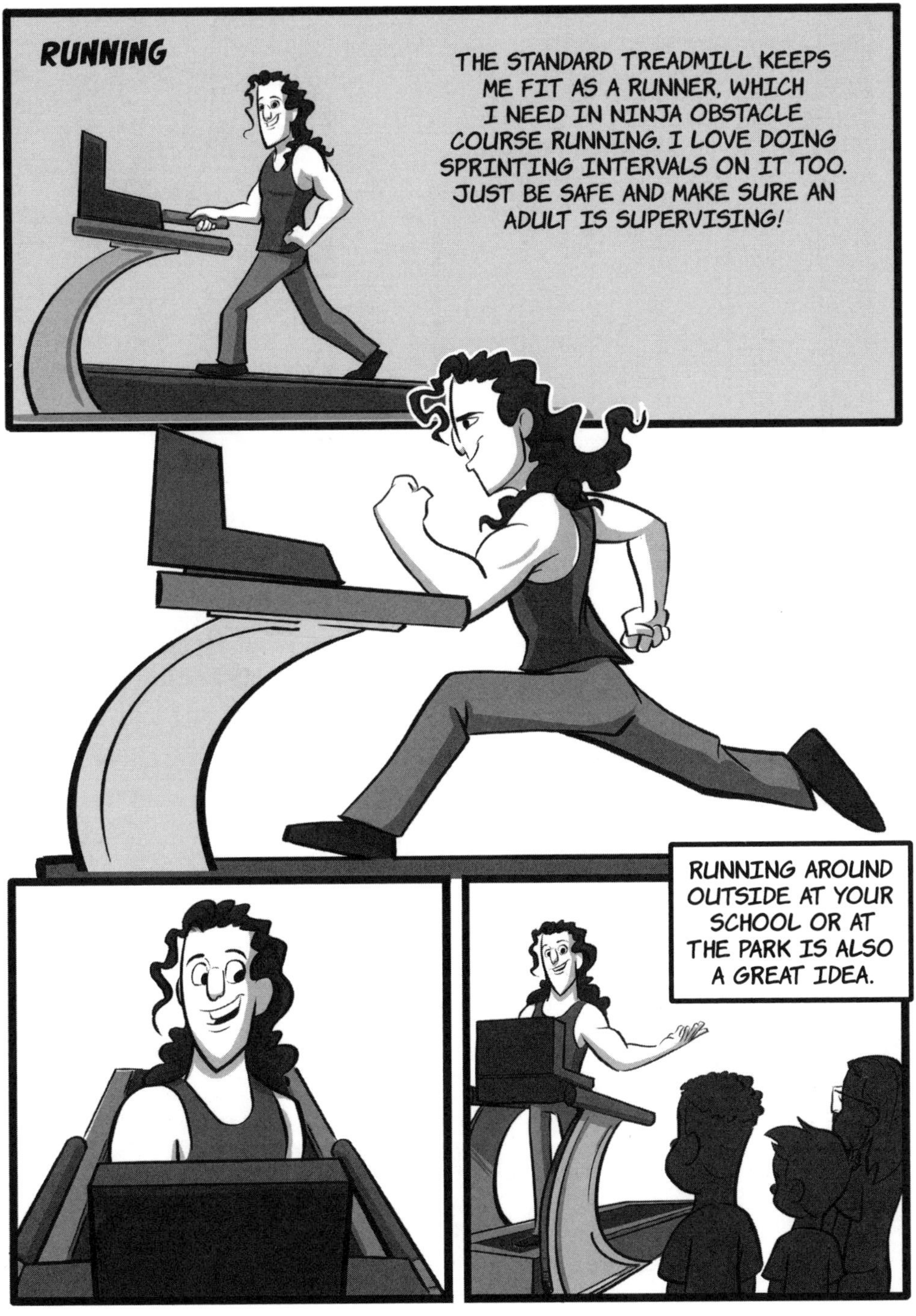
RUNNING
THE STANDARD TREADMILL KEEPS ME FIT AS A RUNNER, WHICH I NEED IN NINJA OBSTACLE COURSE RUNNING. I LOVE DOING SPRINTING INTERVALS ON IT TOO. JUST BE SAFE AND MAKE SURE AN ADULT IS SUPERVISING!
RUNNING AROUND OUTSIDE AT YOUR SCHOOL OR AT THE PARK IS ALSO A GREAT IDEA.

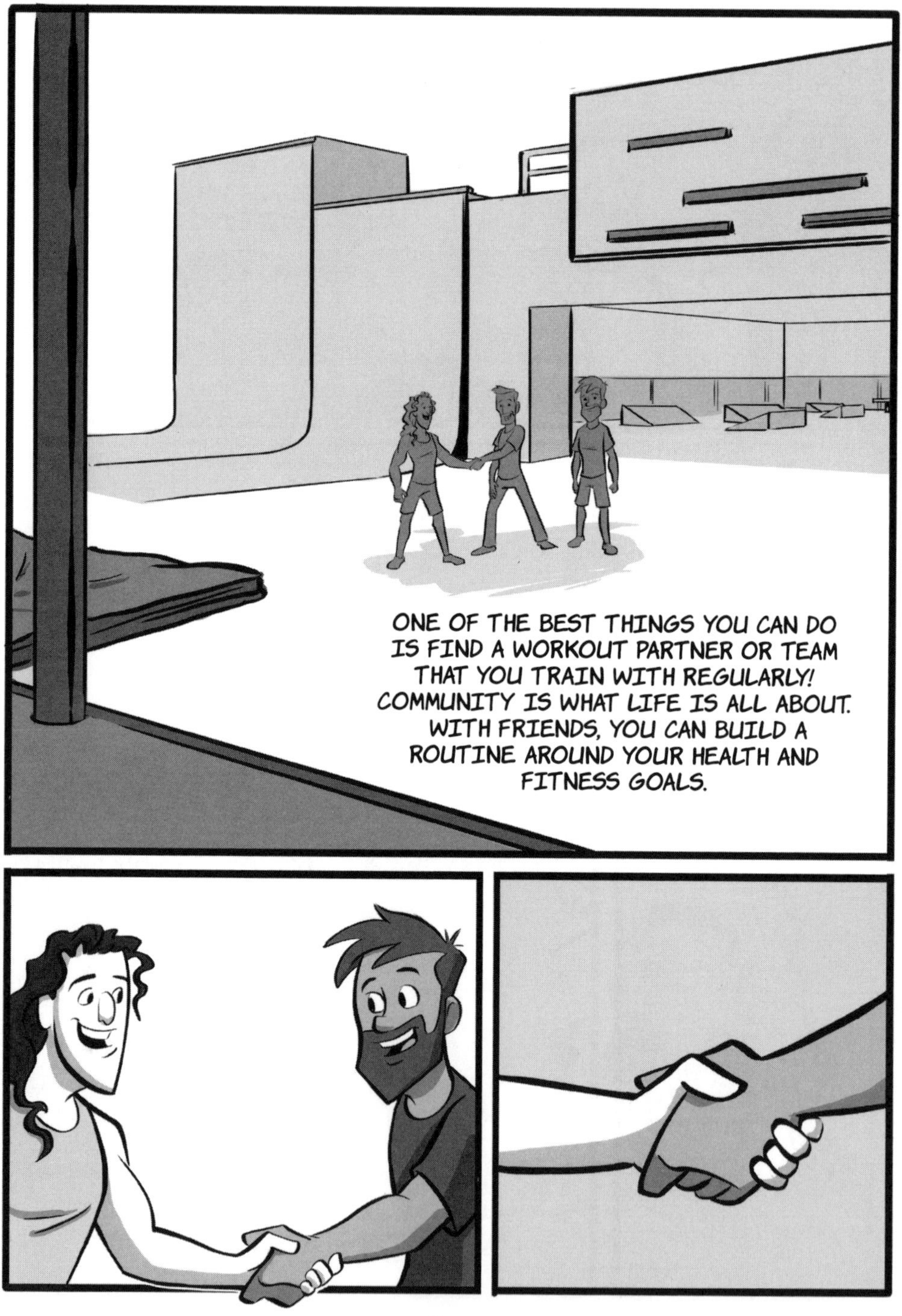
ONE OF THE BEST THINGS YOU CAN DO IS FIND A WORKOUT PARTNER OR TEAM THAT YOU TRAIN WITH REGULARLY! COMMUNITY IS WHAT LIFE IS ALL ABOUT. WITH FRIENDS, YOU CAN BUILD A ROUTINE AROUND YOUR HEALTH AND FITNESS GOALS.

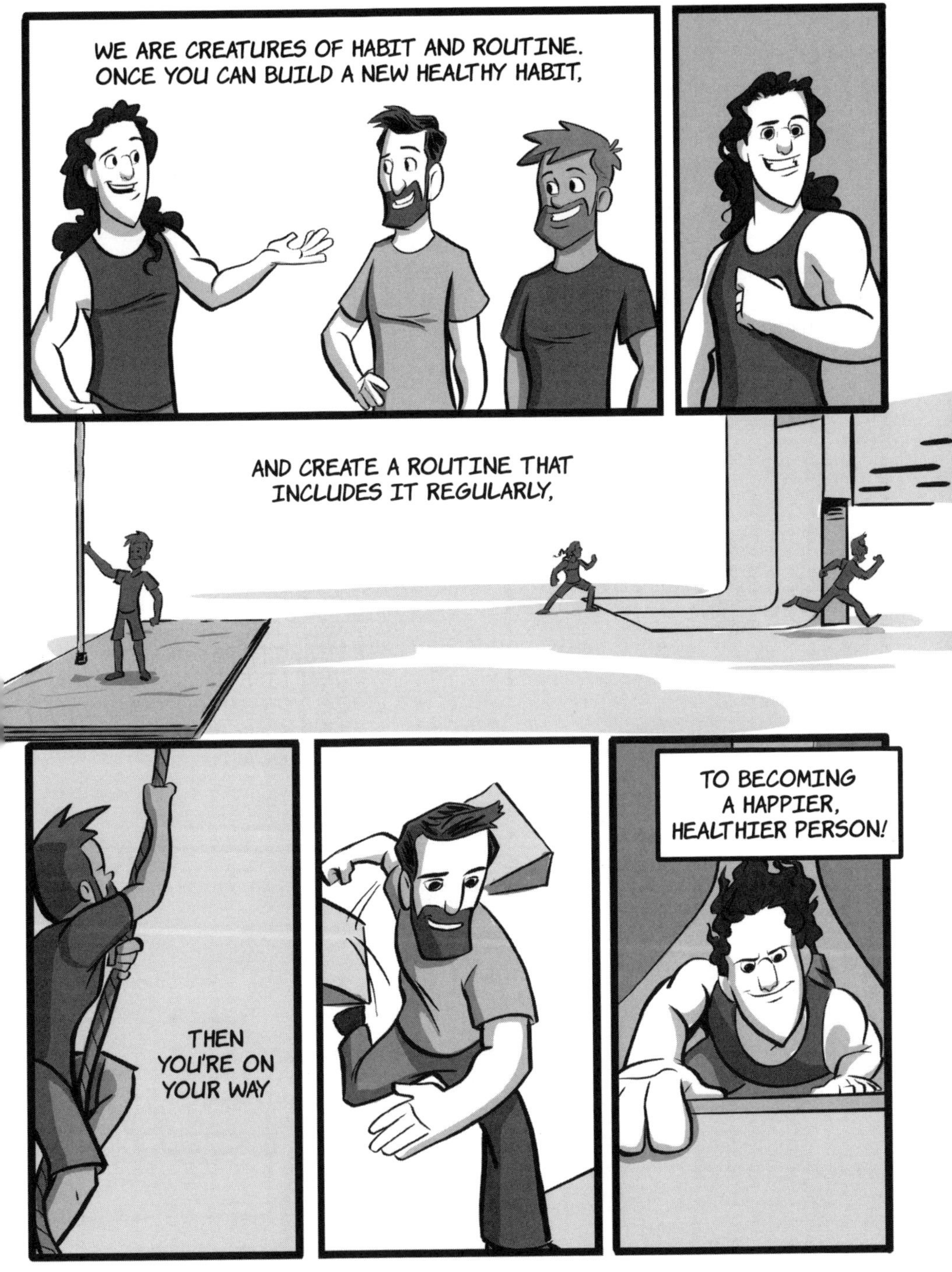
WE ARE CREATURES OF HABIT AND ROUTINE. ONCE YOU CAN BUILD A NEW HEALTHY HABIT,
AND CREATE A ROUTINE THAT INCLUDES IT REGULARLY,
THEN YOU'RE ON YOUR WAY
TO BECOMING A HAPPIER, HEALTHIER PERSON!

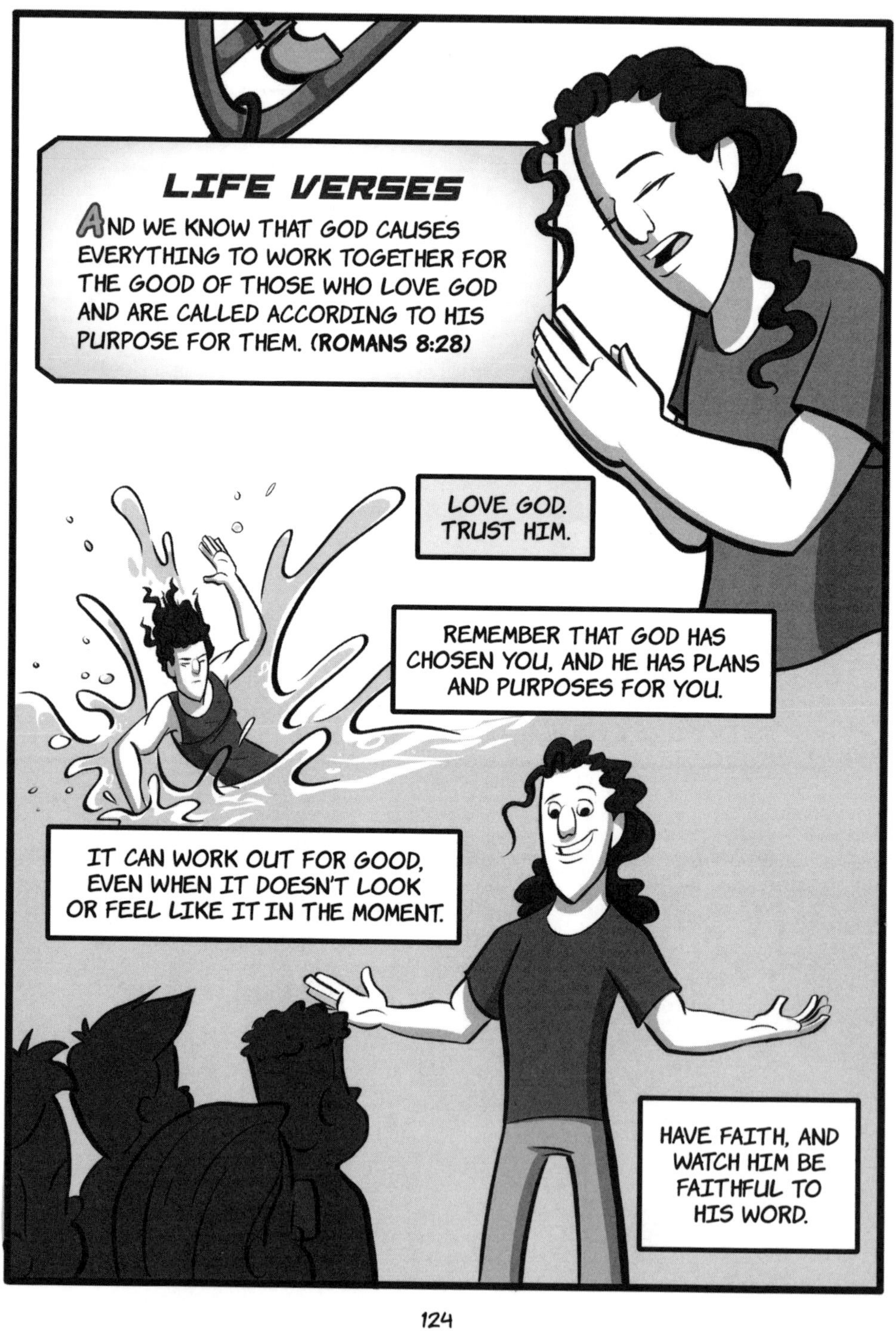
LIFE VERSES
AND WE KNOW THAT GOD CAUSES EVERYTHING TO WORK TOGETHER FOR THE GOOD OF THOSE WHO LOVE GOD AND ARE CALLED ACCORDING TO HIS PURPOSE FOR THEM. (ROMANS 8:28)
LOVE GOD. TRUST HIM.
REMEMBER THAT GOD HAS CHOSEN YOU, AND HE HAS PLANS AND PURPOSES FOR YOU.
IT CAN WORK OUT FOR GOOD, EVEN WHEN IT DOESN'T LOOK OR FEEL LIKE IT IN THE MOMENT.
HAVE FAITH, AND WATCH HIM BE FAITHFUL TO HIS WORD.

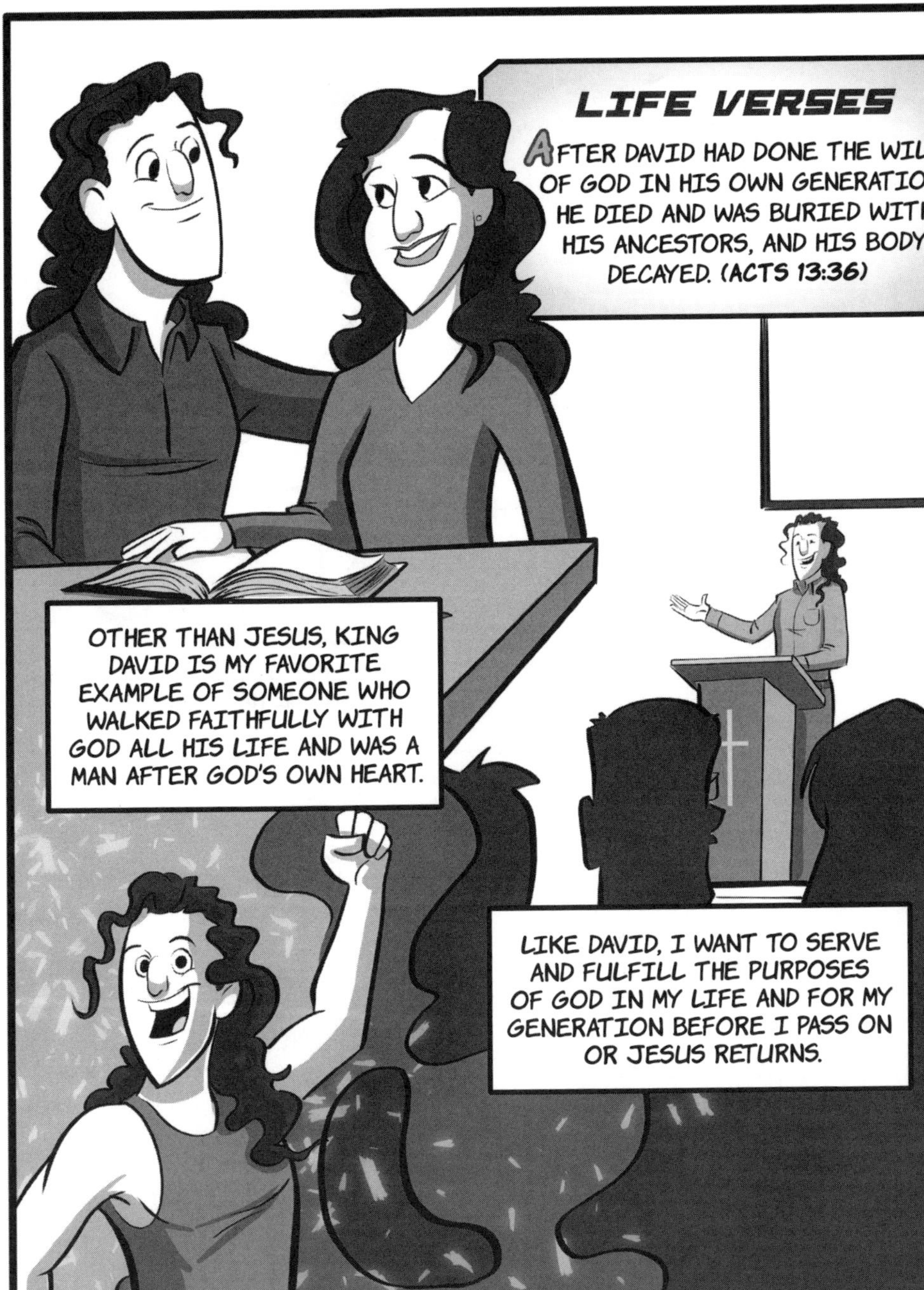
LIFE VERSES
AFTER DAVID HAD DONE THE WILL OF GOD IN HIS OWN GENERATION, HE DIED AND WAS BURIED WITH HIS ANCESTORS, AND HIS BODY DECAYED. (ACTS 13:36)
OTHER THAN JESUS, KING DAVID IS MY FAVORITE EXAMPLE OF SOMEONE WHO WALKED FAITHFULLY WITH GOD ALL HIS LIFE AND WAS A MAN AFTER GOD'S OWN HEART.
LIKE DAVID, I WANT TO SERVE AND FULFILL THE PURPOSES OF GOD IN MY LIFE AND FOR MY GENERATION BEFORE I PASS ON OR JESUS RETURNS.

LIFE VERSES

JOYFUL ARE PEOPLE OF INTEGRITY, WHO FOLLOW THE INSTRUCTIONS OF THE LORD. JOYFUL ARE THOSE WHO OBEY HIS LAWS AND SEARCH FOR HIM WITH ALL THEIR HEARTS. THEY DO NOT COMPROMISE WITH EVIL, AND THEY WALK ONLY IN HIS PATHS. YOU HAVE CHARGED US TO KEEP YOUR COMMANDMENTS CAREFULLY. OH, THAT MY ACTIONS WOULD CONSISTENTLY REFLECT YOUR DECREES! THEN I WILL NOT BE ASHAMED WHEN I COMPARE MY LIFE WITH YOUR COMMANDS. AS I LEARN YOUR RIGHTEOUS REGULATIONS, I WILL THANK YOU BY LIVING AS I SHOULD! (PSALM 119:1-7)

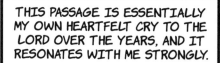

THIS PASSAGE IS ESSENTIALLY MY OWN HEARTFELT CRY TO THE LORD OVER THE YEARS, AND IT RESONATES WITH ME STRONGLY.

IT HIGHLIGHTS SO MUCH OF WHAT I VALUE: CHARACTER, INTEGRITY, INTENTIONALITY, ACTIVE PURSUIT, AND DAILY PROGRESSION TOWARD HIS BEST FOR MY LIFE AND THE LIVES OF THOSE I AFFECT.

LEARN AND GROW EACH DAY THROUGH READING SCRIPTURE. EVERY COMMAND IN SCRIPTURE IS THERE FOR OUR PROTECTION AND IS FULL OF BENEFITS IN THIS LIFE. ARE WE PERFECT? NEVER. CAN WE GET CLOSER EACH DAY?

ABSOLUTELY.

I dedicate this book to all the young ninjas in training! I hope this book encourages you to work hard, give it your all, get back up, and never quit. Every day, learn and grow! As an athlete and as a person, that's the best mentality to have. Trust in the Lord, and be confident both in yourself and in your training. You can do it! Even if nobody else tells you this, remember that I believe in your ability to do great things. Learn to enjoy the process of getting a tiny bit better each day, and watch it pay off over time.

To my students, and my children, and all my nieces and nephews: I truly love you guys. I wrote this book especially with you in mind. My greatest prayer is that you remember the stories within these pages every day so that they strengthen you and fill you with courage to walk by faith and be who the Lord God Almighty has called you to be. The goal is souls, so may you come closer to Jesus through this book.

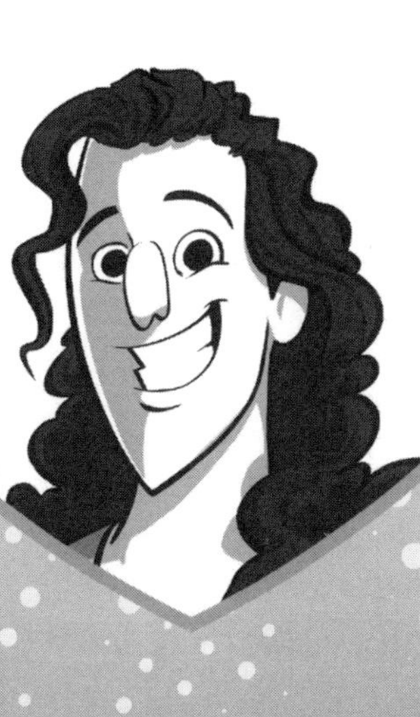

DANIEL GIL is a pro-level *American Ninja Warrior* athlete, a nine-time national finalist, and the season 12 champion. He is an author, a motivational speaker, and a mental wellness coach. For more than a decade, Daniel has trained and coached ninja/OCR students in the Houston area. He is blessed to be a global ambassador for the growing sport and to use his expertise to build and develop the sport as he now travels all over the world for various ninja events, competitions, and speaking engagements.

He is called the "Kingdom Ninja" because of his walk with the Lord Jesus Christ. His mission is to exemplify a holistic lifestyle of health, wellness, and determination while impacting the world for greater purposes. He and his wife, Abby, and their family live in Houston, Texas.

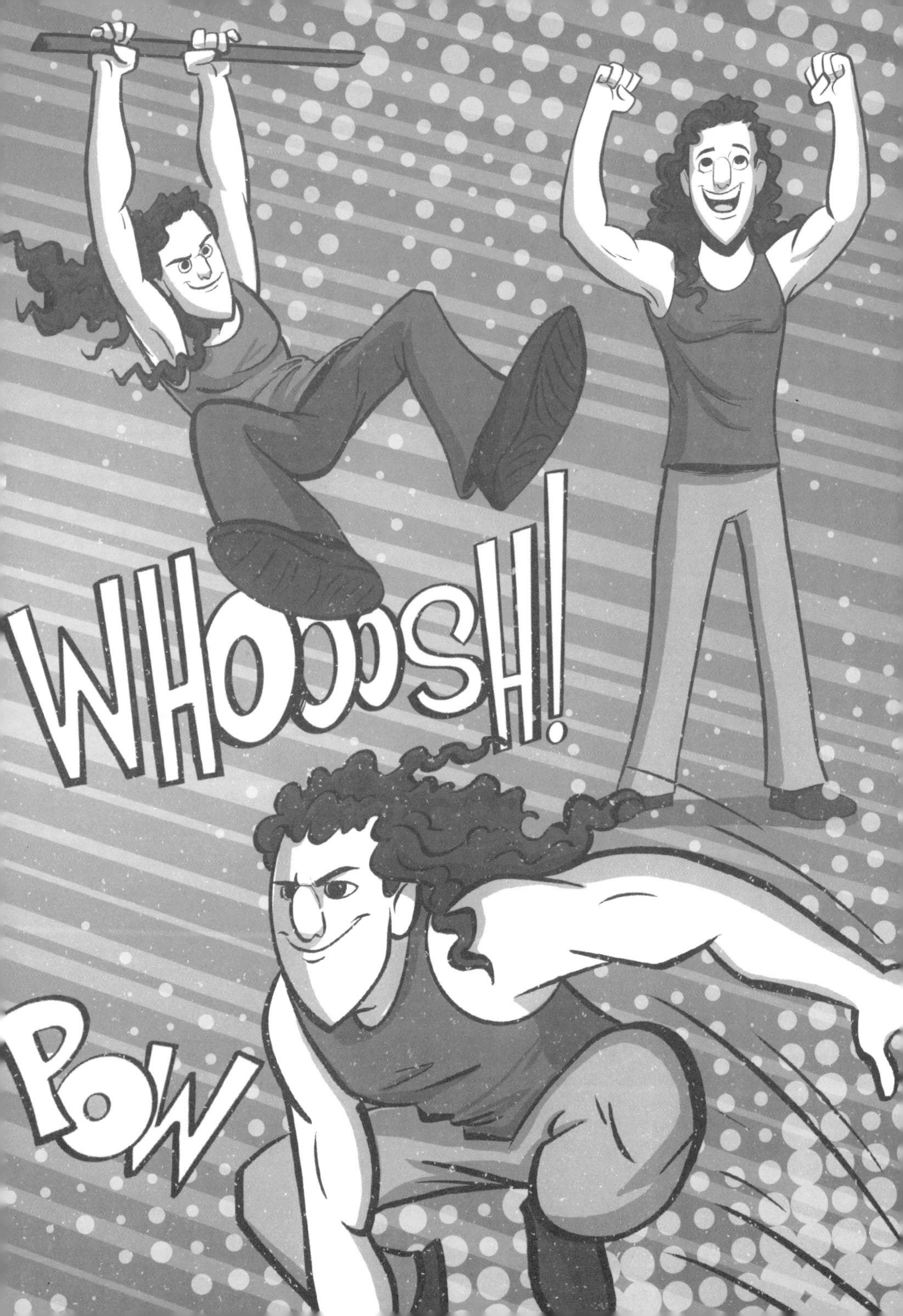
WHOOOSH!
POW

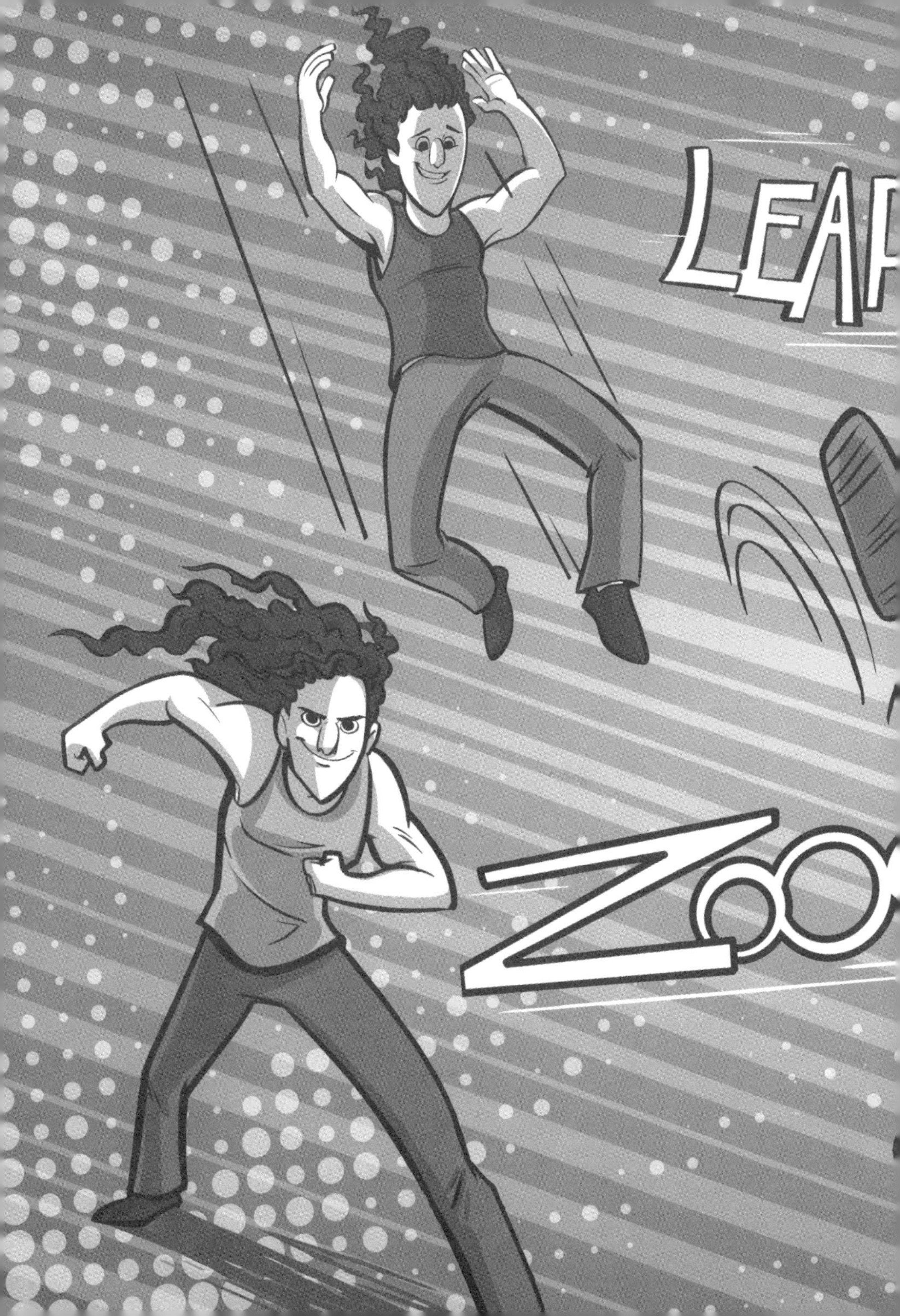
LEA
ZOO